DAYTRIPS
IN
BRITAIN
60
**One Day Adventures
by Rail, Bus, or Car**

D1316396

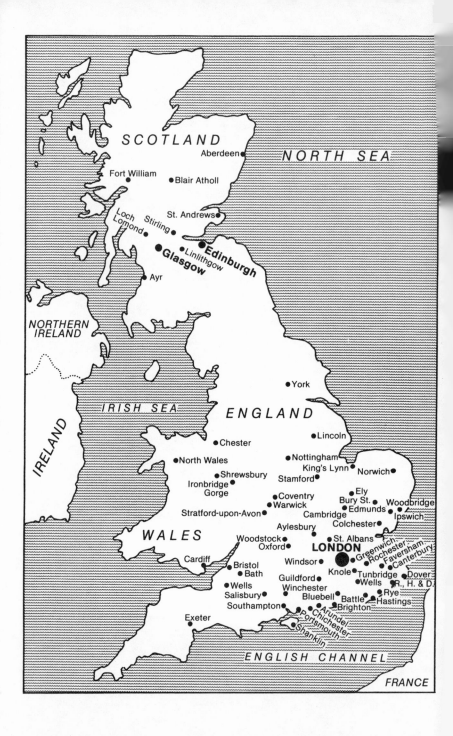

DAYTRIPS
IN
BRITAIN
60

One Day Adventures
by Rail, Bus, or Car

by
Earl Steinbicker

HASTINGS HOUSE / PUBLISHERS
MAMARONECK, NEW YORK

The author would like to thank the following people, whose generous help and encouragement made this book possible.

Robin Prestage, of the British Tourist Authority.

John Lampl, of British Airways.

F. Paul Weiss, President of BritRail Travel International.

All photos are by the author except as noted.

Library of Congress Cataloging-in-Publication Data
Steinbicker, Earl, 1934–
    Daytrips in Britain.

    1. Great Britain—Description and travel—1971–
Guide-books. I. Title.
DA650.S743   1987   914.1'04858   87-81360
ISBN 0-8038-9301-9

Printed in the United States of America
10 9 8 7 6 5 4 3 2

Contents

	Introduction	7
Section I	**Getting Around**	9
Section II	**Daytrips from London**	19
	Greenwich	20
	Rochester	25
	Faversham	30
	Canterbury	34
	Dover	40
	Knole	44
	Romney, Hythe & Dymchurch	48
	Rye	52
	Tunbridge Wells	58
	Battle	62
	Hastings	66
	Bluebell	71
	Brighton	75
	Arundel	81
	Chichester	85
	Guildford	92
	Portsmouth	97
	Shanklin (Isle of Wight)	102
	Winchester	108
	Southampton	114
	Salisbury and Stonehenge	119
	Windsor and Eton	125
	Bath	130
	Wells	138
	Bristol	143

Cardiff (Caerdydd) 150
Exeter 157
Oxford 162
Woodstock 171
Warwick 175
Stratford-upon-Avon 179
Aylesbury 186
Coventry 190
Ironbridge Gorge 195
Shrewsbury 202
North Wales Rail Excursion 207
Chester 212
St. Albans 219
Nottingham 224
Stamford 228
Lincoln 232
York 237
Cambridge 245
Ely 253
King's Lynn 257
Bury St. Edmunds 263
Colchester 267
Ipswich 271
Woodbridge 275
Norwich 279
Section III **Daytrips in Scotland** 285
Edinburgh 286
St. Andrews 297
Aberdeen 302
Linlithgow 309
Stirling 314
Blair Atholl 318
Glasgow 322
Ayr and the Burns Country 330
Loch Lomond 335
West Highland Rail Trip 339
Index 345

Introduction

Britain is by far the favorite European destination for North American travelers, and with good reason. They can choose from an enormous variety of pleasurable experiences within the bounds of one small, compact island. What's more, the overwhelming majority of Britain's most exciting attractions can easily be enjoyed on a daytrip basis with absolutely no need for frequent hotel changes. This book takes a careful look at 60 of the most intriguing destinations and tells you, in step-by-step detail, exactly how to go about probing them on your own.

Daytrips in Britain is an expansion and elaboration of a previous book, *Daytrips from London,* which had gone through three editions and several printings since its first publication in 1983. As was the case with its predecessor, this book is not intended to be a comprehensive guide to the entire nation. It focuses, instead, on the broad scope of daytrip possibilities open to you when you base yourself in London, Edinburgh, or Glasgow.

Daytrips have many advantages over the usual point-to-point touring, especially for short-term visitors. You can sample a far greater range in the same time by seeing only those places that really interest you instead of "doing" the country region by region. They also lead to a more varied diet of sights, such as spending one day in Yorkshire, the next back in London, and the third on an island off the southern coast.

The benefits of remaining in one hotel for a while are obvious. Weekly rates are often more economical than overnight stays, especially in conjunction with airline package plans. You also gain a sense of place, of having established a temporary home-away-from-home in a large city where you can get to know the restaurants and enjoy the nightlife. Then, too, you won't waste time searching for a room every night. Your luggage remains in one place while you go out on carefree daytrips.

There is no need to pre-plan every moment of your vacation since with daytrips you are always free to venture wherever you please. Feel like seeing Salisbury this morning? Ah, but this is Sunday, so maybe it would be better to head for Brighton instead, or take a delightful ride on the old Bluebell steam railway. Is rain predicted for the entire day? You certainly don't want to be on the southern coast in a shower, so why not try the wonderful museums in Nottingham? Is the day just too glorious to spend in Edinburgh, regardless of its many charms? You can always take off for Loch Lomond on a moment's inspiration and enjoy a long, lazy cruise. The operative word here is flexibility, the freedom of not being tied to a schedule or route.

All of the daytrips in this book may be taken by public transportation, and nearly all by car. Full information for doing this is given in the "Getting There" section of each trip. A suggested do-it-yourself tour is outlined in both the text and on the local map provided. Time and weather considerations are included, along with price-keyed restaurant recommendations, background data, and sources of additional information.

The trips have been arranged in a geographic sequence following convenient transportation routes. In several cases it is possible to combine two trips in the same day. These opportunities are noted whenever they are practical.

Destinations were chosen to appeal to a wide variety of interests. In addition to the usual cathedrals, castles, and stately homes there are also country walks, maritime museums, canals, caves, exciting railfan excursions, Roman ruins, places where history was made, places of literary association, quaint fishing villages, great seaports, resorts, elegant spas, and early industrial sites. You should really read through all of them before deciding which intrigue you the most.

Many of the attractions have a nominal entrance fee—those that are free will come as a pleasant surprise. Cathedrals and churches will appreciate a small donation in the collection box to help pay their maintenance costs.

Finally, a gentle disclaimer. Places have a way of changing without warning, and errors do creep into print. If your heart is absolutely set on a particular sight, you should check first to make sure that it isn't closed for renovations, or that the opening times are still valid. Phone numbers for the local tourist information offices are included for this purpose.

Happy Daytripping!

Getting Around

All of the daytrips in this book can be made by rail (with an occasional local bus thrown in), almost all by car, and nearly half by coach. One, to Greenwich, can even be made by boat. Which of these you choose depends purely on personal factors, but you may want to consider the following information before deciding.

BY RAIL:

The British invented passenger trains and, on balance, their system is probably the best in the world. While some of the trains and stations are not quite as sleek as the latest found in, say, France or Germany, British Rail has the decided advantage of taking you exactly where you want to go, when you want to go, and of doing so with a minimum of fuss. With over 2,500 destinations and some 15,000 trains a day, there are few places that cannot be reached quickly and comfortably from London or your base in Scotland. BritRail stations are usually located in the heart of town, so close to the major tourist attractions that most of the walking tours described in this book begin right at the station. Trains have the additional advantage of neatly bypassing traffic going in and out of your base city.

Equipment varies from the swift InterCity 125s, which whisk you to distant places at speeds of 125 mph, to some rather quaint and colorful old commuter trains. Between these extremes are a wide variety of reliable workhorses, including the Sprinter 150s, a new generation of unusually fast and comfortable self-propelled trains now in widespread use.

All but the most local of commuter runs carry both first- and economy (2nd)-class accommodations. Most long-distance trains also have buffet or dining cars serving meals, snacks, and drinks. BritRail's English Breakfast is justly famous, and so huge that it may eliminate the need for lunch. By some odd quirk in the law, trains are allowed to sell alcoholic beverages even during hours when the pubs are closed.

Experienced travelers often consider riding trains to be the very best way of meeting the British people on their home ground. It is not unusual to strike up an engaging conversation that makes your trip all the more memorable. You will also get a good view of the passing countryside from the large windows, and have time to catch up on your reading.

London has many train stations, a legacy from the days before nationalization, when just about every route was operated by a separate company. The map on the opposite page shows the general location of those that are of interest to tourists. All of these are connected to the Underground (subway) system and can be reached easily. Be sure you know which station you are leaving from before starting out on the day's adventure. Some of the stations, most notably Liverpool Street, can be confusing to the uninitiated, so it is always best to allow a little extra time to orient yourself the first time you use them. All have information offices that can give you current schedules. Be sure to check for any possible day-of-the-week variations or temporary service reductions. Information can also be had by calling the following phone numbers in London.

FOR TRAINS LEAVING FROM:	CALL:
Charing Cross, Victoria, Waterloo, Waterloo East, Cannon Street, or London Bridge	(01) 928 5100
St. Pancras, Euston, Broad Street, or Marylebone	(01) 387 7070
King's Cross	(01) 278 2477
Liverpool Street	(01) 283 7171
Paddington	(01) 262 6767

Those going directly from London to **Scotland** can make the journey by train during the day in as little as 4½ hours to Edinburgh or 5 hours to Glasgow. You can also save the better part of a day as well as a night's lodging by taking one of the late-evening sleepers, which travel more slowly and arrive at a civilized hour in the morning. Reservations are needed for this, and there is a rather modest extra charge for the sleeping compartment. This is a very comfortable way to travel the 400-mile distance. Departures are made from either London's Euston or King's Cross station, so be sure to check this when you make the reservation. Sleeper service is also provided to Manchester, Liverpool, and the West Country.

The system-wide **British Rail Passenger Network Map** is highly detailed and extremely useful in planning your trips. It is available free of charge from any office of BritRail Travel International in North America or can be purchased from the Transportation Centre in the larger train stations of Britain. Although you really don't need it, a schedule book of the entire system can also be bought at major sta-

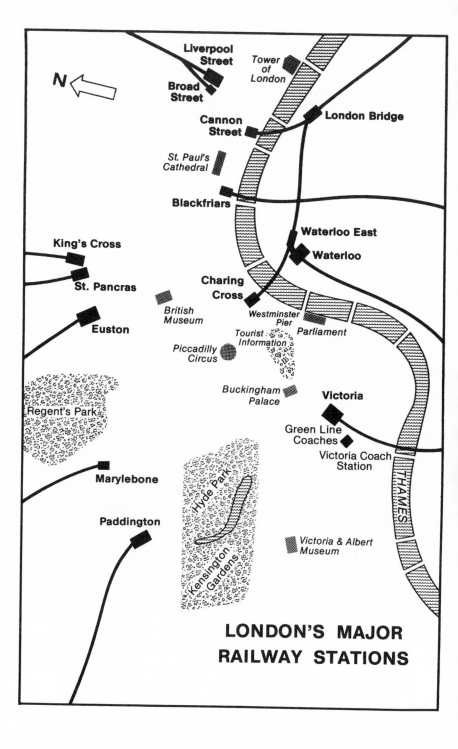

N

Liverpool
Street

Broad
Street

Tower
of
London

London Bridge

Cannon
Street

St. Paul's
Cathedral

Blackfriars

King's Cross

Waterloo East

Waterloo

St. Pancras

Charing
Cross

Euston

Westminster
Pier

British
Museum

Parliament

Tourist
Information

Piccadilly
Circus

Regent's Park

Buckingham
Palace

Victoria

Green Line
Coaches

Marylebone

Victoria Coach
Station

THAMES

Hyde Park

Paddington

Victoria & Albert
Museum

Kensington
Gardens

LONDON'S MAJOR
RAILWAY STATIONS

tions, or you may want to use the handy but somewhat less comprehensive **Thomas Cook Continental Timetable,** covering all of Europe and sold at Thomas Cook travel offices throughout Britain. This is also available at some travel bookstores in America or by mail from the Forsyth Travel Library, P.O. Box 2975, Shawnee Mission, Kansas 66201, phone toll-free 1-800-FORSYTH for credit-card orders.

The **BritRail Pass** is an incredible bargain that should definitely be investigated before going to Britain. It allows unlimited train travel throughout the entire British Rail system (all of England, Wales, and Scotland) for periods of 8, 15, or 22 days, or for one month; and is available in both first- and economy (2nd)-class versions. First class offers more comfort and less crowding for a somewhat higher price, although the economy-class cars get there just as fast. There are also reduced-price passes for children from 5 through 15 years of age, and for youths from 16 through 25; as well as a special deal for senior citizens 60 and over. Another interesting arrangement for short-term visitors is the **London Travel Pak,** which combines a 3-day London Visitor Travelcard (described on page 15) and airport transfers with a special 4-day BritRail Pass. You may also want to ask your travel agent about the Britainshrinker and Great Britain Express touring plans offered by British Rail, which can be taken in conjunction with a BritRail Pass if desired.

If you intend to take several of the daytrips in this book, and especially if at least one of these is to a distant city such as York, Exeter, or Chester—or if you're also going to Scotland—the BritRail Pass will probably save you a considerable sum of money. Even if the savings amount to less than that, the pass should still be considered for the convenience it offers in not having to line up for tickets, and for the freedom of just hopping aboard almost any train at whim. Possession of a BritRail Pass will also encourage you to become more adventurous, to seek out distant and offbeat destinations.

For even more versatility there are also **BritRail/Drive** packages, which include bargain car-rental vouchers valid at 282 Europcar locations throughout Britain, 75 of which are in BritRail stations. These can be very useful on some of the more complex daytrips such as Wells, Stratford-upon-Avon, Cardiff, or Ironbridge Gorge, where you can take a train most of the way and complete the trip by rental car, thus getting better acquainted with the countryside while avoiding traffic and bus schedules.

The BritRail Pass **must** be obtained **before** going to Britain. Specific information about the various plans and prices, as well as the actual purchase, can be handled on the spot by most travel agents, by mail from the Forsyth Travel Library mentioned above, or may be had through the nearest office of BritRail Travel International—located in

New York, Los Angeles, Chicago, Dallas, Toronto, and Vancouver. Written or phone inquiries can be made to:

BritRail Travel International
630 Third Avenue
New York, NY 10017
Phone (212) 599-5400

The BritRail Pass must be validated at any British Rail ticket office within six months of the date of issue. It provides transportation only and does not cover possible additional charges such as reservations, sleeping accommodations, or meals. If you have decided against a BritRail Pass—or live in Britain and cannot buy one—you still have several money-saving options. Before purchasing a full-fare ticket you should always ask about special fares that might be applicable to your journey, including same-day returns, called "Awayday" tickets.

BY COACH:

Coaches are a lower-cost alternative to trains for relatively short distances. The British make a fine distinction between coaches, which travel between towns; and buses, which operate strictly on local routes within towns or rural districts. Although they are slower and generally have less frequent service, there are some advantages to coach travel that trains cannot match. One of these is the opportunity to observe life on the main streets of towns and villages from a more intimate perspective. Many local buses are of the double-deck variety, which afford wonderful panoramic views from their upper level. The main advantage of coaches or buses, however, remains one of price—the fares are often as little as half that of a train.

Most coach services mentioned in this book leave from London's Victoria Coach Station on Buckingham Palace Road, just a five-minute walk from the Victoria train station. Along the way you will pass Eccleston Bridge, the departure point for Green Line coaches, whose schedules can be had by phoning (01) 668-7261. Information about National Express and other services departing from London's Victoria Coach Station is available by calling (01) 730-0202. For similar information in Edinburgh call (031) 556-8464, and in Glasgow (041) 332-9191.

The **Britexpress Card** gives you a one-third discount off normal fares on all National Express, Scottish Citylink, and some other coach services for a period of 30 days. It can be purchased from travel agents in North America or from National Express at Victoria Coach Station in London upon presentation of a passport.

BY CAR:

Car rentals are a good way to see some of the places that are more difficult to reach by train or coach. A particularly attractive plan is to use a BritRail/Drive package (described above) to combine rail and car travel, getting to your first destination by train and then switching to a car, thus avoiding both city traffic and miles of tiresome highways. Cars can also be economical when several people travel together, although it takes more than two passengers to make the cost comparable to rail. If you plan to rent a car and are not considering a BritRail/ Drive package, then by all means check out the various money-saving **fly/drive** deals offered by British Airways and other carriers. Other than getting used to driving on the left, you should have no trouble adapting to British roads, which are usually quite excellent. American and Canadian licenses are valid, although there may be some age or experience restrictions. Ask your travel agent about this as it varies with different rental companies.

BY AIR:

You may prefer air travel for the long haul between major base cities. **British Airways** operates a frequent shuttle service that guarantees seats without reservations between London and either Edinburgh or Glasgow, a fast and easy way to get to Scotland.

As for transatlantic services, British Airways has more flights to London from more North American gateways than any other carrier, 17 departure cities in all, plus a New York-to-Manchester service. Their new Terminal 4 at London's Heathrow Airport was designed for convenience and rivals the best in the world today. It has direct bus and Underground (subway) service to central London, as well as very frequent shuttle buses to terminals 1, 2, and 3. Some other transatlantic carriers land at London's Gatwick Airport instead, which has excellent rail service to Victoria Station in London.

PACKAGES:

Package plans offered by several transatlantic airlines in conjunction with their flights are a superb way to stretch your budget to its limit. The leader in this field is **British Airways,** which has some very enticing packages, including prepaid hotel accomodations in London or elsewhere; car rentals if you wish; guaranteed theater tickets to even the most popular shows; sightseeing tours; or a London Visitor Travelcard—all for considerably less than they would cost if purchased separately. The number of possible combinations is enormous, and can be adjusted to fit the length of your trip, the specific hotel you want, the type of car you prefer, and other idiosyncrasies to suit your fancy. To take maximum advantage of this it is imperative that you consult your travel agent as far in advance as possible and to study the brochures carefully. Please note that these packages require that you fly both ways on the issuing airline and that they can be used with any applicable fare, from the speedy Concorde or first class down to the least-expensive excursion. British Airways offers some very attractive APEX fares that require advance purchase. The situation with airline flights, fares, and package plans is constantly changing, so it will pay you to deal with a reliable agent who keeps abreast of the latest developments. The toll-free number in the U.S.A. for British Airways is 1-800 AIRWAYS.

There are several other money-saving plans that your travel agent can tell you about. One of these, the **Open to View Ticket,** may be of particular interest to readers of this book. This is a pass, valid for one month after its first use, that entitles the bearer to free entry into hundreds of Britain's greatest castles, stately homes, and historic sites. A great many of these are the same ones featured in the 60 daytrips that follow. The pass will save you money if you intend to visit more than just a few of these attractions. Another plan to consider is the **London Visitor Travelcard,** which allows virtually unlimited use of London's Underground and red buses for 3, 4, or 7 days. It is a worthwhile investment if you plan to make extensive use of the system.

WHEN TO GO:

The best time to visit Britain, especially if you're going beyond the big cities, is between mid-spring and early fall. The extra hours of sunlight in these months will greatly enhance your daytrips, as will the mild weather. While periods of rain are fairly frequent, the showers are also brief and usually blow over quickly, often bringing bright sunshine in their wake. The slight inconvenience this causes can easily be remedied by always carrying a folding umbrella with you, no matter how perfect the day appears to be. A light jacket or sweater will often be welcome, sometimes even in the middle of July. As you will quickly learn, Britain's fast-changing weather is utterly unpredictable but rarely given to extremes.

HOLIDAYS:

Legal holidays in Britain are:

January 1 (New Year's Day)
Good Friday
Easter Monday (not in Scotland)
May Day (first Monday in May)
Spring Bank Holiday (last Monday in May)

August Bank Holiday (last Monday in August, first Monday in August in Scotland)
Christmas
December 26 (Boxing Day)

FOOD AND DRINK:

Several choice restaurants, pubs, or other establishments are listed for each destination in this book. Many of these are long-time favorites of experienced travelers and serve typically British food unless otherwise noted. Their approximate price range, based on the least expensive complete meal offered, is indicated by the following symbols:

$ — Inexpensive, but may have fancier dishes available.

$$ — Reasonable. These establishments may also feature daily specials.

$$$ — Luxurious and expensive.

X: — Days closed.

The quality of restaurant food in Britain has been steadily increasing, although there is still plenty of room for improvement, especially in the middle price range. In addition to the well-recommended establishments listed here you may want to consult an up-to-date guide such as the red-cover *Michelin Great Britain and Ireland*, any of the *Egon Ronay* guides, or *The Best Pubs of Great Britain*. It is always wise to check the posted menus before entering, paying particular attention to any daily set meal specials.

Besides restaurants specializing in traditional British fare, you will encounter a great many featuring foreign cuisines, most notably French, Italian, Indian, and Chinese. American favorites such as hamburgers, chili, pizza, and the like have become extremely popular and can be found anywhere.

Having a light lunch at a **pub** will save you a great deal of time and money, and is often a very pleasant experience. Not all pubs serve meals, and of those that do, not all serve particularly good food. A reliable way to judge quality before eating is to size up the other customers and to note whether the pub makes a special point of preparing meals. Some unfortunately consider food as something that fills the stomach between pints of beer. A great many pubs, especially in cities, do not serve evening meals. Virtually all pubs are self-service in that you buy drinks at the bar, usually order food at a separate counter, and take both to a table. Tipping in this case is neither expected nor encouraged. Pub hours vary somewhat, but are frequently something like 11 a.m. to 3 p.m. and 6–10:30 p.m., with shorter hours on Sundays. Scotland has more liberal laws, especially in Edinburgh and Glasgow. The limited hours are a throwback to the times when it was thought best to keep the working classes sober during the day.

Beer, happily, remains the national beverage of Britain. It comes in a bewildering variety of tastes and local specialties. The most common types, at least on tap, are *lager,* which is somewhat similar to American and Continental beers and should be served cool; and *bitter,* the richly flavored traditional British brew, always served at cellar temperature. The latter is an acquired taste, but once you get used to it you'll probably be back for more. The best of these come from small local breweries, and are virtually never exported. "Real Ale," a term sponsored by the CAMRA organization, denotes cask-conditioned beer made the old-fashioned way without chemical additives. It is worth seeking out. A "free house" is a pub not owned by or otherwise associated with a particular brewery—it is free to sell various brands. Asking the bartender for his—or her—advice will not only get you some interesting brews, it will often open the way to spirited conversations as well.

SUGGESTED TOURS:

The do-it-yourself walking tours in this book are relatively short and easy to follow. On the assumption that most readers will be traveling by public transportation, they always begin at the local train station or bus stop. Those going by car can make a simple adjustment. Suggested routes are shown by heavy broken lines on the maps, while the circled numbers refer to major attractions or points of reference along the way, with corresponding numbers in the text.

Trying to see everything in any given town could easily become an exhausting marathon. You will certainly enjoy yourself more by being selective and passing up anything that doesn't catch your fancy in favor of a friendly pub. God will forgive you if you don't visit *every* church.

Practical information, such as the opening times of various attractions, is as accurate as was possible at the time of writing. Everything is, of course, subject to change. You should always check with the local tourist office if seeing a particular sight is crucially important to you.

As a way of estimating the time any segment of a walking tour will take, you can look at the scale on the map and figure that the average person covers about 100 yards in one minute. The maps, by the way, were drawn to best fit the page size. North does not necessarily point to the top, but is always indicated by an arrow.

TOURIST INFORMATION:

Virtually every town of any tourist interest in Britain has its own information office, which can help you with specific questions or perhaps book local accommodations. The locations of these offices are shown on the town maps in this book by the word "**info.**," and repeated along with the phone number under the "Tourist Information" section for each trip. To phone ahead from another town in Britain you must first dial the area code, which always begins with 0 and is shown in parentheses, followed by the local number. Most pay phones use coins and have operating instructions on them.

In **London,** information concerning all of Britain can be had from the **British Travel Centre** on Regent Street, just south of Piccadilly Circus. Open daily, their phone number is (01) 730-3400.

ADVANCE PLANNING INFORMATION:

The **British Tourist Authority** has branches throughout the world, which will provide help in planning your trip. In North America they are located at:

40 West 57th St.,
New York, NY 10019
Phone (212) 581-4700

John Hancock Center
875 North Michigan Ave., Suite 3320
Chicago, IL 60611
Phone (312) 787-0490

Cedar Maple Plaza
2305 Cedar Springs Road, Suite 210
Dallas, TX 75201-1814
Phone (214) 720-4040

World Trade Center
350 South Figueroa, Suite 450
Los Angeles, CA 90071
Phone (213) 628-3525

94 Cumberland St., Suite 600
Toronto, Ont. M5R 3N3
Canada
Phone (416) 925-6326

COMMENTS:

We are always grateful for comments from readers, which are extremely useful in preparing future editions of this or other books in the series. Please write directly to the author, Earl Steinbicker, c/o Hastings House/Publishers, 9 East 40th Street, New York, NY 10016, U.S.A. Thank you.

Daytrips from London

It is absolutely amazing to realize just how much of England, and even Wales, can be explored on a daytrip basis from London. The nation is so compact that most of its major attractions, located as far north as Lincoln and as far west as Cardiff, can be comfortably reached by rail in under two hours—while a slightly longer ride takes you all the way to York or Exeter. The regions to the south and to the east are even closer, with virtually all towns being only 30 to 90 minutes away. Those touring by car will have a somewhat shorter range, but still a very impressive one.

The advantages of staying in one hotel and traveling without the burden of luggage far outweight the additional mileage involved. By departing London around 8 or 9 a.m. you will reach your destination long before noon, leaving the rest of the day free for sightseeing before returning in time for dinner and perhaps an evening's entertainment.

Even your first day in Britain need not be lost to jet lag. Two of the daytrips in this section, those to Greenwich and Windsor, are so simple and relaxing that you can enjoy them even before fully recovering from the flight. In many ways this is more attractive than just wandering around London while waiting for your hotel room to be made ready. Just drop off your luggage and go, returning in the evening for a good night's sleep.

The 50 daytrips described here were chosen to cover a wide variety of interests and experiences. Some are to world-famous destinations, while others will take you well off the beaten path to unusual adventures. A short list of those that have most consistently pleased nearly everyone would include Rye, Bath, Stratford-upon-Avon, York, and Cambridge—all especially good choices for first-time visitors.

Greenwich

Barely five miles east of central London stands the ancient borough of Greenwich, a town exceptionally rich in history and beauty. Once the home of royalty, a great palace stood on the green meadows by the river until the late 1600s. Henry VIII was born there, as were Mary I and Elizabeth I. For centuries, Greenwich remained the center of Britain's naval power. It is best known today, however, as the site of the Prime Meridian, that imaginary line from which all longitudinal distances on earth are measured, and from which the world's time is reckoned. Miraculously, Greenwich was spared the encroachment of a growing London, and it still retains much of its gracious character. There are easily enough fascinating sights to occupy an entire day, although you may prefer to combine this trip with one to nearby Rochester.

GETTING THERE:

Boats depart London's Westminster Pier, just opposite Parliament, at frequent intervals for the 45-minute cruise to Greenwich. Return boats operate until early evening. Refreshments are available on board.

Trains to Greenwich leave from London's Charing Cross, Waterloo East, or London Bridge stations at frequent intervals. The trip takes between 10 and 15 minutes, and return service runs until late evening.

Buses on routes 177, 180, 185, and 188 connect various points in London with Greenwich town center.

By car, take the A-200 direct to Greenwich.

WHEN TO GO:

The Maritime Museum and the Old Royal Observatory do not open on Sundays until 2 p.m., and are closed on some major holidays. The Royal Naval College is closed on Thursdays and some holidays.

FOOD AND DRINK:

There are a great many pubs and restaurants in Greenwich, including a handy one within the Maritime Museum. Some particularly good choices are:

The Cutty Sark

Trafalgar Tavern (Park Row, by the Thames) An old and very popular combination pub and restaurant with traditional English fare. X: Restaurant only—Sun. eve., Mon., Sat. lunch. $ and $$$

Le Papillon (57 Church St., by the *Cutty Sark*) Traditional food. X: Sat. lunch, Sun. eve., bank holidays. $$

Spread Eagle (2 Stockwell St., near St. Alfege's Church) A traditional old tavern. X: Sat. lunch, Sun. eve., bank holidays. $$

The Yacht (Crane St., near Trinity Hospital) A colorful riverside tavern with pub food. $

Bar du Musée (17 Nelson Road, near St. Alfege's Church) A wine bar with simple food. $

TOURIST INFORMATION:

The local tourist office, phone (01) 858-6376, is located between the pier and the *Cutty Sark*.

SUGGESTED TOUR:

Those coming by train will begin at **Greenwich Station** (1). Follow the map to **Greenwich Pier** (2), the arrival point for boats from London. The 19th-century clipper ship *Cutty Sark*, once the fastest in the world, sits in dry dock next to the *Gipsy Moth IV*, a 53-foot ketch in which Sir Francis Chichester single-handedly circumnavigated the globe in 1967. A few yards away stand the tourist office and the entrance to the pedestrian tunnel under the Thames.

A tour aboard the **Cutty Sark** is a must for any visitor to Greenwich. Launched in 1869 for the China Sea trade, she was later used to haul wool from Australia and served as a training ship until the end of World War II. Now honorably retired, the elegant ship is a stirring sight recalling the great days of sail. In her hold there is a fascinating display of nautical items. The *Cutty Sark* may be visited Mondays through Saturdays, from 10 a.m. to 6 p.m.; and on Sundays from 12 noon to 6 p.m. It closes at 5 p.m. in winter, and is closed on a few major holidays. The **Gipsy Moth IV** may also be boarded during the same times, from Easter through September.

From here follow King William Walk to Greenwich Park and climb uphill to the **Old Royal Observatory** (3). No longer used due to London's bright lights and pollution, the observatory buildings now house an intriguing museum of astronomical and time-keeping instruments. Embedded in the courtyard pavement is a brass strip marking 0° longitude, the **Prime Meridian** that separates the eastern and western hemispheres. Be sure to set your watch by the wonderful old clock just outside the gate, probably the most official time you'll ever get. The ornate **Flamsteed House** was built by Sir Christopher Wren in 1675 on instructions from Charles II to provide "for the Observator's habitation, and a little for Pompe." From the adjoining terrace there is a marvelous view of Greenwich, the Thames, and London. The Observatory is open during the same times as the National Maritime Museum, of which it is a part. A combined ticket covering both attractions is available.

A downhill stroll through the park leads to the **East Wing** of the **National Maritime Museum** (4). This part deals with Britain's sea history during the 19th and 20th centuries, including the great migrations to the New World, the development of merchant shipping, and both world wars.

The **Queen's House** (5) is reached via a colonnade. The first Palladian villa in England, it was begun in 1616 by the famous architect Inigo Jones as a summer palace for James I's queen, Anne of Denmark. The entrance hall is an elegant 40-foot cube, from which an outstanding spiral staircase leads to the upper floor where the reconstructed Queen's-bedroom may be visited. The entire house is filled with art treasures worth a careful examination.

Continue along the colonnade to the **Maritime Museum's West Wing** (6), its largest and most interesting part. The huge Neptune Hall

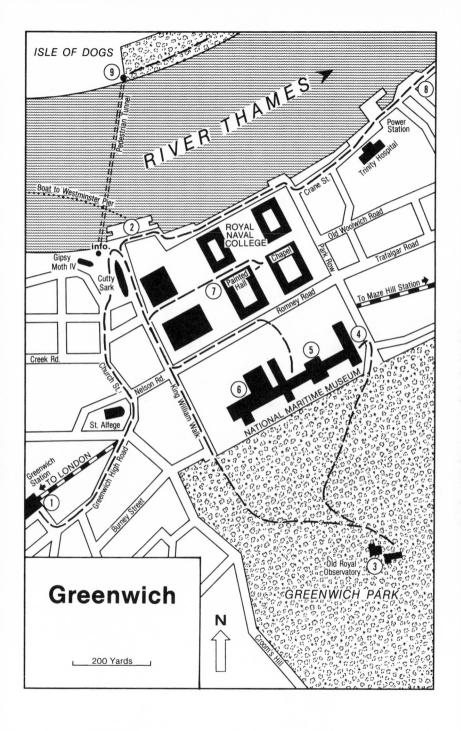

ISLE OF DOGS

⑨

RIVER THAMES

Power Station

Trinity Hospital

Crane St.

Boat to Westminster Pier

Old Woolwich Road

②

ROYAL NAVAL COLLEGE

Chapel

Trafalgar Road

⑧

Gipsy Moth IV

Info.

Painted Hall

Park Row

To Maze Hill Station

Cutty Sark

⑦

Romney Road

④

⑤

Creek Rd.

Church St.

Nelson Rd.

King William Walk

⑥

NATIONAL MARITIME MUSEUM

St. Alfege

Greenwich Station

TO LONDON

Greenwich High Road

Burney Street

①

Old Royal Observatory

③

GREENWICH PARK

Greenwich

N

200 Yards

contains entire boats, including a full-size paddle steamer. Several galleries are devoted to the careers of Captain Cook and Lord Nelson, while others cover the American and French revolutions. The Barge House is particularly intriguing with its collection of elegant royal barges. Both a restaurant and a bookshop are located in this wing. The entire Maritime Museum, including the Royal Observatory and the Queen's House, is open Mondays through Saturdays, from 10 a.m. to 6 p.m.; and on Sundays from 2–6 p.m. It closes at 5 p.m. in winter, and is closed on some major holidays.

Now follow Romney Road and King William Walk to the west gate of the **Royal Naval College** (7). On this site once stood the Tudor palace of Placentia, birthplace of Henry VIII, Mary I, and Elizabeth I. Badly damaged by Cromwell's troops during the Civil War, the palace was torn down following the Restoration and a hospital for retired seamen was erected in its place. These buildings, largely designed by Sir Christopher Wren, became the Naval College in 1873, a function they serve today. You may visit the **Painted Hall** with its glorious ceiling, and the **Chapel,** the only parts of the college open to the public, on any day except Thursdays and some holidays, from 2:30–5 p.m.

A wonderful way to end your visit is to take a walk along the Thames to **Ballast Quay** (8). Just before the pier there is a passageway that leads to the right. Follow this past the front of the Royal Naval College and continue on to the historic Trafalgar Tavern, a luxury restaurant once frequented by cabinet ministers during the reign of Queen Victoria. From here stroll along narrow Crane Street. The Yacht Tavern is a more modest pub that recaptures some of the old riverside charm. In a short distance you will come to Trinity Hospital, an almshouse founded in 1614 and still the home of 20 pensioners. The walk now passes through a power station and leads to the Cutty Sark Tavern on delightful Ballast Quay. Here you can relax at outdoor riverside tables before returning to the pier. Another interesting walk is under the Thames through a **pedestrian tunnel,** reached by an elevator near the tourist office, to the **Isle of Dogs** (9) for a classic panoramic view of Greenwich.

NEARBY SIGHT:

The recently completed **Thames Barrier,** built to protect London from tidal flooding, is the world's largest movable flood barrier and may be inspected at close range from its Visitors' Centre, which also features working models and an audio-visual show. You can get there by boat, train, bus, or car. Ask for details at the Greenwich tourist office.

Rochester

The ancient cathedral town of Rochester is most famous for its close association with Charles Dickens, who spent much of his life nearby and used the town as a locale for many of his stories. A marvelous museum that explores his life and works in stunning audio-visual terms has been opened and is reason enough for the visit. There are several other attractions as well, including a massive Norman castle, a 12th-century cathedral, remains of a Roman wall, the excellent Guildhall Museum, several buildings of historic importance, and an exceptionally attractive main street.

No one knows just how old Rochester is, but it probably dates from prehistoric times. The early Britons called it *Doubris,* which the Romans changed to *Durobrivae* after they built their bridge across the Medway. The present name derives from the Anglo-Saxon *Hrofes-ceaster.* In A.D. 604 the second-oldest bishopric in England was established here, becoming the foundation for the present Norman cathedral.

By getting off to an early start it is possible to combine Rochester with a trip to either Greenwich or Faversham, as there are good rail and road connections between the three.

GETTING THERE:

Trains to Rochester depart at about half-hour intervals from both Victoria and Charing Cross stations in London, with a journey time of about one hour. Return service operates until late evening.

Coaches operated by Invictaway leave London's Victoria Coach Station hourly for the 1½-hour ride to Rochester. Returns operate until mid-evening and service is reduced on Sundays and holidays.

By car, Rochester is 30 miles from London following the A-2/M-2 all the way.

WHEN TO GO:

All of the important sights in Rochester are open daily throughout the year with the exception of major holidays. Some shops close early on Wednesdays.

FOOD AND DRINK:

There are several good restaurants and pubs along High Street. A few fine choices are:

> **Royal Victoria and Bull** (16 High St., opposite the Guildhall) A 400-year-old inn used as a locale by Dickens. $$

> **King's Head** (58 High St., 1 block south of the Guildhall) Serving traditional fare for over four centuries. $$

> **Castle Tea Rooms** (151 High St., near Dickens Centre) Light lunches. $

TOURIST INFORMATION:

The tourist office, phone (0634) 43-666, is in Eastgate Cottage, next to the Charles Dickens Centre.

SUGGESTED TOUR:

Leaving **Rochester Station** (1), turn right on High Street and follow it to the **Charles Dickens Centre** in **Eastgate House** (2). The 16th-century house itself was mentioned in Dickens' novel *Pickwick Papers* as "Westgate House" and in *The Mystery of Edwin Drood* as the "Nun's House." Inside, two floors are filled with life-size models of his characters, reconstructions of scenes from his books, and mementoes of his life. All of this is brought alive through the clever use of sound and light, a unique theatrical experience that is absolutely first rate. The museum is open daily from 10 a.m. to 12:30 p.m. and from 2–5:30 p.m. Upon leaving, be sure to take a look at Dickens' tiny Swiss chalet in the garden, which was moved here from his home at nearby Gad's Hill. The gabled house on the other side of High Street is Uncle Pumblechook's house in *Great Expectations*.

Continue along High Street to the **Six Poor Travellers' House** (3), otherwise known as the Watts Charity. Founded in 1579, it provided lodging for impoverished travelers until 1947. You may visit the little Elizabethan bedrooms from April through October, Tuesdays through Saturdays, from 2–5 p.m. Dickens changed its name to "The Seven Poor Travellers" in his *Christmas Tale* of 1854.

A further stroll down High Street leads to the Corn Exchange of 1706 with its extraordinary moon-faced clock projecting over the street. This was mentioned in Dickens' novel *The Uncommercial Traveller*. Just beyond is the **Guildhall** (4), built in 1687, which now houses a modern town-museum dealing with regional history from the Stone Age onward. The collection of Victorian toys is especially interesting and should not be missed. Opening hours are from 10 a.m. to 12:30 p.m. and from 2–5:30 p.m. daily, except for a few major holidays. Across the street is the Royal Victoria and Bull Hotel, which appears

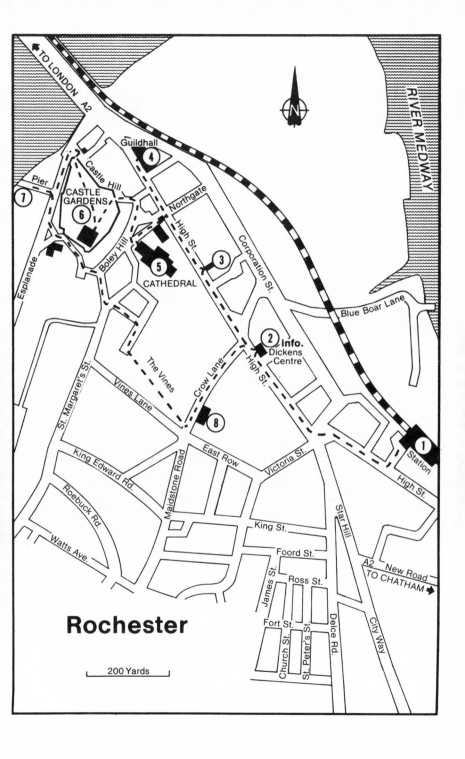

Inside Rochester Castle

as "The Bull" in *Pickwick Papers* and as the "Blue Boar" in *Great Expectations*. Queen Victoria stayed there when she was still a princess.

Now return on High Street to Chertsey's Gate, also known as College Gate, a 15th-century structure that is featured in Dickens' *The Mystery of Edwin Drood*. Pass through it and look to the left. The tombstones in the graveyard of St. Nicholas' Church provided Dickens with names for many of his characters.

You are now at **Rochester Cathedral** (5). An almost perfect example of early Norman architecture, it resembles Canterbury Cathedral and has several of the same features, including double transepts, an elevated choir, and an extensive crypt. The west front, with a magnificent doorway, is among the finest in England. Built on the site of an early-7th-century church, the cathedral was begun in 1080 and consecrated in 1130. Many additions were made through the centuries, making the mixture of styles particularly interesting. The cathedral is open daily from 8:30 a.m. to 6 p.m., closing at 5 p.m. in winter.

Stroll over to **Rochester Castle** (6). The Romans had a fortress here to guard their bridge, and in later centuries Saxons fought Vikings on this hill. Of the great castle begun in 1087 by William the Conqueror, only the massive 12th-century keep remains. One of the finest examples of Norman military architecture, it is 113 feet high and has walls that are 12 feet thick. A climb to the top will reward you with a superb

Miss Havisham in the Charles Dickens Centre
(Photo courtesy of Rochester Tourist Office)

panorama of the town and the Medway estuary. The castle is open Mondays through Saturdays, from 9:30 a.m. to 6:30 p.m.; and Sundays from 2:30–5:30 p.m. It closes earlier in winter.

Descend through the park to the Bridge Warden's Chapel of 1387 and turn left to **Rochester Pier** (7). From here you get a good view of activities on the river. Follow the map past the Satis House, where Queen Elizabeth I was entertained in 1573, and the Old Hall, an early Tudor building. Continue on past Minor Canon Row, mentioned in Dickens' *Edwin Drood*, the King's School, which was founded in 1542 by Henry VIII, and the Archdeaconry of 1661.

Pass through The Vines, a park where monks once had their vineyard. Parts of the old Roman city wall can be seen on the north side. The **Restoration House** (8) on Crow Lane was the home of Miss Havisham in Dickens' *Great Expectations*. Its name derives from the tradition that Charles II stayed here in 1660 on his way to be crowned king following the end of the Commonwealth. A few steps down Crow Lane will return you to High Street and the end of the tour.

Faversham

Located at the end of a tidal creek, the ancient port of Faversham has remained a delightfully unpretentious little town for over a thousand years. Relatively few tourists venture this way, but those who do are enchanted by its simple charms. Settlements have existed on this site since prehistoric times, and Faversham was granted its first charter in A.D. 811. It became a town of some importance during the Middle Ages, when many of its present structures were built. Despite this heritage, the town is not another preserved relic of the past but a growing community with its own thriving industries. A visit to Faversham makes a refreshing change from the usual tourist circuit and can easily be combined in the same day with Rochester.

GETTING THERE:

Trains to Faversham leave London's Victoria Station at least twice an hour, the journey taking about 65 minutes. Return service operates until late evening.

By car, Faversham is linked to London via the A-2 and M-2 highways. The distance is 49 miles.

WHEN TO GO:

Good weather is essential for this outdoor trip. Avoid coming on Sundays, Thursdays, or bank holidays, when the Heritage Centre is closed. The colorful outdoor market is held on Fridays and Saturdays.

FOOD AND DRINK:

Faversham is famous for its two breweries, the last still operating in the whole of Kent. These are Shepherd Neame, founded on the same site in 1698, and Fremlin, dating from the 1760s and now part of the Whitbread group. Both make what is called "real ale." Some choice pubs and restaurants are:

> **La Grillade** (Jacobs Yard, Preston St., just north of Heritage Centre) French cuisine. $$

The Parish Church

Recreation Tavern (16 East St., 2 blocks east of the Guildhall)
Quality food in a 16th-century building, self-service. $
The Sun (West St., 1 block west of the Guildhall) Typical 16th-
century pub and a local favorite. $
Phoenix (99 Abbey St., 1 block north of St. Mary's Church) A
cozy 15th-century pub with home-cooked food. $

TOURIST INFORMATION:

The local tourist office, phone (0795) 534-542, is in the Fleur de Lis
Heritage Centre at 13 Preston Street.

SUGGESTED TOUR:

Leaving the **train station** (1), walk down Preston Street to the tourist office and museum. The **Fleur de Lis Heritage Centre** (2) provides
an excellent introduction to Faversham's past and present. Housed in
a former 15th-century inn, it has colorful displays of life in bygone
days and a good audio-visual presentation of the town's history. The
center is open all year, Mondays through Saturdays, from 9:30 a.m. to
1 p.m. and from 2–4:30 p.m., closing at 4 in winter. It is closed on
Sundays, Thursdays, and bank holidays.

Continue down Preston Street and turn left on Market Street. It was in the house at number 12 that King James II was held prisoner by local fishermen when he tried to flee the country in 1688. In a few yards you will come to the **Guildhall** (3), a rather quaint Georgian building set atop 16th-century pillars. An open-air market is held under this on Fridays and Saturdays. Note the interesting town pump at the rear.

Court Street contains many fine 17th- and 18th-century houses. Follow it to Church Street and turn right to the parish church of **St. Mary of Charity** (4), which has a particularly elegant flying spire. Although restored in the 18th century, it retains some Norman arches and windows from earlier times. The misericords in the choir are among the finest in England. Other features unusual for a parish church are the aisled transepts and the 14th-century frescoed pillar. Stroll around the churchyard, in which sheep freely graze, then follow the footpath to Abbey Place, passing the 16th-century old Grammar School.

The famous 15th-century **Arden's House** on the southeast corner of Abbey Place was the scene of a notorious murder in 1551, which became the basis for the first play in English to use a contemporary event as its theme. Published in 1592, *Arden of Feversham* is still in the national repertory. Abbey Street is lined with well-preserved houses dating from the 16th and 17th centuries. Turn right on it and walk down to **Standard Quay** (5). Going past old warehouses, follow the creek until you come to a dilapidated fertilizer works. Pass through an opening in the fence and continue on. All along here you will see interesting old sailing barges, some of which are restored as houseboats, and which still take part in sailing barge races in the summer.

Now return to Abbey Street and make a right at Quay Lane. Cross the bridge and walk out along Front Brents, from which you get a colorful view of the tiny harbor. Faversham's prosperity has always been closely linked with the creek, where ships were once built for the Royal Navy.

From here follow the map past the austere 12th-century Davington Church and down to **Stonebridge Pond** (6), the source of the creek. A path opposite leads to the restored **Chart Gunpowder Mills** (7), the oldest of their kind in the world. Built in the late 18th century, they are the sole remaining link with a local industry that supplied the navy with gunpowder from 1560 to 1934.

Return to the pond and turn right on West Street. In a short distance this becomes a charming pedestrians-only street leading back to the Guildhall.

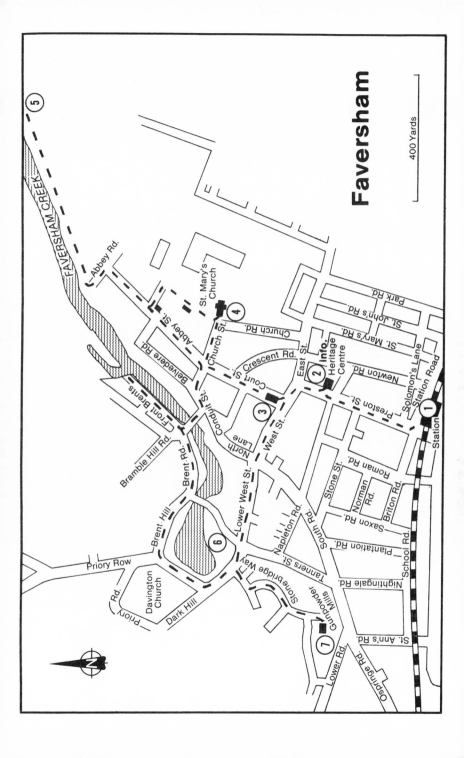

Faversham

400 Yards

Canterbury

Over two thousand years of history have left their mark on Canterbury, a magnet for countless pilgrimages since the 12th century. St. Augustine established the Christian Church in England here as far back as A.D. 597, and in 1170 the martyr Thomas à Becket was murdered in its cathedral. As a convenient place to ford the River Stour, Canterbury was a strategic settlement ever since the Iron Age. Under the name *Durovernum,* the Romans made it an important center of trade in the first century A.D. This status increased during Anglo-Saxon times, when the name was changed to *Cantwarabyrig,* and it became the capital of the Kingdom of Kent. Much of Canterbury's colorful past remains intact today, despite the ravages of Cromwell's troops and the bombs of World War II.

By cutting short the walking tour it is possible to combine this trip with one to Dover, which is nearby on the same highway and rail line.

GETTING THERE:

Trains to Canterbury East Station depart from Victoria Station in London at hourly intervals. The journey takes about 80 minutes. Be sure to get on the right car, as the train splits at Faversham. Return service operates until late evening.

Coaches leave London's Victoria Coach Station twice daily for the two-hour ride to Canterbury.

By car, Canterbury is 58 miles from London via the A-2 and M-2 highways.

WHEN TO GO:

Any day is a good day to visit Canterbury, bearing in mind that the museums are closed on Sundays. A few shops in town close early on Thursdays.

FOOD AND DRINK:

Having attracted pilgrims and their modern counterparts since the Middle Ages, Canterbury has no shortage of restaurants and pubs in all price ranges. Some particularly good choices are:

Seventy-Four (74 Wincheap, 2 blocks southwest of East Station) Regarded as the best restaurant in Canterbury, in a 16th-century house just outside the town center. X: Sat. lunch, Sun. $$$

Tuo e Mio (16 The Borough, opposite the King's School) Noted for its fine Italian cuisine. X: Tues. lunch, Mon. $$$

Waterfield's (5a Best Lane, just northeast of the Weavers' House) In an old house with a view of the river. X: Mon. lunch, Sun. $$

Sweeney Todd's (8 Butchery Lane, near the Roman Pavement) A popular basement restaurant featuring pizza, burgers, salads, and the like. $

Caesar's (46 St. Peter's St., between the Weavers' House and Westgate) A favorite with the young crowd for its salads and burgers. $

TOURIST INFORMATION:

The local tourist office, phone (0227) 66-567, is at 13 Longmarket, just off St. George's Street.

SUGGESTED TOUR:

Leaving **Canterbury East Station** (1), cross the footbridge over the A-2 highway and turn right on the ancient city walls. Dating from the 13th and 14th centuries, these were built on Roman foundations. To your left is Dane John Gardens, a pleasant 18th-century park with a strange mound of unexplained but probably prehistoric origin. Continue atop the walls and turn left by the bus station onto St. George's Street. The tower on the right is all that remains of St. George's Church, where Christopher Marlowe was baptized in 1564.

St. George's Street soon becomes High Street. Stroll down this and make a right into narrow **Mercery Lane,** the traditional pilgrim's approach to the cathedral. During medieval days this was lined with stalls selling healing water from Becket's Well, medallions of St. Thomas, and other mementoes of the pilgrimage. At its far end is the Butter Market, an ancient center of trade. The magnificent **Christchurch Gate,** opposite, dates from the early 16th century and is the main entrance to the cathedral grounds.

Pass through the gate and enter the grounds of **Canterbury Cathedral** (2), the mother church of the Anglican faith throughout the world. For centuries it has been a center of pilgrimage and in a sense still is, although today's visitors are more likely to be tourists. Neither the largest, the tallest, nor the most beautiful of English cathedrals, it nevertheless has an attraction that is second to none.

A cathedral was built on this site by St. Augustine, the first Archbishop of Canterbury, in A.D. 602. This lasted until 1067, when it burned down. The present structure was begun in 1070 and completed in 1503, although little of the earlier work remains.

Enter the cathedral by way of the southwest porch. The lofty nave was built in the Perpendicular style during the 14th century, replacing an inadequate Norman original. Above the crossing you can see up the entire height of the magnificent **Bell Harry Tower,** whose bell is rung every evening for curfew and tolled on the death of a sovereign or an archbishop. A flight of steps to the right of the screen leads to the elevated **choir,** one of the longest in England.

Behind the high altar is the **Trinity Chapel,** which held Becket's tomb until Henry VIII had it demolished and the bones scattered in 1538. The tomb of the only king to be buried at Canterbury, Henry IV, and that of Edward, the Black Prince, are also in this chapel. At the extreme east end is a circular chapel known as the **Corona,** or Becket's Crown. The marble chair in its center is used for the enthronement of every archbishop.

The north aisle leads past the choir to the northwest transept, the scene of the martyrdom. It was here that Archbishop Thomas à Becket was murdered on December 29, 1170. The four knights who committed the deed thought they were carrying out the desire of their king, Henry II, although his part in it is disputed by historians. Henry certainly had reason to get rid of "this turbulent priest," his former friend and ally who had challenged the power of the State. Whatever the rationale behind the killing, it led to the canonization of Becket, the chastisement of Henry II, the role of Canterbury as a place of pilgrimage, and helped further the cause of individual freedom.

The spacious **crypt** is the oldest part of the cathedral, dating from Norman times. Along its south aisle there is a Huguenot chapel where services in French are still held. Becket was first buried at the east end, which was also the scene of Henry II's penance.

Stroll into the early-15th-century **cloisters** by way of the northwest transept. Adjoining it is the chapter house and library. Follow the passageway and turn left into the grounds of the **King's School** (3). Although it was refounded by Henry VIII, the school claims an ancestry going back to the time of St. Augustine, which would make it the oldest in England. The 12th-century Norman staircase near the northwest corner of the Green Court is truly magnificent, as are the views of the cathedral from this point.

Returning, bear left and walk around the rear of the cathedral to the Kent War Memorial Gardens. Go through the gate in the far corner and follow the map to the ruins of **St. Augustine's Abbey** (4). Originally founded in A.D. 598 and rebuilt several times since, it was destroyed by Henry VIII following the Reformation. Excavations have

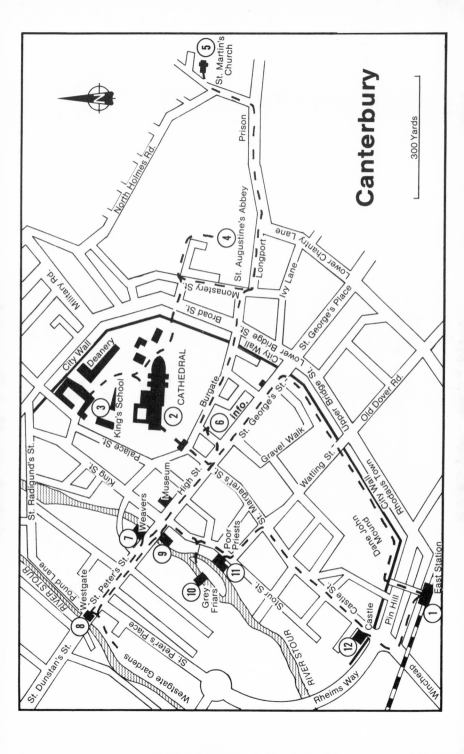

Canterbury

300 Yards

revealed the layout of several buildings including the church, monk's dormitory, kitchen, refectory, and cloisters. The abbey is open Mondays through Saturdays, from 9:30 a.m. to 6:30 p.m.; and on Sundays from 2–6:30 p.m. It closes at 4 p.m. in winter.

Walk back around St. Augustine's College and turn left on Monastery Street, then left again on Longport. Just past the jail make another left to **St. Martin's Church** (5), said to be the oldest church in England still in use. Parts of it date from before the time of St. Augustine and were used by Queen Bertha, Christian wife of King Ethelbert. Explore the interior, noting in particular the Saxon font, then stroll through the tranquil graveyard.

Returning to town via Longport and Church Street, walk down Burgate and turn left into Butchery Lane. In a basement below a modern shopping center is an excavated **Roman pavement** (6), once part of a large villa erected around A.D. 100. It may be seen Mondays through Saturdays, from 10 a.m. to 1 p.m. and from 2–5 p.m., with shorter hours in winter.

Continuing along High Street, you will pass Queen Elizabeth's Guest Chamber, a Tudor house on the left in which the queen entertained her French suitor, the Duke of Alençon. It is now a restaurant. Farther along on the right is the **Royal Museum and Art Gallery,** otherwise known as the Beaney Institute. It has a fine collection of Roman and other antiquities as well as local art, and may be visited Mondays through Saturdays, from 10 a.m. to 5 p.m. The famous **Weavers' House** (7) on the edge of the River Stour was occupied by Huguenot weavers who settled in Canterbury after fleeing France in the 17th century. Now a gift shop, it is open to visitors, who may inspect the old looms and ducking stool, or even take a boat ride on the river.

Walk along St. Peter's Street to the **Westgate** (8). Built in the late 14th century, this imposing fortification once guarded the western approach to Canterbury. Its upper floor served as the city jail until 1829. Now a museum of arms and torture instruments, it is open daily except on Sundays, from 10 a.m. to 1 p.m. and from 2–5 p.m.; with winter hours being 2–4 p.m. There is a superb view from the top.

A stroll through Westgate Gardens is very inviting. Return to St. Peter's and turn right. Opposite the Weavers' is the **Eastbridge Hospital** (9), a well-preserved 12th-century hostel for poor pilgrims. Its crypt, chapel, and hall are open to visitors Mondays through Saturdays, from 10 a.m. to 1 p.m. and from 2–5 p.m.

Turn right on Stour Street and then right again into a tiny lane marked "to Greyfriars." Follow the path onto a small island. The extremely picturesque 13th-century **Greyfriars** (10) is all that remains of the first Franciscan friary in England. From inside you can get a feeling of what monastic life in medieval Canterbury was like.

Interior of Canterbury Cathedral

Just beyond this, also on Stour Street, is the **Poor Priests' Hospital** (11). This 14th-century hostel is now the Canterbury Heritage Museum. Turn left on Beer Cart and right on Castle Street. At its end, opposite the city wall, are the ruins of an 11th-century **Norman castle** (12). Never very effective as a defensive bastion, it was later used as a jail, a coal dump, and a water tank. Take a look inside the doorway and then return to the train station.

Dover

The white cliffs of Dover have marked the gateway of England for over two thousand years. Iron Age men settled on these shores, and so did the Romans, who built their port of *Dubris* in A.D. 43. Strategically, Dover is of paramount importance to Britain, being the closest point to the Continent and only 22 miles from France. It was inevitable that a great fortress would rise here, one that has defended the island nation down to our own times. Today, this massive 12th-century castle is among the leading tourist attractions of England, while the harbor it overlooks is the busiest passenger port in the land.

By getting off to an early start and rushing a bit, a visit to Dover could be combined with one to Canterbury.

GETTING THERE:

Trains to Dover's Priory Station leave at least hourly from either Victoria or Charing Cross stations in London. The journey time is about 1½ hours. Be sure to board the correct car as some trains split en route. Return service operates until mid-evening.

Coaches from London's Victoria Coach Station takes about 2½ hours to reach Dover.

By car, Dover is 74 miles from London either by way of the A-2 and M-2 highways, or the A-20 and M-20 highways.

WHEN TO GO:

Good weather is important for this largely outdoor trip, which may be taken anytime except on major holidays. The castle is closed on Sunday mornings in winter, and some shops close early on Wednesdays. The Roman Painted House is closed on Mondays and from November through March.

FOOD AND DRINK:

Dover has a fairly good selection of restaurants and pubs in all price ranges. Among the better choices are:

Dover Castle

Queen's Moat House (Townwall St., near the tourist office) A modern restaurant in a large hotel. $$
White Cliffs (Marine Parade, on the seafront below the castle) In a pleasant old hotel with a good view of the port. $$
Britannia (Townwall St., near the tourist office) Both a downstairs pub and an upstairs restaurant. $ and $$
Arlington (Snargate St., near the Western Docks) A pub with tasty meals at lunch only. $

TOURIST INFORMATION:

The local tourist office, phone (0304) 205-108, is on Townwall Street, just inland from Marine Parade.

SUGGESTED TOUR:

Leaving **Priory Station** (1), walk down St. Martin's Hill and follow the map to the **bus station** (2) on Pencester Road. Here you can board a bus to the castle, perched dramatically atop a nearby hill.

Dover Castle (3) is by far the finest and most fascinating military structure in England. While it is essentially of Norman construction, parts of its date from Saxon and even Roman times. Brutally strong, its 20-foot-thick walls have withstood sieges during its entire history.

Begin your visit with the **Pharos,** a Roman lighthouse erected about A.D. 50. This is probably the oldest intact building in England. Directly adjacent to it is the Saxon **Church of St. Mary de Castro,** which was heavily restored during the 19th century. Its exact age is unknown, but it may date as far back as the 7th century.

The main part of the castle is its mighty **keep.** Built in 1180 by Henry II to replace earlier structures, it has been continually modified down through the centuries. You can easily spend hours exploring the many rooms and passageways. Be sure to get to the roof, from which there is a fabulous view extending all the way to France in clear weather. A visit to the **tunnel system** beneath the castle, reached from outside the keep, completes your tour. Dover Castle is open daily from 9:30 a.m. to 6:30 p.m., closing at 4 p.m. between mid-October and mid-March. It is also closed on Sunday mornings between October and March.

Return to the town by bus or, since it is downhill, on foot. To do this just follow the path opposite the bus stop, which leads through Victoria Park. Laureston Place and Castle Hill Road will bring you to Castle Street, at the end of which is the Market Square, built over the site of the ancient Roman harbor. From here take King and Bench streets to Marine Parade. Along the way you will pass Townwall Street, where the tourist office is located.

There are splendid views of the harbor from **Marine Parade** (4). For an even closer look, turn right and stroll out on **Prince of Wales Pier** (5). By walking around the Western Docks you can reach **Admiralty Pier** (6), which has the best panorama of all.

Return to Market Square and visit the **Roman Painted House** (7) on New Street. Britain's answer to Pompeii, this excavated 2nd-century ruin has beautifully painted walls and an intact underfloor heating system. It is open from April through October, every day except on Mondays, from 10 a.m. to 5 p.m.

From here follow Cannon Street and Biggin Street to the **Maison Dieu** (8), a 13th-century Pilgrims' hostel that is now part of the Town Hall. It contains some interesting weapons, armor, and stained-glass windows depicting the town's history. Attached to it is the **Dover Museum,** displaying ancient coins and archaeological finds. Visits may be made Mondays through Saturdays, except Wednesdays, from 10 a.m. to 4:45 p.m.

St. Edmund's Chapel (9) on Priory Road is on the way back to the train station. Dating from the 13th century, it ceased religious services in 1544 and was later used as a forge. In 1968 the tiny wayside chapel was re-consecrated and is thought to be the smallest in England in regular use.

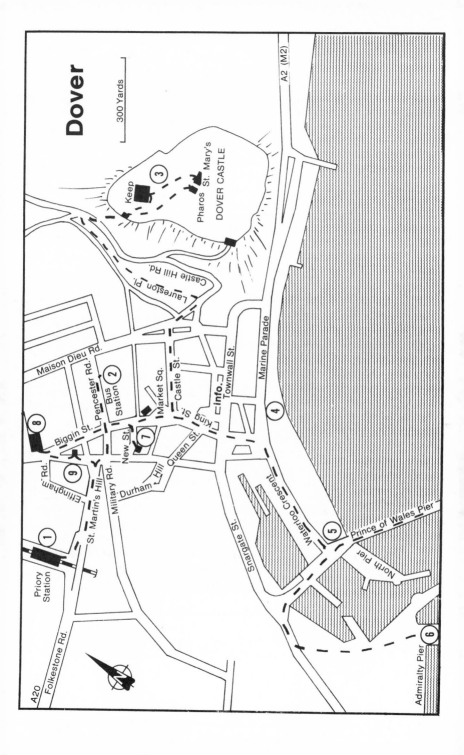

Knole

Knole ranks as one of the largest and most famous of England's stately homes. It is also among the oldest. The building as it stands today was largely begun by Thomas Bouchier, Archbishop of Canterbury in the mid-15th century. It remained a palace for the archbishops until being appropriated by Henry VIII for the Crown. In 1566 Queen Elizabeth I presented the estate to her cousin, Thomas Sackville, whose descendants have lived there ever since.

Sometimes called the "Calendar House," Knole has 365 rooms, 52 staircases, and seven courtyards. Those parts that are open to the public contain a large number of paintings by various artists, magnificent tapestries, and furnishings dating from Elizabethan times. The surrounding park covers a thousand acres of pleasant countryside where tame deer freely roam.

As a bonus to this trip, a short side excursion can be made to nearby Ightham Mote, a very different and thoroughly enchanting early-14th-century moated manor house. Alternatively, you can visit Chartwell, the home of Sir Winston Churchill for over 40 years. If you plan to take either of these options, please note the opening hours carefully. Minibus tours to two or three of the attractions are operated every day except Mondays, between April and October. These depart around 10 a.m. from the Sevenoaks train station. Details and reservations are available by calling the Sevenoaks tourist office.

This trip can easily be combined in the same day with one to Tunbridge Wells by visiting only Knole and then continuing about 11 miles south on the same rail or highway route.

GETTING THERE:

Trains leave London's Charing Cross Station at frequent intervals for Sevenoaks, the town in which Knole is located. The journey time is about 32 minutes, and return service operates until late evening.

By car, follow routes A-20 and A-225 direct to Sevenoaks, a distance of 25 miles southeast of London.

WHEN TO GO:

Knole is open from April through October, on Wednesdays through Saturdays plus bank holidays, from 11 a.m. to 5 p.m.; and on Sundays from 2–5 p.m.

Knole House

Ightham Mote is open from late March until the end of October; on Mondays, Wednesdays, Thursdays, Fridays, and Sundays, from 11 a.m. to 5 p.m.

Chartwell is open from March through November on Wednesdays, Saturdays, and Sundays, from 11 a.m. to 4 p.m. Between April and the end of October it is also open on Tuesdays and Thursdays from 12 noon to 5 p.m., and on Saturdays, Sundays, and bank holidays from 11 a.m. to 5 p.m.

The above times should be confirmed with the Sevenoaks tourist office.

FOOD AND DRINK:

No food is available at either Knole or Ightham Mote, but you could bring along a picnic lunch. There is a restaurant at Chartwell, and there are a few restaurants and pubs in Sevenoaks, of which the following are recommended:

> **Royal Oak** (Upper High St., just beyond the turn into Knole Park) Intimate dining, with French cuisine. X: Sat. lunch, Sun. eve. $$

> **Le Chantecler** (43 High St., not far from the tourist office) Continental dining in the town. X: Sat. lunch, Sun., Mon. $$

Ightham Mote

TOURIST INFORMATION:

For all details contact the Sevenoaks Tourist Information Centre on Buckhurst Lane, just off High Street, between the train station and Knole Park. Their phone number is (0732) 45-03-05.

SUGGESTED TOUR:

Leaving the **Sevenoaks train station** (1), you can either walk or take a taxi the one-mile distance to **Knole.** If you walk, just turn right and continue straight ahead until you come to a sign pointing to Knole Park on the left. Go through the park to the **manor house** (2) and take the hour-long guided tour. A leisurely stroll in the surrounding deer park and gardens is absolutely delightful.

Those wanting to visit **Ightham Mote** (3) can get there by walking the four-mile distance, which is completely over pleasant country lanes, or by returning to Sevenoaks and taking a bus or taxi. If you go by bus, take one that follows route A-25 and get off at Ightham Common, then walk the remaining mile-and-a-half. The map shows the way on foot or by bus.

If you would rather see **Chartwell** (4), take bus number 483 from Sevenoaks to Westerham, then walk 1½ miles to the estate by following the map. You could, of course, take a taxi all the way. The house contains many personal mementoes of the great prime minister in rooms that remain as he left them. There is also a good selection of Churchill's paintings in his garden studio.

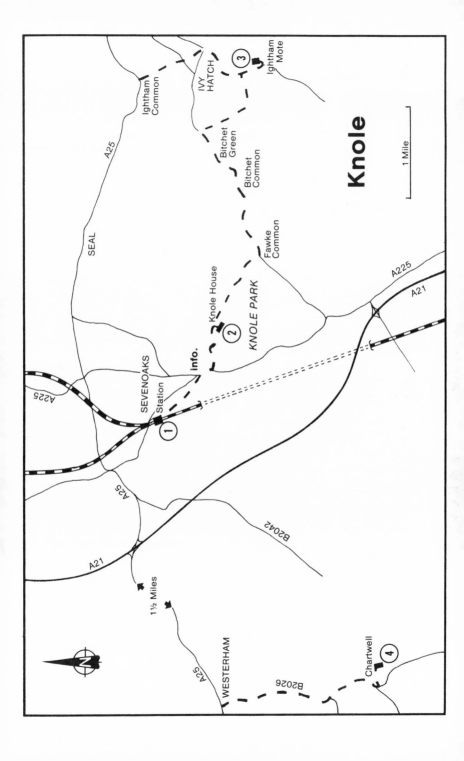

Knole

1 Mile

Romney, Hythe & Dymchurch

A ride on the Romney, Hythe & Dymchurch Railway is a pure delight. There are no famous sights along its 14-mile length, just the exhilarating joy of being hauled across the Romney Marshes aboard a miniature steam train. This fun-filled daytrip is the perfect antidote to a steady diet of cathedrals, castles, and stately homes.

Opened in 1927, the railway is one of the most popular attractions in southern England. Its one-third-scale locomotives are faithful replicas of famous engines that once served on the main lines. Over 300,000 passengers, not all of them children by any means, are carried each year in the diminutive coaches. Join them in the fun and you'll be glad you did.

GETTING THERE:

Trains leave twice an hour from London's Charing Cross Station for Folkestone Central Station. The journey time is about 80 minutes, and service is reduced on Sundays. Some trains split en route. Return trains run until mid-evening. From Folkestone you can travel the five miles by bus or taxi to Hythe, where the steam line begins.

Coaches go directly to Hythe from London's Victoria Coach Station. The ride takes about 2½ hours.

By car, take the A-20 and M-20 roads to Newingreen/Stanford, then the A-261 to Hythe. The total distance is about 68 miles southeast of London.

WHEN TO GO:

Good weather is necessary to really enjoy this trip. The Romney, Hythe, & Dymchurch Railway operates daily from Easter to the end of September, and on weekends in March and October. Service is more frequent during the peak summer months.

FOOD AND DRINK:

Snacks are available at the Hythe and New Romney stations, and drinks are served at any time on the miniature bar car attached to some of the trains. Some choice restaurants and pubs in Hythe, New Romney, Dungeness, and Folkestone are:

> **Butt of Sherry** (5 Theatre St., Hythe) A wine bar with traditional English fare. X: Sun., Mon. eve. $

Steaming Along on the R, H & D
(Photo courtesy of R, H & D Railway)

Country Kitchen (18 High St., New Romney) Light lunches not far from the station. X: Sun. $

The Pilot (on the beach at Dungeness) An unusual pub noted for fish and chips. $

La Tavernetta (Leaside Court, Clifton Gardens, near Castle Hill Ave. and The Leas in Folkestone) Italian cuisine. X: Sun. $$

Emilio's Portofino (124a Sandgate Rd., 3 blocks southwest of the bus station in Folkestone) Another Italian restaurant. X: Mon. $$

TOURIST INFORMATION:

For information about the miniature rail line call their office in New Romney at (0679) 62-353. The tourist office in Folkestone, phone (0303) 58-594, is near the harbor, with a branch on Sandgate Road, phone (0303) 53-840.

SUGGESTED TOUR:

Those coming by train will begin their trip at **Folkestone Central Station** (1). From here follow the map to the **Folkestone bus station** (2), a few blocks away. Board a bus for Hythe and ask to be left off at the Light Railway Station. You could, of course, take a taxi directly from Folkestone Central to Hythe, a distance of about five miles.

The Romney, Hythe & Dymchurch Light Railway Station in **Hythe** (3) is next to the Royal Military Canal, which was built as a defense

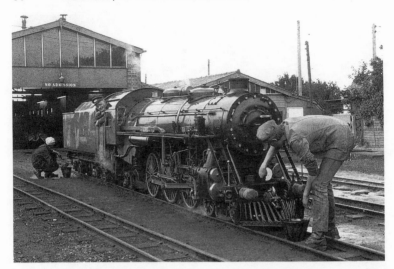

A Locomotive Being Serviced at New Romney
(Photo courtesy of R, H & D Railway)

during the Napoleonic Wars. A short walk along its banks is a pleasant way to while away some time if you have a wait before the next train departure. Take careful look at the posted schedule and decide whether you want to go just to New Romney or make a stop there and then continue on all the way to Dungeness. The fares vary with the distance traveled. Be sure to purchase a round-trip ticket. Note also that a very few of the miniature trains are hauled by diesel traction, so you might want to wait for steam.

The ride from Hythe to New Romney takes about 35 minutes, stopping at Dymchurch and Jefferstone Lane along the way. **New Romney** (4) is the headquarters of the railway and has several interesting things to see, including yards, engine shops, and a fascinating model-train exhibition. There is also a snack bar with hot meals, and a gift shop.

Continuing on to **Dungeness** (5), the rails follow very close to the sea. This is a lovely and sparsely inhabited region, a perfect spot for the nuclear power plant at the end of the line. Getting off there, you may visit the lifeboat station and perhaps climb to the top of the old lighthouse.

Those traveling back to London via Folkestone will probably want to see a bit of that town before they leave. From the bus station it is an easy walk to **The Leas** (6), a promenade with magnificent maritime views. The **harbor** (7) is in the oldest part of town. Return via the quaint and narrow High Street, then head back to Central station by bus, taxi, or on foot.

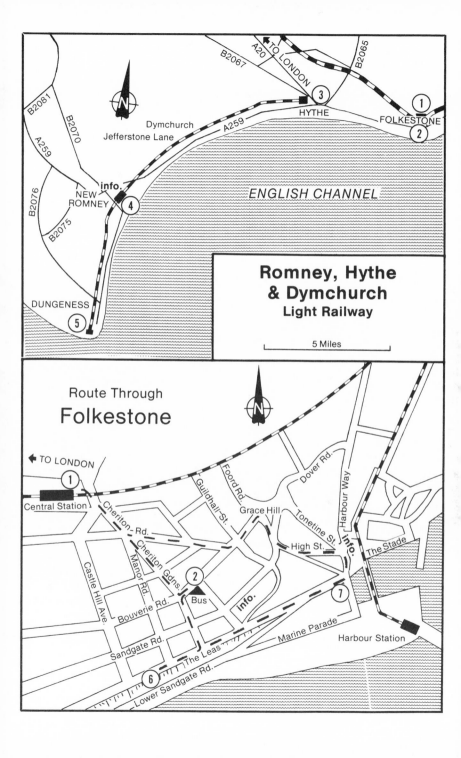

Rye

A relic from the Middle Ages, the once-great seaport of Rye has been stranded ever since its harbor silted up in the 16th century. Today, only small craft can sail the two miles up the River Rother to the town's docks. In a way this is fortunate, as it left England with a well-preserved medieval port that still clings to its salty past. Rye is alive with the smell of the sea, and working fishermen still walk its ancient streets, side by side with their many visitors. It easily ranks among the prettiest towns in Britain, and is one of the most enjoyable for tourists.

This trip can be combined with one to nearby Hastings, easily reached by rail, bus, or car.

GETTING THERE:

Trains depart London's Charing Cross or Victoria stations frequently for Ashford, where you change to a local for Rye. The total journey takes less than two hours. Return trains run until mid-evening. It is also practical to go by way of Hastings. Service is reduced on Sundays and holidays.

By car, the shortest route is to take the A-21 from London to Flimwell and change to the A-268. Rye is 63 miles southeast of London.

WHEN TO GO:

Rye may be savored on a fine day in any season. Many of the shops close early on Tuesdays.

FOOD AND DRINK:

As you would expect of such an ancient and frequently visited place, Rye has plenty of quaint old inns, tea shops, and pubs. Some choices are:

> **Flushing Inn** (Market St., near the Town Hall) A 15th-century inn noted for its seafood. X: Mon. eve., Tues., Jan. $$ and $$$

> **Mermaid Inn** (Mermaid St.) An old smugglers' haunt from the 15th century. World famous. $$

Along Church Square

Simmons (68 The Mint) An elegant restaurant in a 15th-century house. X: Sat. lunch, Sun. eve., Mon., Feb. $$

Fletcher's House (Lion St., just north of St. Mary's Church) Light meals in an historic medieval house. $$

Elizabethan Restaurant (Cinque Ports St., near the tourist office) A Tudor setting for lunch and teas. X: Sun. $

Standard Inn (The Mint, near Needles Passage) A delightful pub with meals. $

TOURIST INFORMATION:

The local tourist office, phone (0797) 22-22-93, is at 48 Cinque Ports Street.

SUGGESTED TOUR:

Leaving the **train station** (1), walk straight ahead and turn left on the Cinque Ports Street. In a few yards you will pass the tourist office on the left and, on the right, remnants of the original 14th-century town walls, just behind a parking lot. Continue on to the **Land Gate** (2), the only remaining town gate of the three that once protected Rye. It was probably constructed about 1340 and originally contained machinery for a drawbridge over the town ditch.

Walk uphill along Hilder's Cliff. From here there are marvelous views across the Romney Marsh. Much of this lowland was once an open ocean, but that was before the sea receded as the River Rother silted up and the tides washed countless pebbles onto the shore.

At the intersection make a right and walk down Conduit Hill a few yards to the **Augustine Friary** (3), commonly known as The Monastery. Originally built in 1379, it was used in the 16th century as a refuge for persecuted French Huguenots. Today it houses a pottery that you can visit. Now return to High Street and follow it one more block past the Old Grammar School, erected in 1636 and immortalized by Thackeray. Opposite this is the 400-year-old George Hotel.

A left onto Lion Street leads past Fletcher's House, once a vicarage and now a tea shop. The dramatist John Fletcher was born here in 1579. At the corner of Market Street stands the **Town Hall** (4), which contains some interesting artifacts, including the gruesome gibbet cage with the remains of a notorious 18th-century murderer who was executed in the town. Ask to be shown these.

In a few more steps you will come to **St. Mary's Church** (5), first erected between 1150 and 1300. Facing the top of Lion Street is the church clock, the oldest in England still functioning with its original works. Two figures above the clockface strike the quarter hours but not the hours. Between them is a plaque that proclaims, "For our time is a very shadow that passeth away." A climb to the top of the tower is absolutely fascinating and well worth the effort. The extremely narrow stairway leads to the bell-ringing room where various combinations of changes are posted. In the same room is the venerable clock mechanism, from which hangs an 18-foot-long pendulum. A ladder goes to the bell room itself, and another to the roof. From here there is an unsurpassed view of the entire area. A visit to the church interior is also worthwhile.

Across from the churchyard there is a curious oval-shaped brick **water reservoir,** built in 1735 but no longer used. Bear right and stroll down to **Ypres Tower** (6). Pronounced *Wipers*, this is the oldest existing structure in town. Largely unchanged since it was first constructed as a defensive fortification around 1249, it ceased to have any military value in later years and was sold to one John de Ypres who used it as a private habitation. The town bought it back in 1513 for use as a jail, a function it served until 1865, when it became a mortuary. The tower is now the **Rye Museum,** housing artifacts of the town's history. A visit to its various rooms and cells is very interesting and may be made between Easter and mid-October, any day from 10:30 a.m. to 1 p.m. and from 2:15–5:30 p.m. Just below this is the **Gun Garden,** an emplacement for artillery pieces that once helped defend England's shores.

Walk down Church Square, an exceptionally lovely cobbled street. This leads to Watchbell Street, whose name derives from the warning

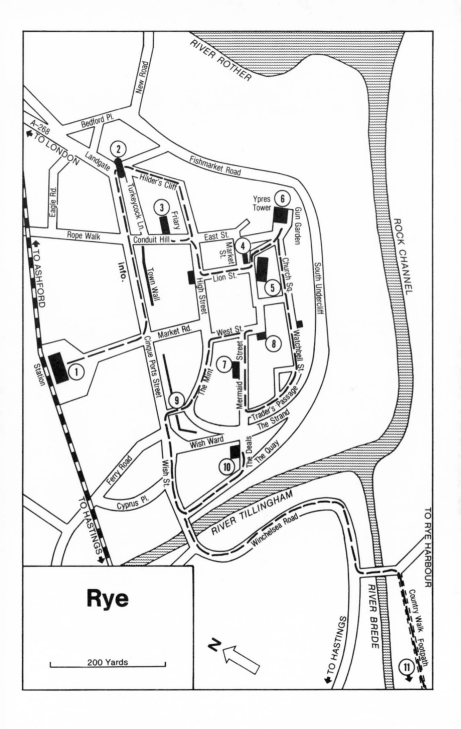

St. Mary's Church

bell once housed there. Along the way you will pass a Spanish-style Catholic church. At the end is the Lookout, overseeing the harbor.

From here, Traders Passage leads to Mermaid Street, quite possibly the most picturesque thoroughfare in all England. Go uphill to the **Mermaid Inn** (7), a famous hiding place for smugglers and highwaymen, first built in the late 15th century and much altered over the years. It is now a hotel and restaurant. Walk through a passage into the courtyard. Now continue up Mermaid Street and turn right on West Street. Here, where the street bends, you will find the **Lamb House** (8), formerly the residence of the Lamb family, which for a long time provided many of the mayors of Rye. Henry James lived in this house from 1897 until 1916, writing many of his best-known novels there. It is now owned by the National Trust and receives visitors on Wednesdays and Saturdays, April through October, from 2–5:30 p.m.

Stroll back down West Street to High Street and turn left to The Mint, then make a right into **Needles Passage** (9). This narrow path takes you through a gap in the old town wall and down a few steps to Cinque Ports Street. Turn left here and follow Wish Street.

Another left, just before the bridge, leads onto The Strand, where you will find an interesting group of 19th-century **warehouses** (10)

Mermaid Street

that bear testament to the town's past as a trading port. The **Rye Town Model,** a highly entertaining sound-and-light show, is held in one of these every half-hour, daily from 10:30 a.m. until 12:30 p.m. and from 2–4:30 p.m. Don't miss this special treat. From here it is only a few steps back to Mermaid Street.

Before leaving Rye you may want to take a delightful walk in the countryside. From the bridge at the foot of Wish Street it is only about 1½ miles to **Camber Castle** (11), built by Henry VIII in the 16th century. To get there just follow the map to the public footpath along the River Brede. This trail leads through some pleasant sheep-grazing land and is well marked.

Tunbridge Wells

You won't find any medieval or even Tudor buildings in Tunbridge Wells, which remained a forest until the discovery of its mineral springs in 1606. Soon after that, however, the nobility from London began coming in droves. An elegant spa developed, attracting aristocrats down through the days of Queen Victoria. Like Bath, Tunbridge Wells reached its peak under the guidance of that 18th-century dandy, Richard "Beau" Nash, who as Master of Ceremonies organized balls, concerts, and other entertainments for the smart set. Alas, fashion is fickle, and by the time of the Regency many of its patrons had switched their allegiance to upstart Brighton.

Today's Tunbridge Wells is still a very lovely place, retaining much of the style that made it famous. The Pantiles, a delightfully romantic 18th-century promenade adjoining the springs, could very well be considered the most beautiful urban street in England. For the more adventurous, there are numerous possibilities for walks in the nearby countryside. Though its days of greatness have faded, the town offers a fascinating glimpse into a gracious past.

This trip can easily be combined with one to Knole, Battle, or Hastings, which are on the same rail line.

GETTING THERE:
Trains to Tunbridge Wells leave frequently from London's Charing Cross Station, with reduced service on Sundays and holidays. The trip takes about one hour. Return trains run until mid-evening.

Coaches operated by the Green Line depart from Buckingham Palace Road by Victoria Station in London for the two-hour trip to Tunbridge Wells.

By car, Tunbridge Wells is 36 miles southeast of London via the A-21 and A-26 roads.

WHEN TO GO:
You can make this trip at any time when the weather is good. Most of the shops close early on Wednesdays.

FOOD AND DRINK:
Tunbridge Wells has a fairly good selection of restaurants and pubs.

The Pantiles

Some choices are:

Thackeray's House (85 London Road, 5 blocks northwest of the train station) Located in an historic house and regarded as the best in town. X: Sun., Mon., late Aug. $$$

Buster Browns (155 Camden Road, a few blocks northeast of the art museum) American-style food from burgers to steaks. $ and $$

Delicious (14 Mount Pleasant Road, between the station and the art museum) A popular self-service place for light meals. $

TOURIST INFORMATION:

The tourist office, phone (0892) 26-121, is in the Town Hall on Mount Pleasant Road.

SUGGESTED TOUR:

Leaving **Central Station** (1), turn right and follow High Street to Chapel Place. This leads to **The Pantiles** (2), an 18th-century pedestrian walk sheltered by lime trees that has scarcely changed since Regency days. Its name derives from the square clay tiles with which it was paved in 1700. The original chalybeate (iron-impregnated) spring

The Bath House

is under the porch of the Bath House at the northern end. You may sample its faintly rusty-tasting water, served from a traditional dipper. There are many elegant shops in the area selling antiques, books, gifts, and the like.

Strolling along, you will come to the delightful Musick Gallery above a small shop; the Corn Exchange with its statue of Ceres, the goddess of agriculture; and the Royal Victoria, once an inn and now the Assembly Rooms. Queen Victoria stayed there while still a princess. It was her visits as well as those of other royalty which allowed the town to be known as Royal Tunbridge Wells, a title it still affects.

Return to Chapel Place and visit the **Church of King Charles the Martyr** (3), whose name reflects the local Stuart sympathies. Built in 1678, it is the oldest in town and has an outstanding ceiling of ornamental plasterwork.

From here follow the map to **Calverley Grounds** (4), a beautiful town park. Calverley Park Crescent, just beyond, is somewhat reminiscent of Bath when seen from the garden side.

Walk over to the **Museum and Art Gallery** (5) on Mount Pleasant Road. Here you will see an excellent collection of Victoriana, local crafts, toys, costumes, and assorted bygones. It is closed on Sundays. The tourist information office, in the Town Hall, can furnish you with maps for nearby country walks. A fine way to spend the remainder of your time is to take a stroll through **The Common** (6), a 250-acre park with unusual rock formations.

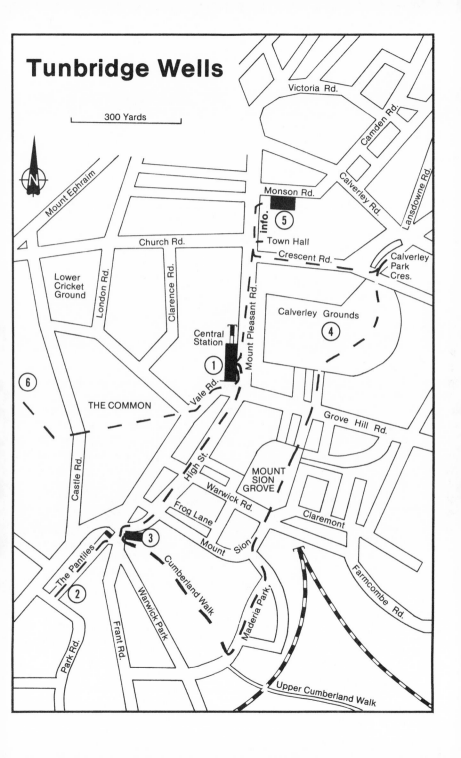

Battle

The Battle of Hastings was probably the most significant event in English history. It was fought on that fateful day in 1066, not at Hastings, but on a hill six miles inland where the attractive village of Battle now stands. Visitors may wander around the fields and, with the help of explanatory signs, re-create in their minds the conflict that signaled England's entry into European civilization. Also waiting to be explored are the ruins of the great abbey begun by William the Conqueror to commemorate the event.

The story of the Battle of Hastings is well documented by the famous Bayeux Tapestry, a replica of which is in the Battle Museum. Briefly, what happened is that the childless King Edward of England promised the throne to his cousin, Duke William of Normandy. He even sent Harold Godwinson, his brother-in-law, to France to confirm the pledge. Upon the death of King Edward, however, Harold took the crown himself. Feeling betrayed, William assembled a mighty army and invaded England. Meanwhile, Harold was successfully fighting off a third claimant to the throne, the king of Norway, at Stamford Bridge near York. On hearing of Duke William's invasion, he rushed his tired troops 200 miles south and engaged the Normans at Battle. The two armies were nearly matched in strength. Harold, occupying the higher ground, might have won except for a brilliant ruse on the part of William, who feigned retreat and trapped the English on the lower ground. By the end of that long, bloody day of October 14th, 1066, Harold lay dead and the sun set forever on Anglo-Saxon England.

It is possible to combine this daytrip with one to either Hastings, Tunbridge Wells, or Knole.

GETTING THERE:

Trains to Battle depart London's Charing Cross station at least hourly, with slightly reduced service on Sundays and holidays. The journey takes about 75 minutes, and return trains run until mid-evening.

Ruins of Battle Abbey

Coaches leave London's Victoria Coach Station once a day during the summer, arriving in Battle 2½ hours later.

By car, Battle is 57 miles southeast of London via the A-21 and A-2100 roads.

WHEN TO GO:
You can visit Battle at any time during good weather. The abbey and battlefield are open daily all year round, except for a few major holidays, closing only on off-season Sunday mornings.

FOOD AND DRINK:
Battle has a good selection of restaurants and pubs, including:

Bayeux (31 Mount St., north of the abbey) Noted for its fine food. X: Mon. lunch, Sun. $$$

Blacksmiths (43 High St., north of the abbey) A friendly ambiance in a medieval building. X: Mon., early Sept. $$

Pilgrims' Rest (opposite the Abbey Gatehouse) Lunch in a 15th-century half-timbered house. $$

Chequers (Lower Lake, between the station and the abbey) A restaurant and pub in a 16th-century inn. $ and $$

TOURIST INFORMATION:
The tourist office, phone (04246) 37-21, is at 88 High Street.

SUGGESTED TOUR:
Leaving the **railway station** (1), a Victorian Gothic structure dating from 1853, turn right and follow Lower Lake and Upper Lake to The Green. On your left you will pass the abbey wall. The **Abbey Gatehouse** (2), one of the finest in England, was built in 1338.

Enter the grounds to the right of the gatehouse and follow the sign marked for a one-mile country walk around the **Battlefield** (3). The trail is exceptionally lovely and would be worth taking even without its historic significance. All along the way there are signs explaining the progress of the battle.

The origins of the **Abbey** (4) date from a vow made by William the Conqueror on the day of the battle to build a church on the site if God led him to victory. This promise was kept, with the high altar erected on the very spot where Harold fell. The abbey continued to grow until being disbanded by Henry VIII in 1539 and given to his Master of the Horse, who destroyed most of the buildings. The only structure still fully intact is now used as a girls' school and cannot be visited. Of the ruins, the most interesting is the **Dorter,** or monks' dormitory. Walk out on the nearby terrace for a good overall view of the battlefield. The abbey and battlefield are open Mondays through Saturdays, from 9:30 a.m. to 6:30 p.m.; and on Sundays from 11 a.m. to 6:30 p.m. They close at 4 p.m. between mid-October and mid-March, and do not open on Sundays until 2 p.m. between October and the end of March. They are also closed on a few major holidays.

Across The Green is the **Battle Museum** (5), which has models explaining how the battle was fought. Also on display are a copy of the Bayeux Tapestry, several ancient coins, and various other historical items. It is open from Easter to early October, Mondays through Saturdays, from 10 a.m. to 1 p.m. and from 2–5 p.m.; and on Sundays from 2:30–5:30 p.m.

A stroll up High Street is worthwhile for a look at the changing house styles, some of which date from the Middle Ages. Returning to the train station, you will pass **St. Mary's Church** (6), with its Norman nave and fine 15th-century tower.

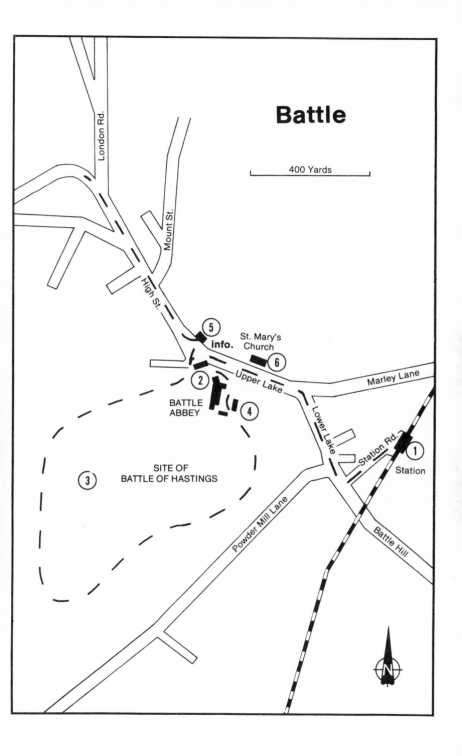

Hastings

An intriguing combination of past and present, Hastings has managed to maintain its heritage while prospering as a modern resort. In a sense it is really two towns split neatly down the middle.

With origins going back to the 7th century, Hastings became one of the Cinque Ports during the time of Edward the Confessor. It had a harbor then, which silted up during the 12th century, never to be successfully rebuilt. William the Conqueror invaded the town in 1066 after landing his Norman troops at nearby Pevensey Bay. The famous Battle of Hastings was fought a few days later on a hill six miles to the northwest, the site of today's village of Battle. During the Hundred Years War of the 14th century the town was repeatedly pillaged by the French. It survived as a fishing village, a role it still plays, and in the 19th century became the popular resort it is today.

This trip can easily be combined with one to either Rye, Battle, Tunbridge Wells, or Knole as there are excellent rail and road connections.

GETTING THERE:

Trains to Hastings leave from London's Charing Cross Station at hourly intervals. The journey takes about 1½ hours, and return service operates until mid-evening.

Coaches leave at least daily from Victoria Coach Station in London for the 2½-hour ride to Hastings.

By car, Hastings is 63 miles southeast of London via the A-21 highway.

WHEN TO GO:

Being a seaside resort, Hastings is best visited during the summer. Most of the sights are open from Easter to late September. Good weather is essential to enjoy this trip fully.

FOOD AND DRINK:

You can find any kind of food in Hastings. Some choice establishments are:

> **Röser's** (64 Eversfield Place, near Hastings Pier) Elegant dining, with luncheon specials. X: Sat. lunch, Sun. $$ and $$$

Beached Fishing Boats

Judge's (51 High St., in the Old Town) A cozy place with traditional English fare. X: Sun., Mon. $

First In, Last Out (14 High St., in the Old Town) A pub with
meals and a good selection of beers. X: Mon. lunch. $

TOURIST INFORMATION:

The local tourist office, phone (0424) 42-42-42, is at 4 Robertson
Terrace, between the pier and the castle. During the summer there is
also a branch near the net shops.

SUGGESTED TOUR

Leaving the **train station** (1), follow Havelock Road and Castle Street
to Marine Parade. Continue up George Street to the **West Hill Lift,**
which will spare you a climb to the castle. From the top of the hill,
bear left to the cliff overlooking the beach for a marvelous view.

Hastings Castle (2) was built by William the Conqueror shortly
after the Battle of Hastings. Now little more than a romantic ruin, it is
still very much worth exploring. Be sure to take the guided tour through
the underground dungeons. The castle is open daily from Easter until
the end of September, from 10 a.m. to 5 p.m.

Stroll over to **St. Clement's Caves** (3), an extensive and somewhat
bizarre network of rambling subterranean passages that are partly
natural and partly man-made. They were reputedly used in centuries

past by smugglers, and played a role as bomb shelters during World War II. A guide will lead you through the labyrinth during about the same hours that the castle is open.

The most interesting part of Hastings is its **Old Town,** a picturesque fishermen's quarter of narrow streets and ancient buildings. Descend into it via Exmouth Place and turn left on Hill Street. **St. Clement's Church** (4) dates from the 14th century. Two cannon balls are lodged in the south wall of its tower, the one on the right being the result of a French bombardment in the late 17th century. The other one was put there just to balance things off. Inside, there are some fine stained-glass windows and two superb old brasses.

Walk down to High Street and turn left to the Old Town Hall, now the **Museum of Local History** (5). Life-size mannequins provide a touch of the past while other displays are concerned with the Battle of Hastings, the story of the Cinque Ports, and smuggling—once a major vocation in these parts. The museum is open between Easter and the end of September, Mondays through Saturdays, from 10 a.m. to 1 p.m. and from 2–5 p.m.

Continuing up High Street with its Tudor homes on the left, you will come to the Stables Theatre, which at one time housed horses for the 18th-century Old Hastings House at the top of the street.

Return by way of All Saints' Street. Destroyed by the French in 1377, All Saints' Church was rebuilt in the 15th century. Inside, there is a well-preserved mural from that time depicting the Last Judgement. Farther along, on the left, is the Piece of Cheese, a peculiar wedge-shaped house that resembles its name.

Probably the best-known sight in Hastings is of its **Net Shops** (6), an extraordinary group of tall black wooden sheds used by fishermen to store their nets. The unusual shape, unchanged since Elizabethan times, was dictated by high rents on the available ground between the sea and cliff. Next to this is the fishmarket, a place where local fishermen sell the day's catch right off the boat.

The **Fishermen's Museum** (7) on Rock-a-Nore Road houses the *Enterprise,* the last fishing vessel to be built in Hastings before the local shipyards closed in 1909. It is typical of the luggers, a style of wide boats with thick bottoms designed to be beached in these harborless waters. Like most of the Hastings luggers, she ferried men back from Dunkirk in that heroic rescue of 1940. There are other fascinating items in the museum, which is open daily except Saturdays, mid-May through September, from 10:30 a.m. to 12:30 p.m. and from 2:30–5:30 p.m.

Just up the road a few yards is the **Shipwreck Heritage Centre,** where over 3,000 years of maritime history are illustrated with exhibitions of underwater treasures. There is a spectacular audio-visual show

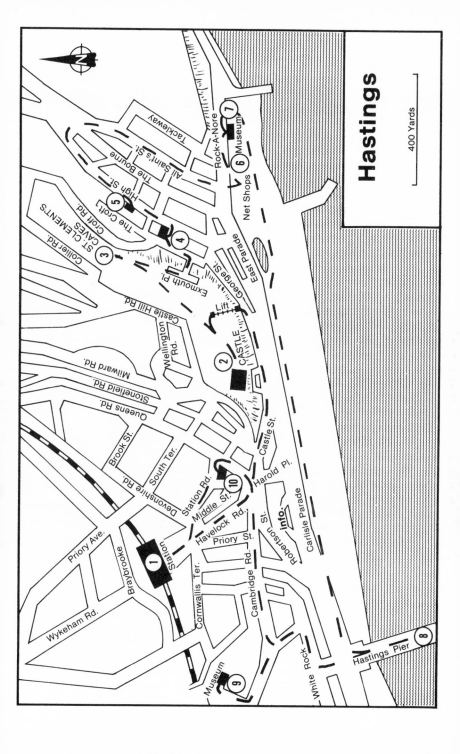

Hastings

400 Yards

The Net Shops at Hastings

and working radar equipment allowing you to monitor shipping activity in the English Channel. Visits may be made daily between the beginning of March and the end of October, from 10 a.m. to 6 p.m., closing at 5 p.m. in March, April, May, and October.

From here you can stroll back along the shore. The character quickly changes to that of a resort as you pass a small boating lake and amusement area. **Hastings Pier** (8) has the usual fun and games. Beyond it, to the west, lies the more elegant St. Leonards, which developed in the early 19th century.

The **Museum and Art Gallery** (9), on the way back to the train station, is worth a stop. It has interesting collections of Sussex ironwork, local ceramics, and a fantastic pavilion from a 19th-century Indian Colonial palace. It is open Mondays through Saturdays from 10 a.m. to 1 p.m. and from 2–5 p.m.; and on Sundays from 3–5 p.m.

The **Town Hall** (10) on Queens Road displays the renowned 80-yard-long **Hastings Embroidery,** depicting events in British history from the Battle of Hastings to modern times. There is also a scale model of the battle and a collection of dolls in period costumes. You can see them all Mondays through Saturdays, from 10 a.m. to 5 p.m., during the summer; and Mondays through Fridays, from 11:30 a.m. to 3:30 p.m. the rest of the year. From here it is only a short stroll back to the train station.

Bluebell

The glorious Age of Steam is alive and well on the Bluebell Railway! People who love old trains will rejoice in this delightful daytrip as they ride across the unspoiled countryside in antique coaches hauled by locomotives that date as far back as 1872.

No mere amusement, the Bluebell was a working standard-gauge branch line from 1882 until 1958, when it closed for economic reasons. Preservation by a dedicated band of amateurs began the following year, and since 1960 the railway has become one of the most popular attractions in southeastern England. Being a non-profit organization staffed largely by volunteers has allowed it to devote much of its income to improvements. The Bluebell's growing collection of locomotives and rolling stock is equaled only by the National Railway Museum in York. Its two stations are beautifully restored relics of another era. You may have seen these before since they are frequently featured in film and television productions. As an extra bonus, the National Trust's magnificent 18th-century Sheffield Park Garden is within easy walking distance.

GETTING THERE:

Trains leave frequently from London's Victoria Station for the 50-minute ride to Haywards Heath, with returns until late evening. From there you can take a local bus or taxi to Sheffield Park Station, where you board the Bluebell Railway. A special bargain combination ticket covering both the bus and the steam train is available at certain times between Easter and September. Details concerning this or other information about the Bluebell schedules can be had at the British Rail information office in London's Victoria Station, phone (01) 928-5100.

Coaches make special excursions in summer from London's Victoria Coach station directly to Sheffield Park Station. For details, call the coach station in London at (01) 730-0202.

By car, take the A-23 and A-22 south from London, going past East Grinsted, then the A-275 to Sheffield Park Station. The total distance is about 45 miles.

WHEN TO GO:

Open all year, the Bluebell Railway operates daily in summer; on Saturdays, Sundays, and Wednesdays in spring and fall; and on Sun-

Locomotive at Sheffield Park Station

days only, in winter. This is a particularly nice trip to make on a week-end, when steam activity is at its peak.

FOOD AND DRINK:

Complete inexpensive meals and snacks are available at the new buffet ($) at Sheffield Park Station. The wonderful Victorian refreshment room ($) on platform 2 at the Horsted Keynes Station serves draft beer and other beverages during pub hours, and has snacks and other refreshments at all times.

TOURIST INFORMATION:

For current information about the Bluebell Railway and connecting bus services, call the railway at (082-572) 23-70. You can also check the British Rail information office in London's Victoria Station, phone (01) 928-5100. BritRail Passes are not accepted on the steam train.

SUGGESTED TOUR:

Those coming by train will begin at the **Haywards Heath Station** (1), where a special inclusive bus and Bluebell Rail ticket can be purchased. Buses on route 769 leave from the front of the station or nearby and go direct to Sheffield Park Station. These operate on Sundays from Easter to late September, and daily from late July to late August. Inquire at the train station. At other times you can take route 169 (week-

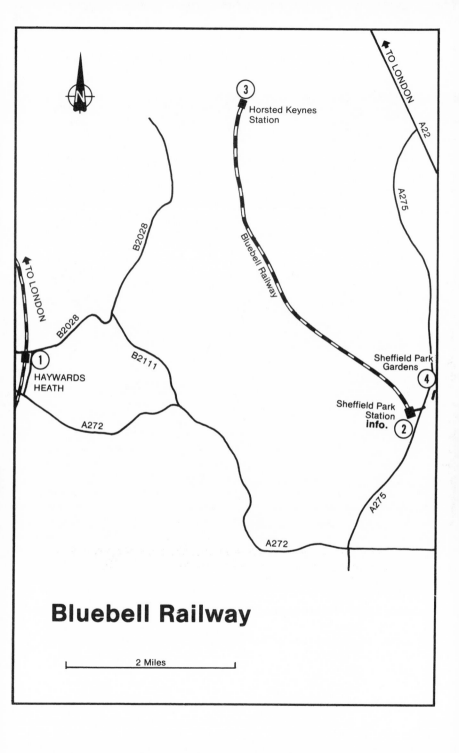

Bluebell Railway

Horsted Keynes Station

days only, marked for Uckfield) from the bus stop on Perrymount Road, one block away on the hill to the right. A walk of over one mile may be necessary as not all of these go to Sheffield Park Station. Ask the driver. Alternatively, you could take a taxi for the eight-mile trip.

Sheffield Park Station (2) was erected in 1882 and is typical of Victorian country stations. Its locomotive sheds, which you may visit, house a large collection of steam engines ranging in age from over 100 years old to some built as late as 1952. On the far platform there is a museum of railway relics.

Now board the train and enjoy the five-mile ride to **Horsted Keynes** (3), a former junction station where two lines once met. There is constant activity here as cars are shunted about. The carriage shed is usually busy with restoration projects on the large stock of vintage coaches. Other old cars are parked on a siding nearby and may be inspected.

Returning on the train, you may be interested in taking a half-mile walk to the **Sheffield Park Garden** (4), a lovely place with rare trees and shrubs spaced among five lakes at different levels. It was laid out by the famous landscape architect Capability Brown during the 18th century and can be visited from the beginning of April to mid-November. It is open Tuesdays through Saturdays from 11 a.m. to 6 p.m.; and on Sundays and holidays from 2–6 p.m., but not on Tuesdays following a bank holiday.

Brighton

Londoners have been tripping down to Brighton in search of amusement since the mid-18th century, when a local doctor first promoted his famous sea cure. What made the town fashionable, though, was the frequent presence of naughty George IV, then Prince of Wales, who began construction on his Royal Pavilion in 1787. Brighton remained an aristocratic resort until the coming of the railway turned it into the immensely popular "London-by-the-Sea" that it is today.

The town itself is actually very old, dating from at least Roman times. It was mentioned in the famous Domesday Book of 1086 as *Brighthelmstone,* then a tiny fishing village. Traces of what Brighton looked like before becoming a resort can still be found in the area of The Lanes, a colorful district between the Pavilion and the sea.

Brighton has no equal as an easy and fun-filled daytrip from London. Here you will mix with every sort of Englishman, from aristocrats to cockneys, and visit elegant places as well as popular amusements. Because of its superb facilities and transportation, Brighton also makes a good base for exploring southeast England.

GETTING THERE:

Trains leave London's Victoria Station at least hourly for Brighton, a ride of about one hour. Return service operates until late evening.

Coaches for Brighton depart London's Victoria Coach Station hourly, with a journey time of about one hour and forty-five minutes.

By car, the most direct route is via the A-23, bypassing Gatwick on the M-23. Brighton is 54 miles south of London.

WHEN TO GO:

Most of the major sights are open daily, with the exception of the art museum, which closes on Mondays. A bright, warm day will add to your enjoyment.

FOOD AND DRINK:

Brighton offers the widest range of restaurants this side of London. From simple fish and chips to the most elegant French cuisine, the choice is up to you and your pocketbook. Some outstanding selections are:

> **English's Oyster Bar** (29 East St., in The Lanes) Considered to have the best seafood in town. $$$
>
> **Wheeler's Restaurant** (64 King's Rd., in the Sheridan Hotel, near The Lanes) Renowned for its seafood. $$$
>
> **Le Grandgousier** (15 Western St., north of King's Rd., between Montpelier and Waterloo streets) French cuisine in a casual setting. X: Sat. lunch, Sun. $$
>
> **Stubbs** (14 Ship St., in The Lanes) A popular place in the middle of an historic district. X: Mon. lunch, Sat. lunch. $$
>
> **Brown's Café** (3–4 Duke St., in The Lanes) Steaks, grills, spaghetti, chili, and the like. $
>
> **Food for Friends** (17 Prince Albert St., in The Lanes) Vegetarian food in a simple atmosphere. $
>
> **Cricketers** (15 Black Lion St., in The Lanes) A friendly old pub with good food. $

TOURIST INFORMATION:

The tourist office, phone (0273) 23-755, is in Marlborough House at 54 Old Steine. During the summer there is a branch kiosk on the seafront opposite West Street.

SUGGESTED TOUR:

Leaving the marvelously Victorian **train station** (1), follow the map to **Old Steine** (2), an easy stroll of about ten minutes. You could also get there by bus or taxi. Along the way you will pass the Royal Pavilion, a treat best saved for the end of the tour. The Old Steine (pronounced *Steen*) is the center of activity in Brighton and is probably named after a stone on which fishermen dried their nets in those quiet centuries before the town became England's playground. The main tourist office is located here, and this is also the spot from which most bus services operate.

Continue straight ahead to the **Palace Pier** (3), a gaudy Victorian structure dating from 1899 that juts out some 1,717 feet, nearly a third of a mile, into the English Channel. On it you will find a fantastic variety of fun houses, rides, shows, shops, and people from all over Britain, with accents ranging from pure North Country to London Cockney.

The best way to explore the beach is to take a ride on **Volk's Railway** (4). This quaint, open train has been operating since 1883, the first in Britain to run on electricity. It follows right along the edge of the beach from near Palace Pier to the new marina at Black Rock, a distance of about a mile. Volk's Railway operates from Easter to the

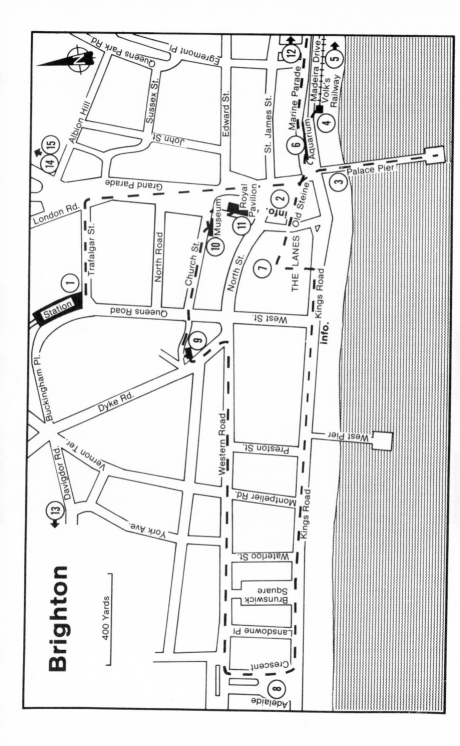

On the Palace Pier

end of September.

Brighton Marina (5) is the largest in Europe and can accommodate over 2,000 yachts. There are several interesting things to see, including a chandlery, old boats, and H.M.S. *Cavalier*, a World War II destroyer that can be visited. Just west of this is the "naturist" beach, where—as the tourist office so tactfully puts it—clothes need not be worn.

Return by walking along Marine Parade with its attractive 19th-century terraces, squares, and crescents. The distance is only a bit over a mile, but you could, of course, take a bus or Volk's Railway. At the end, near the Palace Pier, is the **Aquarium** (6), which features performing dolphins and over 10,000 fish from all over the world. Opened in 1872, this is Britain's largest aquarium. Its subterranean galleries alone are worth the visit. The Aquarium is open daily.

Just beyond Old Steine lies the original Brighton, now known as **The Lanes** (7). No longer inhabited by fishermen, this warren of narrow traffic-free alleyways has become a fashionable center of boutiques, antique shops, pubs, and restaurants. The Lanes are a good spot for aimless strolling, although you should not miss Brighton Square and Duke's Lane, the most attractive of the tiny byways.

Continuing on, walk out onto King's Road and turn right along the beach. This is the main promenade of Brighton, a stretch of seaside lined with the traditional entertainments. Fish-and-chips shops, ice

The Royal Pavilion

cream stands, the famous Brighton rock candy—it's all here. As you approach the adjoining town of Hove the atmosphere changes to one of sedate elegance.

Make a right at **Adelaide Crescent** (8), a beautiful open area of green surrounded by Regency town houses from the early 19th century. From here you can either return along King's Road or take Western Road back to Brighton. Your next stop should be the **Church of St. Nicholas** (9) on Dyke Road. Originally built in 1380 and reconstructed in 1853, it has a remarkable 12th-century Norman font. The churchyard is a perfect spot to rest before pressing on.

A short stroll down Church Street leads to the **Art Gallery and Museum** (10), a very worthwhile stop. Its collection of art nouveau and art deco pieces is probably the best in Britain. In addition, there are several Old Masters, superb porcelains, silver, furniture, and a fascinating display of local history—along with a gallery of fashion history. The museum is open Tuesdays through Saturdays, from 10 a.m. to 5:45 p.m.; and on Sundays from 2–5 p.m. It is closed on Mondays and some major holidays.

Saving the best for last, you are now ready to visit Brighton's stellar attraction, the **Royal Pavilion** (11), which is just around the corner. King George IV, known as "Prinny," began this hedonistic pleasure palace when he was still Prince of Wales, and over the years from 1787 to 1822 it evolved from a classical structure into the bizarre pseudo-

Oriental fantasy that it is today. The final design, from 1815 on, was the work of John Nash, the greatest architect of the Regency period. Before entering the pavilion you should stroll around it as the best views face Pavilion Parade.

The interior of the palace, every bit as extravagant as the outside, may be visited on any day except Christmas and Boxing Day, from 10 a.m. to 6 p.m. (until 4:30 p.m. from October through May). The king used the pavilion until 1827, and it was also visited by his brother, King William IV and, in turn, by Queen Victoria. Its end as a royal residence came in 1850 when Victoria, not amused by the theatricality of it all, sold the pavilion to the town for a fraction of its value. Another century passed before the palace was fully restored to its former splendor as a result of a permanent loan, made by Queen Elizabeth II, of original furnishings.

NEARBY SIGHTS:

Brighton has several other interesting attractions that may easily be reached by local bus or car. Ask for directions at the tourist office on Old Steine. The best of these are:

Rottingdean Village (12), a picturesque spot four miles east of Brighton on a cliff top overlooking the sea. Rudyard Kipling lived here and mementoes of his life can be seen at The Grange, a former vicarage that is now a museum.

British Engineerium (13), located in a former pumping station on the edge of Hove Park on Nevill Road, has a magnificent collection of stationary steam engines and mechanical inventions from the Victorian era.

Preston Manor (14), two miles from Old Steine on London Road, is an 18th-century Georgian mansion in a lovely setting. The manor is open several days a week.

Stanmer Village (15) preserves a turn-of-the-century atmosphere of rural England and is located four miles from central Brighton along Lewes Road.

Arundel

Like a vision from a fairy tale, the picture-book town of Arundel nestles snugly at the base of its massive castle. Both date from the time of the Norman Conquest, and possibly even earlier. Arundel was mentioned in the Domesday Book of 1086 as a port of some consequence, which it remained throughout the Middle Ages. There is still a good deal of boating activity on its river, the Arun, which flows into the sea at nearby Littlehampton. Delightful country walks can be made along its banks and to the Wildfowl Reserve, or through peaceful Arundel Park. Those who prefer more sedentary activities will find excellent antique and craft shops, charming pubs, and three interesting small museums. The main point of the visit remains, of course, the castle—one of the finest in all England.

GETTING THERE:

Trains to Arundel leave hourly from London's Victoria Station. The journey takes about 80 minutes, with return service until mid-evening.

By car, Arundel is 56 miles south of London via the A-24 and A-29 roads.

WHEN TO GO:

Avoid coming on a Saturday or between late October and the end of March, when the castle is closed. Some shops close early on Wednesdays.

FOOD AND DRINK:

Arundel has a number of good places to eat and drink, including:

Norfolk Arms (22 High St., near the tourist office) Traditional English dishes in a charming old coaching inn. $$

Swan (29 High St.) A popular pub with good food. $

General Abercrombie (Queen St., near the river) A 16th-century pub with atmosphere and good food. $

TOURIST INFORMATION:

The local tourist office, phone (0903) 882-419, is at 61 High Street, below the castle.

SUGGESTED TOUR:

Leaving the **train station** (1), turn left and follow The Causeway and

Queen Street to the River Arun. Because the castle is not open in the mornings it is recommended that you begin with a short **country walk** of a bit over one mile.

Cross the bridge and turn right on Mill Road, passing a parking lot. Continue on until you come to a recreation ground on the right. Just beyond this turn right on a well-defined track that leads to the river. There are purple markers along the way, as well as occasional stiles that must be stepped over. When you get to the river, turn right and follow the path along the embankment. From here there are gorgeous views of the town and its castle. Back near the bridge are ruins of the **Maison Dieu** (2), an almshouse for poor men founded in 1395. It was disbanded in 1532 during the Reformation and destroyed in the Civil War of the 17th century.

Arundel Castle (3) is everything a great fortress should be. Built in the late 11th century, it was besieged by Henry I in 1102 and again by King Stephen in 1139. After severe damage caused by Parliamentary forces during the Civil War in 1643, it fell into a dilapidated state until restoration began in the 18th century. What you see today is mostly a romantic Victorian vision, a stately home with all the trappings of a medieval stronghold. Throughout most of its history, the castle has been the seat of the dukes of Norfolk and their ancestors, the Fitzalans. This family, among the highest nobility in England, has always remained Roman Catholic despite centuries of persecution, a fact that explains much of what you will see in Arundel.

Enter the castle grounds and walk around to the **Barbican Tower** of 1295. Once inside, turn hard right and follow the marked route to the 11th-century keep, which was occupied only during a siege. A banner is flown from its top when the duke is in residence. Return and enter the living quarters by way of the chapel. The immense **Barons' Hall** has some interesting paintings, including a double portrait by Van Dyck. This leads past the dining room and the drawing room, which has an appealing lived-in quality and several fine portraits by Gainsborough, Reynolds, and Van Dyck. The elaborate bed in the **Victoria Room** was made for the queen's visit in 1846. From here the route takes you through the handsome library and several smaller rooms to an exit near the keep. Arundel Castle is open from April 1st until the last Friday in October, Sundays through Fridays, from 1–5 p.m. During June, July, and August it opens at 12 noon. The last admission is always at 4 p.m., and it is always closed on Saturdays.

Before leaving the castle grounds, take a walk over to the 14th-century **Fitzalan Chapel** (4). Many of the earls of Arundel and dukes of Norfolk are buried here. A wrought-iron grill-and-glass wall separates this Catholic chapel from the Anglican parish church, another part of the same building.

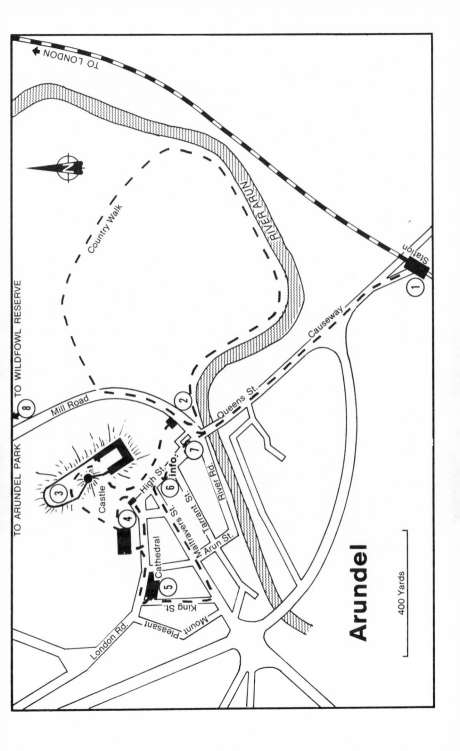

Arundel

TO WILDFOWL RESERVE

TO ARUNDEL PARK

TO LONDON

Country Walk

RIVER ARUN

Station

Causeway

Queens St.

Mill Road

High St.

Info.

Castle

Cathedral

Maltravers St.

Tarrant St.

River Rd.

Arun St.

King St.

London Rd.

Mount Pleasant

400 Yards

Arundel Castle

Exit through the gate and stroll up London Road. On your right is the Protestant part of the church, which makes an interesting contrast and should be visited.

Just beyond is the Roman Catholic **Cathedral** (5), built in a grandiose Gothic style in 1869 as a parish church. It became a cathedral only in 1965, when a new bishopric was created for the region.

Follow the map to the **Arundel Museum and Heritage Centre** (6), in the same building as the tourist office. Open from Easter through October, its displays of bygone times makes it an interesting place to visit. The **Dolls' House and Toy Museum,** just down the street, is also worth a stop.

Don't leave Arundel without seeing **Potter's Museum of Curiosity** (7), an enchanting but very weird collection of Victorian taxidermy opened in 1861. Its rooms and halls are stuffed to overflowing with strange sights, including a series of tableaux in which nursery rhymes are acted out by stuffed cats, rats, rabbits, and the like. You will never forget this place. It is open between April 1st and November 1st, from about 11 a.m. to 1 p.m. and from 2:15–5:30 p.m.

Two other places in Arundel may interest you, both just off the map but within easy walking distance along **Mill Road** (8). They are **Arundel Park,** a gorgeous 1,100-acre spread of natural beauty beginning at Swanbourne Lake, and the **Wildfowl Reserve** where you can observe a great variety of waterfowl from strategically placed hides. It is open daily from 9:30 a.m. to 6:30 p.m., or until dusk if that is earlier.

Chichester and Bosham

The coastal region of West Sussex is unusually rich in history as well as natural beauty. Its location on the English Channel has long made it the doorstep to the Continent, a place where battles were fought and trade flourished. Three aspects of its character are explored in this delightful daytrip—the medieval town of Chichester, the Roman ruins at Fishbourne, and the Saxon hamlet of Bosham.

For hundreds of years the Celts had occupied this territory. One of their tribes had a king named Cogidubnus, who ruled the area near what is now Chichester. When the Romans invaded Britain in A.D. 43, Cogidubnus—no fool—submitted without a fight, became a Roman citizen, and retained his local power. The palace at Fishbourne was probably built for him as a reward. The invaders also built him a proper Roman capital, *Noviomagus,* later to become Chichester. Cogidubnus played a pivotal role in English history, for it was his defection that allowed the legions of Claudius to conquer Britain so swiftly and easily.

With the departure of the Romans about A.D. 410, the region was overrun by barbaric Saxons. Their conversion to Christianity first occurred at Bosham in the 7th century. Bosham also figured in the Norman Conquest of 1066, its church being pictured on the famous Bayeux Tapestry.

William the Conqueror brought peace and unity to Britain, and Sussex prospered as a trading center. By medieval times, Chichester had become an important town. Many of its fine structures still survive, side by side with those of later eras. Bosham, now a yachting center, preserves the feeling of bygone days in a sublimely beautiful setting, the perfect place to end this day's wonderful outing.

GETTING THERE:

Trains leave London's Victoria Station hourly for Chichester, arriving there about 1½ hours later. Be careful to board the correct car, as they split en route. Return service operates until mid-evening.

By car, Chichester is 63 miles southwest of London. Take the A-3 to Guildford and then switch to the A-286.

WHEN TO GO:

Good weather is essential for this largely outdoor trip. Most of the attractions are open daily, except a few museums that close on Sundays and Mondays. The Roman Palace at Fishbourne is open every day from March through November, and on Sundays in winter.

FOOD AND DRINK:

Being a festival town, Chichester has an unusually good selection of restaurants and pubs in every price category, including:

Hole in the Wall (1 St. Martin's St., near St. Mary's Hospital) A casual place with a loyal clientele. $$

The Noble Rot (41 Little London, near the District Museum) A wine bistro and restaurant located in old wine vaults. $ and $$

Clinch's Salad House (14 Southgate, near the station) Healthy food, mostly vegetarian. X: Sun. $

Carter's (South St., near Canon Lane) Light lunches in an ancient crypt. X: Sun. $

Royal Arms (East St., by the Market Cross) A popular pub with good food. $

And in Bosham, you may want to try:

Millstream Restaurant (Bosham Lane) A lovely place for French and English cuisine. $$$

Berkeley Arms (near Bosham Lane) A friendly local pub with meals. $

TOURIST INFORMATION:

The Chichester tourist office, phone (0243) 775-888, is in St. Peter's Market on West Street, near the cathedral.

SUGGESTED TOUR:

Leaving the **train station** (1), walk up Southgate and South Street to the **Market Cross** (2). This medieval shelter, the most elaborate in England, was erected in 1501 by a local bishop. The town's Roman origins become obvious at this point, with the four main streets meeting at right angles in the center.

Stroll down West Street to the tourist office and turn left at the cathedral's detached bell tower, the only one of its kind in the country. The **Cathedral** (3) itself, predominantly Norman, was consecrated in 1108. Its 277-foot spire, recalling that of Salisbury, collapsed in 1861 and was rebuilt in 1866.

Inside, the cathedral has a remarkably comfortable, almost cozy atmosphere. For nearly 900 years it has been the repository of a vast collection of art objects. The nave has two aisles, an unusual arrangement. A carved stone screen from 1475 separates this from the choir. Note the modern pulpit, installed in 1966. The beautifully carved misericords and Bishop's Throne in the choir are outstanding, but the

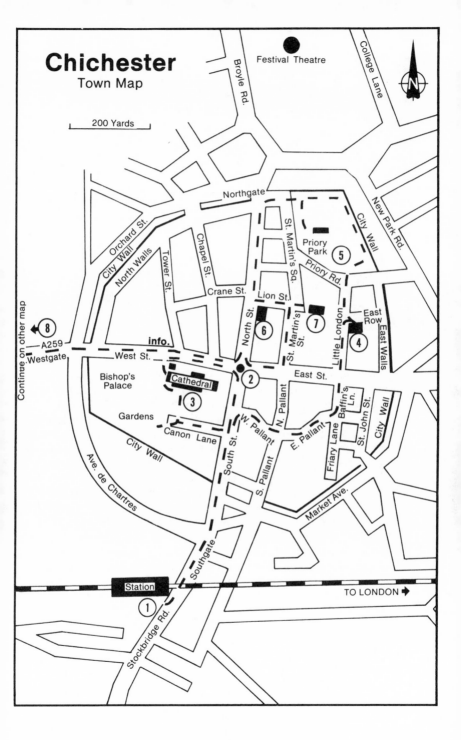

The Market Cross

best works here are the two **Romanesque wall carvings** just opposite them in the south aisle. They depict the *Raising of Lazarus* and *Christ at the Gate of Bethany* and are the finest of their kind in England.

A visually exciting point of focus is provided by the vivid tapestry of abstract design behind the contemporary high altar. Roman floor **mosaics** from a much earlier structure can be seen in the south aisle near the retro-choir. Not to be missed is the window by Marc Chagall and the modern Graham Sutherland painting.

Leave by the main entrance and turn left into the **Cloisters.** Their irregular 15th-century walls enclose a garden known as the Paradise. From here follow St. Richard's Walk, a narrow and very charming passage, to Canon Lane. To the right, a 14th-century gateway leads to the Bishop's Palace and the public gardens. Return on quiet Canon Lane, which has an intriguing collection of old houses, to South Street and turn left. In a few yards make a right onto West Pallant. The **Pallants** are a miniature version of the town itself, reflecting a distinctly Roman layout. Once a special preserve of the bishop, these four streets are lined with outstanding 18th- and 19th-century buildings. The most notable of these is the **Pallant House** of 1712 at the intersection with North Pallant, now home to an interesting public art gallery with mostly changing exhibitions.

Continue along East Pallant and turn left at Baffin's Lane. Once

In the Roman Palace at Fishbourne

across East Street this becomes Little London. The **District Museum** (4) at the corner of East Row is housed in an 18th-century corn store. Its collection includes objects relating to the district that date from prehistoric to modern times, and include a Roman soldier in full armor. The museum is open Tuesdays through Saturdays, from 10 a.m. to 5:30 p.m.

Now follow Little London into **Priory Park** (5). A shady footpath runs along the top of the medieval city walls, built on original Roman foundations. The 13th-century Greyfriars Church in the middle of the lawn houses the **Guildhall Museum,** featuring archaeological finds, open on summer afternoons, Tuesday through Saturday.

Walk down Priory Lane and turn left on North Street. A few blocks to the north lies the Festival Theatre, built in 1962 for the world-famous Chichester Festival, held annually from April to September. Stop at the intersection of Lion Street and visit the elegant **Council House** (6) of 1731. On its outer wall is mounted a Roman stone, found nearby, which reads: *By the Authority of Tiberius Claudius, Cogidubnus, King Legate of Augustus in Britain.* Inside, there is a fine assembly room and council chamber, which may be inspected.

Lion Street leads to St. Martin's Square and **St. Mary's Hospital** (7), built in 1290. Since 1528 it has been an almshouse for the aged, a function it still serves. Its well-preserved medieval interior can be seen Tuesdays through Fridays, from 11 a.m. to noon and from 2–5 p.m.

Follow St. Martin's Street and turn right on East Street, passing the Market Cross. Continue along West Street to Westgate. From here it is about 1½ miles to Fishbourne following the route on the map. You can also get there by a number 700, 276, or 266 bus; or by hourly train from the station to Fishbourne Halt.

The **Roman Palace at Fishbourne** (8), the largest building of that era in Britain, was discovered in 1960 by workmen laying a water main. Those parts of it that survived the centuries of destruction and burial can only hint at the grandeur it must have had in the time of Cogidubnus. A museum and protective structure has been erected over a large part of the remains. In order to understand these it is helpful first to see the short film shown frequently in the museum's theater, and to study the scale model. A **Roman dining room** has been reconstructed, and there is now a **farming display** outside with live Roman-type animals and crops. The palace is open daily between March and November, from 10 a.m. to 6 p.m.; and on Sundays the rest of the year. It closes at 5 p.m. in March, April, and October; and at 4 p.m. from November through February. There is a cafeteria on the site.

Return to Portsmouth Road and cross it. From here you can get a bus to nearby Bosham. Walking the two-mile distance, however, is much more attractive. To do that, turn right on Portsmouth Road. When you get to a pub called the Black Boy, bear left on Old Park Lane. At the end of this you will find a public footpath going straight ahead, which follows a row of trees to the left. Walk along this until you cross a private road. Climb over a stile and continue on the footpath, which soon runs into a paved road. Walk straight ahead, ignoring the sign to Bosham Hoe, and pass the Berkeley Arms Inn. The street now becomes Bosham Lane, which makes a left and leads to the harbor.

It was from **Bosham** (pronounced *Boz-zum*) that Harold set sail in 1064 on that fateful journey that ended in the Norman Conquest. This delightfully dreamy village is, however, much older than that, going back at least as far as the Romans. Turn right on High Street and follow it to **Bosham Church** (9). Begun around 1020, it incorporates parts of a Roman basilica of A.D. 350. The young daughter of King Canute, an 11th-century ruler of England and Denmark, is believed to be buried here.

Step outside and wander around past the old mill, then return along the water's edge to Bosham Lane. A stroll along **The Trippet** to the opposite bank reveals the full nautical flavor of Bosham, while a visit to **Bosham Walk,** a local arts and crafts center, is a pleasant diversion. At the post office on High Street you can get information concerning bus service back to Chichester. If you prefer to take the train, just follow the map to the **station** (10), about a mile away. Trains to Chichester leave hourly from the platform on the far side of the tracks.

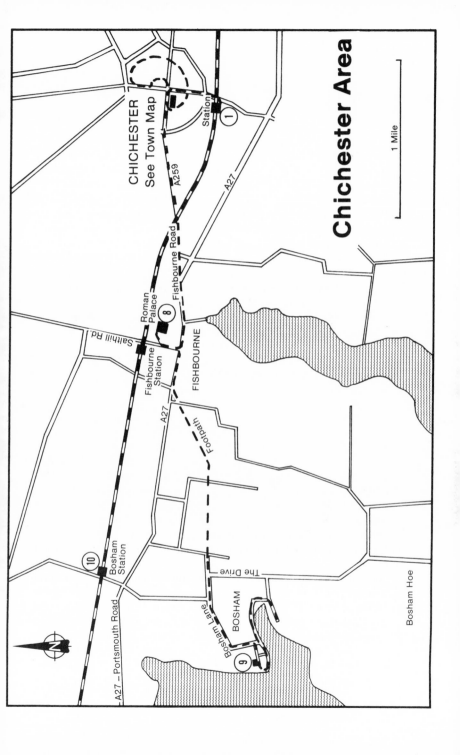

Chichester Area

1 Mile

CHICHESTER
See Town Map

Station

A259

A27

Fishbourne Road

Roman Palace

Salthill Rd.

Fishbourne Station

FISHBOURNE

A27

Footpath

Bosham Station

A27 – Portsmouth Road

The Drive

Bosham Lane

BOSHAM

Bosham Hoe

N

①

⑧

⑨

⑩

Guildford

Dating back at least a thousand years, Guildford is an unusually attractive old town with a rich architectural heritage. The Saxons named it *Gyldeford*—the ford of the golden flowers—after its strategic position on the River Wey. A Norman castle was built here which remained a favorite royal residence for centuries. During medieval times, Guildford was made the county town of Surrey, a status it still holds. Throughout the Middle Ages the peaceful and prosperous town had a thriving woolen industry that died out in the 17th century, only to be replaced by another source of wealth, the shipping of goods by barge along its newly navigable river.

Guildford today is a remarkable blend of past and present. While it has done a good job of preserving the old, it also has some first-rate modern structures. The town is particularly rich in parks, gardens, and open spaces.

This trip can easily be combined with a visit to Portsmouth, which is on the same road and rail line.

GETTING THERE:

Trains to Guildford leave London's Waterloo Station at least every half-hour, with a journey time of less than one hour. Return service operates until late evening.

Coaches operated by the Green Line leave from their Victoria terminal by Eccleston Bridge in London. They arrive in Guildford about 75 minutes later.

By car, Guildford is 33 miles southwest of London via the A-3 road.

WHEN TO GO:

Guildford may be visited at any time. The museums are open Mondays through Saturdays, and the castle daily from April through September.

FOOD AND DRINK:

There are numerous restaurants and pubs on High Street and all along the walking route. Some good choices are:

Angel Inn (High St., opposite Chapel St.) A very romantic 16th-century coaching inn. $$

Guildford Boathouse

Café de Paris (35 Castle St., near the castle) French cuisine. X: Sun., Mon. eve., Sat. lunch. $$

The Star (Quarry St., at High St.) Have lunch at a very old pub, alleged to be haunted. $

Spread Eagle (Chertsey St., near Abbot's Hospital) A pub with home-cooked lunches. $

Richoux (in the Friary Shopping Centre) Light meals and grills. X: Sun. $

TOURIST INFORMATION:

The local tourist office, phone (0483) 57-58-57, is in the Civic Hall on London Road.

SUGGESTED TOUR:

Leaving the **train station** (1), follow Park Street and Millmead to the River Wey, which was converted into a navigable waterway as early as 1653. Through a series of canals and locks it is joined with the Thames to the north, and at one time was open all the way to the south coast. Now owned by the National Trust, the Wey Navigation is very popular with pleasure boaters, who have replaced the commercial barges of old.

Cross the footbridge to Millmead Lock. From here you can stroll down along the water past the **Guildford Boathouse** (2), which offers river cruises and boat rentals. To reach it, use the footbridge and return via Millbrook.

The **Yvonne Arnaud Theatre** (3), delightfully located by Millmead Lock, is a modern circular structure from 1965. Just beyond it is the town mill, built over the millrace and now used as a scenery workshop for the theater.

Cross Millbrook and follow Mill Lane to **St. Mary's Church** (4), the oldest building in Guildford. Its Saxon tower dates from about 1050, with the rest being completed by the 13th century.

Continuing along Quarry Street, take a look down Rosemary Alley, a steep medieval path to the river. Just beyond it is the **Guildford Museum** (5), which has exhibits of local archaeology and history as well as items connected with Lewis Carroll, author of *Alice in Wonderland,* who spent a great deal of time in Guildford. It is open Mondays through Saturdays, from 11 a.m. to 5 p.m.

Pass through the adjacent Castle Arch, which dates from 1265. To the right, on Castle Hill, is a private house called The Chestnuts, that was leased by Lewis Carroll as a home for his six spinster sisters. This is where he died in 1898.

A path leads up to the **Castle Keep** (6). Built in 1170 on an earlier mound, this is all that remains of the great Norman castle that was once a favorite royal residence until it fell into neglect in the 15th century. Later used as a jail, the keep is open to visitors daily from April through September. There is a marvelous view from the top.

Leave the grounds and follow the map to Milk House Gate, a quaint narrow passageway that leads to High Street. Across this, to the left, is the **Guildhall** (7) with its protruding clock, easily the most photographed sight in Guildford. Its dramatic façade was erected in 1683, but the main structure is Elizabethan.

Turn right on High Street and visit the **Guildford House** (8) at number 155. Now used for art exhibitions, it was built in 1660 and is worth seeing for its beautifully molded plaster ceilings and carved wooden staircases. Just beyond it is **Abbot's Hospital** (9), or Hospital of the Blessed Trinity, an old almshouse with an interesting history. It was founded in 1619 by George Abbot, a poor local boy who was given a free education by the town. He rose to become the Archbishop of Canterbury and repaid the people of Guildford by building this home for their elderly poor, which is still used for that purpose. A guided tour of its splendid interior is available at stated times.

The **Royal Grammar School** (10) is a little farther up High Street. Its modern buildings are on the left side, but those on the right date from 1586. Enter the old courtyard and look around. Visitors are occasionally admitted to the library, which contains priceless old chained books. Two blocks beyond, on London Road, is the Civic Hall, home of the Guildford Philharmonic Orchestra. The tourist office is in the same building.

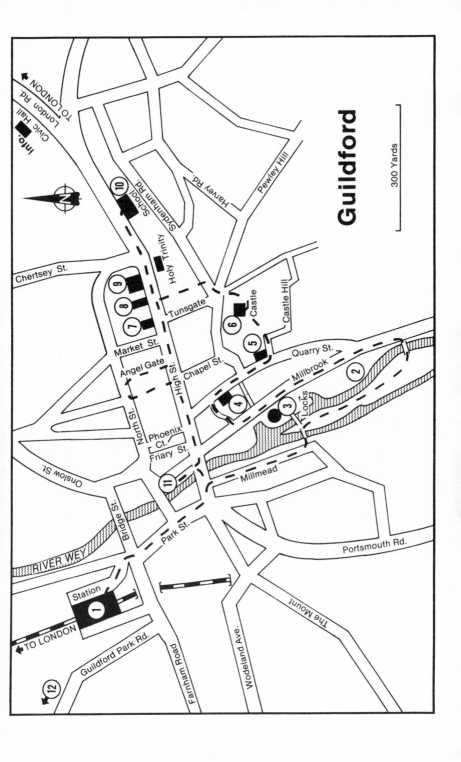

Guildford

300 Yards

High Street in Guildford

Return down High Street, passing Holy Trinity Church on the left. This classical building was erected in 1763 on the site of a medieval church that collapsed in 1740. It was used as a cathedral from 1927 to 1961. Another classical structure, the Tunsgate Arch, directly opposite the Guildhall, fronted the corn market when it was built in 1818. A road now passes beneath it.

Turn right on Angel Gate, a narrow lane by the side of the ancient Angel Inn. This leads to North Street, scene of a colorful farmers' market held on Fridays and Saturdays. Make a left and return by Swan Lane to High Street, which you follow to the river.

The restored late-17th-century **Treadwheel Crane** (11) on the old town wharf is a relic of the Wey Navigation. Up to ten men worked it, unloading the barges that were the backbone of Guildford's prosperity. From here you can stroll back to the station via Friary Bridge or through the Friary Shopping Centre, a well-designed enclosed mall.

There is one more sight in Guildford that may interest you. It is the modern **Cathedral of the Holy Spirit** (12) on Stag Hill, reached via Guildford Park Road and Ridgemount, about one mile from the station. The first Anglican cathedral to be build on a new site in the south of England since the Reformation, it was begun in 1936 and consecrated in 1961.

Portsmouth

There is one very compelling reason to visit Portsmouth, and that is to go aboard H.M.S. *Victory*, Nelson's flagship at Trafalgar. Here you can relive one of the proudest moments in British history. Located on a naval base, the ship has been perfectly restored to the condition she was in on October 21, 1805, when she won the most decisive battle ever fought at sea.

Portsmouth, long known to sailors as "Pompey," has many other attractions as well, including the recently raised *Mary Rose*, a Tudor warship sunk in 1545, and H.M.S. *Warrior*, the sole survivor from the Royal Navy's ironclad era. There are also forts and fortifications, splendid harbor views, several museums, a cathedral, and best of all, Old Portsmouth, which retains much of its nautical atmosphere despite heavy bombing during World War II. The town was originally founded in 1194 by Richard the Lionhearted but did not achieve real importance until 1495, when the first dry dock in the world was established there by Henry VII. Since then, Portsmouth has grown to become one of the major naval bases in the world, a position it still holds. By skipping some of the sights, it is possible to combine this trip in the same day with one to Guildford.

GETTING THERE:

Trains to Portsmouth Harbour Station, the end of the line, leave frequently from London's Waterloo Station. The journey takes about 1½ hours, with return service operating until mid-evening. Those making the suggested tour will probably be returning from Portsmouth and Southsea Station, in the newer part of town.

Coaches leave hourly from London's Victoria Coach Station for the two-hour trip to Portsmouth.

By car, Portsmouth is 71 miles southwest of London via the A-3 road. You may want to drive around the town instead of walking or taking buses.

WHEN TO GO:

Portsmouth may be visited at any time except during the Christmas holidays. Most of the sights are open daily.

FOOD AND DRINK:

Portsmouth has a wide variety of pubs and restaurants in all price ranges. Some good choices, in walking tour sequence, are:

George (84 Queen St., near H.M.S. *Victory*) A colorful old pub serving lunches. $

Le Talisman (123 High St., Old Portsmouth, near the cathedral) Excellent meals in the old town. X: Sun., Mon. $$$

Pembroke (Pembroke Rd., Old Portsmouth, near the cathedral) A pub with meals in a nautical ambiance. $

The Lone Yachtsman (at The Point in Old Portsmouth) A pub restaurant with traditional fare. $

Bistro Montparnasse (103 Palmerston Rd., 2 blocks north of Southsea Castle) A popular French-style restaurant. X: Sun. $$$

Pendragon (Clarence Parade, 2 blocks northeast of Southsea Castle) Fine dining in a small hotel. $$

TOURIST INFORMATION:

The local tourist office, phone (0705) 826-722, is on The Hard, near the entrance to the naval base and H.M.S. *Victory*.

SUGGESTED TOUR:

Leaving **Portsmouth Harbour Station** (1), turn left on The Hard and enter the main gate of the naval base. Continue straight ahead to **H.M.S. Victory** (2), where you join the queue for guided tours aboard the ship. Each group is escorted through the entire vessel by a sailor who is well versed in its history. Built in 1759, H.M.S. *Victory* has been in continuous commission since 1778, and is still manned by serving officers and men. Visits may be made on any day except Christmas, from 10:30 a.m. to 5 p.m., but not before 1 p.m. on Sundays.

The **Royal Naval Museum,** occupying three old storehouses just a few steps away, is an interesting place to visit after the tour. In addition to the expected material relating to Lord Nelson and the Battle of Trafalgar, there are exhibits of more contemporary naval matters, including a mock-up of a modern frigate's operations room. The museum is open daily, except for one week at Christmas, from 10:30 a.m. to 5 p.m., closing at 4:30 p.m. in winter.

The **Mary Rose** was the flower of Henry VIII's fleet, a revolutionary warship lost while defending Portsmouth in 1545. Long forgotten, its oaken hull lay preserved in the seabed mud for four centuries. In 1979, a team led by Prince Charles began recovery work and in 1982 the remains of the ship were raised. These are now on display in a covered dry dock next to H.M.S. *Victory*. There is also a fascinating exhibition of *Mary Rose* artifacts in a boathouse close to the naval base

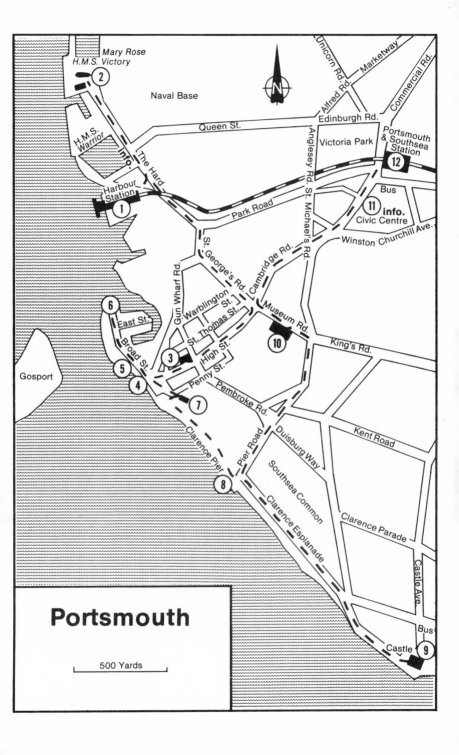

Portsmouth

500 Yards

entrance. Both may be seen daily except on Christmas, from 10:30 a.m. to 5 p.m.

A new addition to the naval base, just west of the entrance gate, is **H.M.S. Warrior.** This iron-hulled warship was built in 1860 as the world's fastest and best protected. She is the only remaining 19th-century capital ship in existence, the sole survivor of the Royal Navy's ironclad era. Visitors to the naval base will be happy to know that there is an inexpensive cafeteria next to the museum, offering lunches, snacks, and refreshments.

Now follow the map to High Street in Old Portsmouth. The **Cathedral of St. Thomas** (3) is a rather odd structure. It was begun in 1188 as a chapel, became a parish church in 1320, and a cathedral only in 1927. The old church now forms the choir and sanctuary, with a new, still unfinished nave having been started in 1935. Although not a great cathedral by any standard, it is certainly interesting and well worth a visit.

At the end of High Street, next to the sea, is the 15th-century **Square Tower** (4), one of the first forts specially designed for cannon warfare. On its side is a gilded bust of Charles I that mysteriously survived the Civil War.

Turn right on Broad Street and pass the **Sally Port,** the traditional point of embarkation for Britain's naval heroes. Just beyond this is the **Round Tower** (5). Begun in 1415, it was the first permanent defensive work to be built in Portsmouth. You can climb up on it for a good view. An iron chain ran across the harbor from here to prevent unfriendly ships from entering.

The Point (6) still retains some of the flavor of Old Portsmouth. Once known as Spice Island, this small peninsula fairly teemed with bawdy pubs and brothels. To this day it remains a colorful place for eating and drinking.

Return on Broad Street and continue to the **Garrison Church** (7). Now in ruinous condition, it was founded in 1212 as a hospice but was disbanded in 1540. It then became an armory and later a residence for the military governors. Charles II was married here in 1622. The building was restored as a church in the 19th century and badly damaged during World War II. It may be visited.

Stroll down to **Clarence Pier** (8), a popular amusement area with the usual seaside amenities. From here you can walk or take a bus past the beautiful gardens of Southsea Common to **Southsea Castle** (9), built in 1545 by Henry VIII. Inside the fort is a museum of local military history and archaeology, which may be visited daily from 10:30 a.m. to 5:30 p.m. Nearby is the new **D-Day Museum,** featuring the 272-foot-long Overlord Embroidery, audio-visual shows, vehicles, weapons, and the like. The only museum in Britain devoted solely to

H.M.S. Victory

the Normandy Invasions, it is open daily from 10:30 a.m. to 5:30 p.m.

Return to Pier Road and follow it to Museum Road. You can also take a bus from the front of Southsea Castle if you're tired. The **City Museum** (10) displays decorative and fine arts from the 16th century to the present, and is open daily from 10:30 a.m. to 5:30 p.m. At this point you could return directly to Portsmouth Harbour Station (1), or follow Cambridge Road to the **Civic Centre** (11). The Guildhall there is an outstanding Victorian structure flanked by modern glass buildings. Another tourist office is in one of these. To the north is the main shopping area along Commercial Road. This street leads, off the map, to the **Charles Dickens Birthplace Museum** at 393 Old Commercial Road. It is open from March through October, every day from 10:30 a.m. to 5:30 p.m. The **Portsmouth and Southsea Station** (12) is a convenient place to get a train back to London.

Shanklin
(Isle of Wight)

Just off the southern coast of England lies the Isle of Wight, a delightful island whose bracing air and spectacular scenery combine to form an unusual and very enjoyable daytrip destination. A favorite holiday retreat ever since the days of Queen Victoria, it remains relatively unknown to foreign travelers. Although the Isle of Wight shares a common heritage with the rest of England, its friendly people regard themselves as somehow different from the mainlanders. Here, British sophistication yields to simpler charms and London seems far away.

GETTING THERE:

Trains leave London's Waterloo Station hourly for Portsmouth Harbour Station, the ride taking about 1½ hours. On arrival there, follow the crowds to the pier, a part of the station complex, and board the Sealink ferry to Ryde. BritRail Passes are not accepted on the boat, so you may have to buy a ticket. Fifteen minutes later you will disembark at Ryde Pier Head. Get on the waiting train marked for Shanklin and take it as far as Sandown, a ride of 17 minutes. You will probably be returning from Shanklin, so be sure to get a round-trip ticket from London to there if you do not have a BritRail Pass. Check the return schedule on arrival to avoid missing the last evening connection back to London

Coaches leave several times in the morning from London's Victoria Coach Station for the two-hour trip to Portsmouth Harbour. From there take the Sealink passenger ferry to Ryde, then the train or a local bus to Sandown.

By car, follow the A-3 from London to Portsmouth Harbour, a distance of 71 miles. Continue on by passenger ferry and rail or bus, as above. It is impractical to take a car to the Isle of Wight for only one day.

The Old Village

WHEN TO GO:

The Isle of Wight is most attractive between mid-spring and early fall. Good weather is absolutely essential to enjoyment of this trip.

FOOD AND DRINK:

Being a popular tourist area, the Isle of Wight is well endowed with restaurants and pubs. Some choice establishments in the area covered by this daytrip are:

Crab Inn (in the Old Village section of Shanklin) A quaint thatched-roof pub with meals. $$

The Cottage (8 Eastcliff Rd., off High St. in Shanklin Old Village) A very popular restaurant. X: Sun. eve., Mon. lunch, Oct. $$

Queensmead (12 Queens Rd., Shanklin, 2 blocks inland from the pier) A small hotel with bar lunches and full dinners. X: Nov. through Mar. $ and $$

Bourne Hall (Luccombe Rd., near Rylstone Park) Light lunch and full dinners in a small hotel. X: Dec., Jan. $ and $$

Biskra House Restaurant (17 St. Thomas' St., in Ryde, near the ferry pier) Fine food in an old mansion with a view of the sea. X: Sun. eve., Mon. $$$

Shanklin
ISLE OF WIGHT

½ Mile

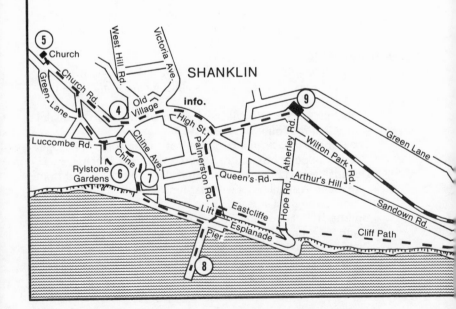

SHANKLIN

5 Church

West Hill Rd.

Victoria Ave.

Green Lane

Church Rd.

4 Old Village

info.

High St.

Luccombe Rd.

Chine Ave.

Chine

Rylstone Gardens

6 7

Palmerston Rd.

Queen's Rd.

Atherley Rd.

Wilton Park Rd.

Green Lane

Arthur's Hill

Hope Rd.

Eastcliffe

Lift

Esplanade

Sandown Rd.

Pier

8

Cliff Path

9

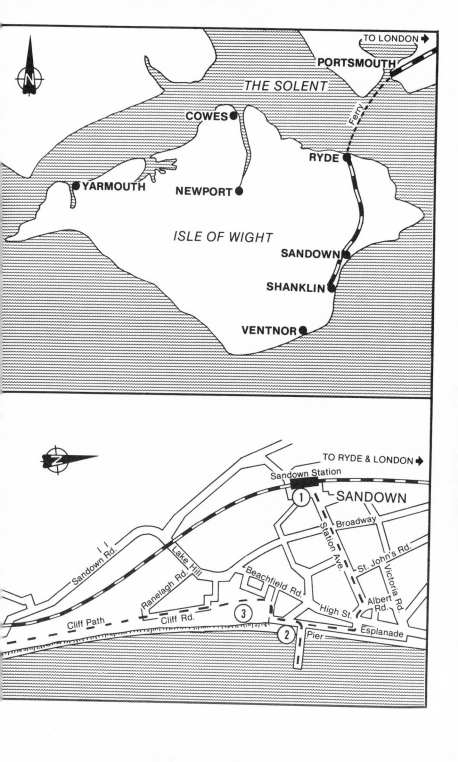

TOURIST INFORMATION:

The local tourist office for Shanklin is at 67 High Street, near the Old Village. You can phone them at (0983) 862-942.

SUGGESTED TOUR:

Leaving **Sandown station** (1), walk straight ahead down Station Avenue and make a right on Albert Road. This leads to The Esplanade, a road built atop a sea wall, which is crowded with vacationers during the season. The beach here is perhaps the best in England, with fine sand and a long, gradual slope. Ahead lies the **Pier** (2), an attractive modern structure owned by the town. A stroll to its far end will reward you with a lovely panorama of sea, cliffs, and rolling hills.

Just beyond the pier turn right off The Esplanade and climb Ferncliff Crescent, which begins as steps. At the top make a left into **Battery Gardens** (3). Amble through this to Cliff Walk and follow the trail that leads to Shanklin. For the next 1½ miles the pathway, sometimes becoming a road, clings to the upper edge of a steep precipice. Far below, tiny bathing huts make a tenuous hold on the narrow strip of sand between sea and cliff. Midway, you will pass the settlement of Lake. Shanklin now opens into view and beyond it lie the hills that define the southern end of Sandown Bay.

Below, Shanklin Pier (8) juts out into the sea. Just beyond this, turn right on Palmerston Road and follow it to the center of town. At High Street make a left, passing the tourist office, right out of the present century. The **Old Village** (4), oozing with quaintness, is just about everyone's vision of that imagined England of long ago. Thatched-roof cottages line the streets, many of them now restaurants, pubs, and gift shops. A more romantic place to stop for lunch could hardly be desired.

Continue straight ahead on Church Road to the **Old Parish Church** of St. Blasius (5), one of the most beautifully situated country churches you'll ever encounter. Architecturally undistinguished and of uncertain age—parts of it may date from the 14th century—it nevertheless works a strange charm on the visitor. Be sure to see its interior and graveyard.

Return on Church Road and turn right on Priory Road, then left on Popham Road to **Rylstone Public Park** (6). This lovely spot of sylvan splendor overlooking the sea is a delight to explore and the perfect place to sit down for a rest.

From here, Chine Hollow leads to the upper entrance of **Shanklin Chine** (7). Paying a small admission charge, descend into the deep and narrow ravine with its plunging waterfalls. The word *chine* is peculiar to this area and derives from the Anglo-Saxon *cine*, meaning fissure. A path leads through the heavily wooded glen, passing a stone bridge

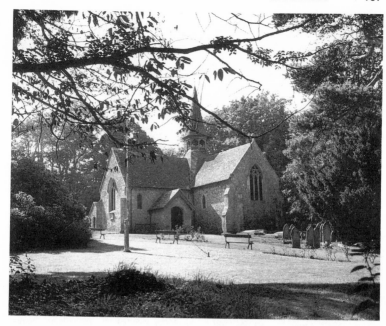

The Old Parish Church

and an aviary along the way. Following the right-hand trail after a fork
near the lower end will reveal traces of Pluto, a secret pipeline built
during World War II, which carried fuel from England down the chine
and across the channel to the Normandy beachhead.

At the end, where the stream runs into the sea, turn left and climb
up onto The Esplanade, a road along the beach. **Shanklin Pier** (8) is
worth a visit as it is quite different from the one in Sandown, having a
honky-tonk atmosphere more reminiscent of Brighton.

From here you can follow the map to **Shanklin Station** (9) and
begin the return journey. The nearby lift will save an uphill climb. If
you would rather walk some more, a particularly nice route to follow
is along the beach to Sandown. There is a surfaced path going all the
way.

Winchester

Winchester wears its history gracefully. The first "capital" of England, it was an important town from Roman times until the 12th century, when it lost out to rival London. Despite this decline, it remained a major religious and educational center, a role it still plays today. There are few places in England where the past has survived to delight the present quite so well.

The history of Winchester goes back to the Iron Age, when the Belgae, a Celtic tribe, settled in the valley of the River Itchen. This became the Roman town of *Venta Belgarum,* the fifth-largest in Britain. Following the collapse of the empire, the Anglo-Saxons took over and, changing the name to *Wintanceaster,* made it the capital of their kindgom of Wessex. Threats from marauding Danes caused the rival kingdoms of England to unite behind Egbert, the king of Wessex, in the mid-9th century, an act that made Winchester the effective capital of all England. A few decades later, under Alfred the Great, the town reached its peak of importance, and afterwards became the seat of such kings as Canute, Edward the Confessor, and William the Conqueror. Winchester's time had passed, however, and during the Norman era the center of power was gradually transferred to London.

By getting off to an early start it is possible to combine this trip with one to Southampton, which is on the same rail line and highway.

GETTING THERE:

Trains to Winchester leave London's Waterloo Station hourly. The trip takes about 70 minutes, and return service operates until late evening.

Coaches leave Victoria Coach Station in London several times in the morning for Winchester, a trip of about two hours.

By car, Winchester is 72 miles southwest of London via the M-3 Highway.

WHEN TO GO:

This trip can be made at any time, although some sights are closed on Sundays, and on Mondays from October through March. Good weather is important if you intend to take the lovely walk to St. Cross Hospital.

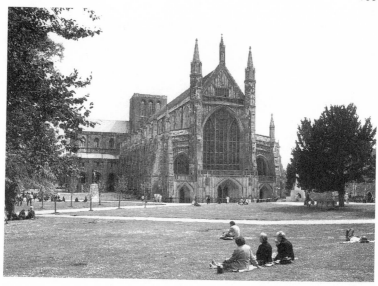

Winchester Cathedral

FOOD AND DRINK:

Winchester has a wide selection of restaurants and pubs in all price ranges. A few good choices are:

Old Chesil Rectory (1 Chesil St., near the City Mill) Traditional English food in a 14th-century rectory. X: Sun. eve., Mon. $$

The Elizabethan (18 Jewry St., near High St.) A Tudor house with traditional English fare. $$

Mr. Pitkin's (4 Jewry St., near High St.) Buffet meals in the wine bar and full meals in the restaurant. $ and $$

Spys (9 Great Minster St., near the City Cross) A wine bar for snacks and a restaurant for full meals. X: Sun. $ and $$

Wykeham Arms (75 Kingsgate St., near Winchester College) An 18th-century inn, now a pub with meals. X for food: Sun., Mon. eve. $

Royal Oak (Royal Oak Passage, just off High St.) Lunch in an ancient pub with plenty of atmosphere. X for food: Sun. $

TOURIST INFORMATION:

The friendly local tourist office, phone (0962) 65-406, is in the Guildhall on The Broadway. It stocks a wide selection of maps and brochures.

SUGGESTED TOUR:

Starting at the **train station** (1), follow Sussex Street to the **Westgate** (2), one of Winchester's two remaining medieval gatehouses. Built in the 12th century, its upper floor was added in 1380 and later served as a debtors' prison. It is now a small museum with an interesting collection of ancient armor and related objects. The view from its roof is excellent. Visits may be made Mondays through Saturdays, from 10 a.m. to 5 p.m.; and on Sundays from 2–5 p.m. From October through March it is closed on Mondays, and closes on Sundays at 4 p.m.

Strolling down High Street, you will pass the Old Guildhall on the right. Its projecting clock and figure of Queen Anne were given to the town to commemorate the Treaty of Utrecht in 1713. On the roof there is a wooden tower that houses the curfew bell, still rung each evening at eight. The 16th-century God Begot House, opposite, occupies the site of a manor given by Ethelred the Unready to his Queen Emma in 1012.

A few more steps will bring you to the **City Cross** (3). Also known as the Butter Cross, it was erected in the 15th century. Make a right through the small passageway leading to The Square. William the Conqueror's palace once stood here. The **City Museum** (4) has fascinating displays of local archaeological finds, including Celtic pottery, a Roman mosaic floor, and painted walls. It is open during the same times as the Westgate, above.

Winchester Cathedral (5) is among the largest in Europe. It was begun in 1079 on the site of earlier Saxon churches. During the 14th century the cathedral was altered with a new Gothic nave, resulting in a mixture of styles ranging from robust Norman to graceful Perpendicular. Several of England's earliest kings are buried here, including Ethelwulf, Egbert, Canute, and William II Rufus, son of the Norman conqueror.

Enter the nave through the west doorway. The windows retain some of the original 14th-century stained glass, most of which was destroyed by Puritan zealots during the Civil War. About halfway down the nave, on the right, is the magnificent **Wykeham's Chantry,** dedicated to Bishop William of Wykeham, who was also the founder of Winchester College and New College at Oxford, as well as a noted statesman. Almost opposite this, on the north aisle, is an outstanding 12th-century **font,** carved with the story of St. Nicholas. Jane Austen's tomb is nearby in the north aisle.

The massive transepts are almost unchanged since Norman times. Near the southeast corner is a chapel containing the tomb of Izaak Walton, author of *The Compleat Angler,* who died here in 1683. A doorway in the south wall leads to the **Library,** which has a 10th-century copy of the Venerable Bede's *Ecclesiastical History* as well as a

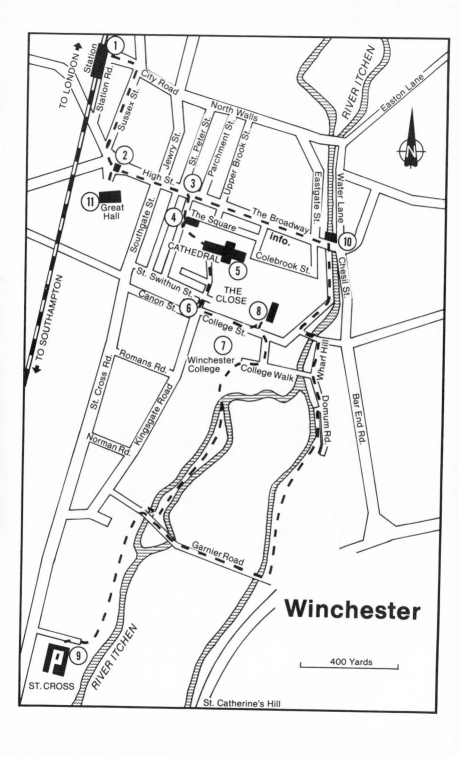

rare 12th-century illuminated Bible. During the summer it is open every day except on Sundays, and in winter on Saturdays and Wednesdays.

Continue up the south aisle and enter the **Presbytery.** Above the screens are six mortuary chests containing the bones of early English kings. Behind the high altar is a magnificently carved 15th-century ornamental screen. Adjoining this is the choir with some outstanding early-14th-century stalls and misericords. The tomb of William II Rufus is under the tower. At the east end of the cathedral is the 12th-century **Chapel of the Guardian Angels,** and the modern **Shrine of St. Swithun.** Other sights include the crypt and the treasury.

Leave the cathedral and stroll through the Close, partially surrounded by the ancient monastery's walls. An arcade of the former Chapter House links the south transept with the Deanery. Dome alley has some particularly fine 17th-century houses. Pass through the **Kingsgate** (6), the second of the two surviving medieval town gates. Above it is the tiny 13th-century Church of St. Swithun-upon-Kingsgate, which should definitely be visited.

Winchester College (7), the oldest "public" school in England, was founded in 1382 and is associated with New College at Oxford. You may visit the chapel or wander around the courtyards on your own whenever the college is open. Guided tours are available from April through September for those who would like to see more.

Continue down College Street to the ruins of **Wolvesey Castle** (8), begun in 1129 and destroyed in 1646 by Cromwell's forces during the Civil War. They are enclosed by part of the old city wall, but you can enter and take a look from April through October, Tuesdays through Saturdays, from 2–5 p.m. The adjacent Wolvesey Palace, thought to have been designed by Christopher Wren, is now the bishop's residence.

From here there is a wonderfully picturesque riverside walk to the venerable Hospital of St. Cross, the oldest functioning almshouse in England. It is about one mile away and can be reached by bus along St. Cross Road, but the delightful stroll along the stream is too lovely to miss. You can always ride back. To get there, just follow the map.

The **Hospital of St. Cross** (9) has always had a tradition of providing a dole of bread and ale to weary wayfarers, which includes you. Ask and ye shall receive. Founded in 1136 by Bishop Henry de Blois, grandson of William the Conqueror, the institution cares for 25 brethren who live in 15th-century quarters and wear medieval gowns. There is a 12th-century Norman chapel and a 15th-century hall and kitchen that can be visited. It is open all year, except on Sundays and Christmas Day, from 9 a.m. to 12:30 p.m. and from 2–5 p.m., with shorter hours in the winter. Don't miss this.

Those returning on foot can take the alternate route via Garnier Road. St. Catherine's Hill, across the river, has an Iron Age fort

The Hospital of St. Cross

and the foundations of an early chapel at its summit, as well as an excellent view.

Back in Winchester, the footpath leads across the River Itchen alongside the medieval walls to the **City Mill** (10), now a youth hostel. There has been a mill at this location since Anglo-Saxon days. The present one, built in 1744, may be visited between April and mid-October, Tuesdays through Saturdays, from 2–5 p.m.

Turn left and follow The Broadway past the statue of King Alfred, who made Winchester a center of learning over a thousand years ago. The huge Victorian Guildhall of 1873 houses the tourist office. From here, High Street leads to The Castle, an administrative complex that includes the **Great Hall** (11), the sole remaining part of Winchester Castle. Dating from the early 13th century, the hall was the scene of many important events in English history. Go inside and take a look at the famous Roundtable, once associated with King Arthur but now known to be of 14th-century origin. It is open daily from 10 a.m. to 5 p.m., closing at 4 p.m. on winter weekends. There are three military museums in the immediate vicinity that may interest you, the **Royal Hussars,** the **Royal Greenjackets,** and the **Royal Hampshire Regiment.** From here it is only a short stroll back to the train station.

Southampton

Great seaports are exciting places, having been touched by the world in ways that inland cities never experience. Despite the decline in passenger traffic, Southampton has maintained its cosmopolitan character and continues to thrive on international trade. There is a certain fascination to watching its ever-changing harbor scene and another to exploring its colorful past.

Southampton's recorded history begins with the Roman garrison of *Clausentum*. This was followed by the Saxon town of *Hamwih* where, in 1016, Canute was offered the crown of England. Large-scale trade with the Continent developed after the Norman Conquest, and in the 12th century the port became an embarkation point for many of Richard the Lionhearted's Crusaders. During the Hundred Years War the town was often raided by the French, most notably in 1338. A serious decline, lasting 200 years, began in the 16th century. The Pilgrims departed from here in 1620, making a stop at Plymouth on their way to the New World. A few decades later, in 1665, Southampton was decimated by the plague.

Great places have a way of bouncing back. At its low point, Southampton suddenly discovered the spa business, becoming a fashionable seaside resort, a position it held until losing out to Brighton during the Regency. But there was still the harbor with its deep channels and four high tides a day. In the 1840s the railway came and vast docks were built. Southampton had become England's gateway to the world. Millions of troops left from here during both world wars. The city was devastated by bombs in the early 1940s, and largely rebuilt in the decades that followed. Miraculously, most of its ancient treasures survived and are now incorporated in the fabric of the modern, thriving city that Southampton is today.

It is possible to combine this trip with one to Winchester in the same day by making an early start. They are both on the same highway and rail line.

GETTING THERE:

Trains depart London's Waterloo Station at least hourly for Southampton. The trip takes 70 minutes or so, and return service operates until late evening.

Coaches leave from London's Victoria Coach Station hourly for the 2¼-hour run to Southampton.

South Side of Bargate

By car, Southampton is 87 miles southwest of London via the M-3 and A-33 highways.

WHEN TO GO:
Avoid coming to Southampton on a Monday, when virtually all of the sights are closed.

FOOD AND DRINK:
There are plenty of restaurants and pubs in the central business area. Some good choices are:

La Brasserie (33 Oxford St., 2 blocks north of the main gate to the docks) One of Southampton's best restaurants; French cuisine. X: Sat. lunch, Sun. $$

The Solent (Herbert Walker Ave., opposite Mayflower Park) Good food in the modern Post House Hotel. $$

Golden Palace (17 Above Bar St., just south of the tourist office) An upstairs Chinese restaurant specializing in seafood and dim sum. $ and $$

The Star (26 High St., near Holy Rood Church) Bar lunches and full dinners in an 18th-century inn. $ and $$

The Red Lion (High St., near the Holy Rood Church) A famous old historic pub with lunches. $

Duke of Wellington (Bugle St., near the Tudor House) Lunch in an ancient pub. $

TOURIST INFORMATION:

The local tourist office, phone (0703) 22-11-06, is in the middle of Above Bar Street, north of the Bargate.

SUGGESTED TOUR:

Leaving the **train station** (1), follow Civic Centre Road to Above Bar Street and turn right. The tourist office is straight ahead. You may want to inquire here about getting permission to go out on the docks.

Continue on to **Bargate** (2), a particularly fine example of an early medieval fortification, once part of the ancient town walls. There is an interesting museum of local history inside, which can be seen Tuesdays through Fridays, from 10 a.m. to 12 noon and from 1–5 p.m.; on Saturdays from 10 a.m. to 12 noon and from 1–4 p.m.; and on Sundays from 2–5 p.m.

From here, Bargate Street leads along remnants of the walls to the Arundel Tower. The western section of the ramparts, originally dating from Norman times, is still in good condition. Take a look at it, then follow the map to Bugle Street.

The **Tudor House** (3) is a handsome half-timbered 16th-century structure that now houses a museum of life in old Southampton. Be sure to see the 12th-century Norman merchant's house in its garden, adjoining the town wall. The museum is open during the same times as the Bargate Museum, above. On the other side of the square is St. Michael's Church, also dating from Norman times but heavily altered in the 19th century.

Follow Bugle Street to Westgate Street and turn right. The 14th-century West Gate opens onto Western Esplanade, once the quay from which the Pilgrims departed in 1620. Turn left and enter **Mayflower Park** (4). There are good views of the harbor here.

Return to Town Quay and visit the **Maritime Museum** (5) in the old 14th-century Wool House, once a warehouse and later a jail. Its attractions include a maritime history of Southampton, models of famous ships, and an interesting collection of seafaring artifacts. Visits may be made during the same times that the Bargate Museum, above, is open. From here you can explore the nearby piers.

God's House Tower (6) on Platform Road is a 15th-century fortification that is now used as a museum of archaeology. Step inside to see the fine displays of prehistoric, Roman, Saxon, and medieval finds. Again, the hours are the same as those of the Bargate Museum, above.

From here you can walk to the **Itchen Bridge** (7), a modern high-level span offering incomparable views of the entire harbor complex all the way out to the Isle of Wight. Along the way you will pass Gate 4 to the Ocean Dock, where the big liners call, just opposite Latimer Road. Permission to enter the dock area is usually given without any

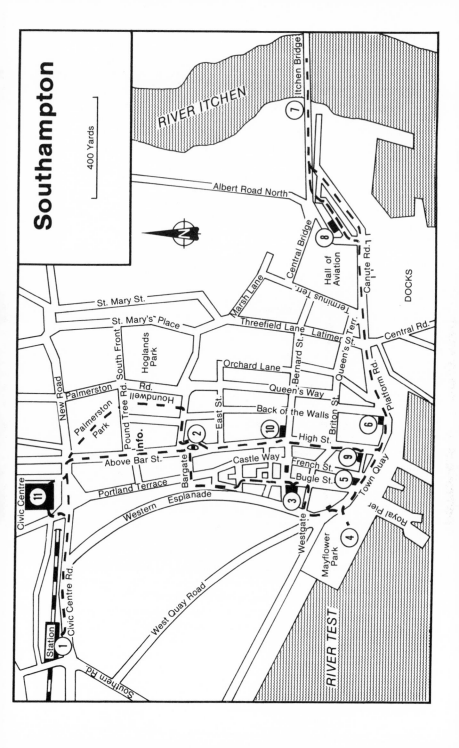

In the Hall of Aviation

problem.

Return and follow the map to the **Hall of Aviation** (8) on Albert Road South. The fascinating displays here include a World War II Spitfire and an actual Sandringham flying boat, once used for passenger service in the Pacific, that may be boarded. Ask for permission to climb up into the flight deck. These marvelous old airplanes may be seen Tuesdays through Saturdays, from 10 a.m. to 5 p.m.; and on Sundays from 12 noon to 5 p.m. Refreshments are available inside.

Continue on and make a right up High Street. The remains of a long Norman structure incorrectly known as "**Canute's Palace**" (9) are in Porter's Lane. High Street leads past the historic Red Lion Inn to the ruined **Holy Rood Church** (10) of the 14th century.

Now follow the route through Houndwell and Palmerston Park to the **Art Gallery** (11) in the massive Civic Centre. One of the very best art museums in all of Britain, it specializes in British painting, and also has an excellent collection of Old Masters, Impressionist, and Post-Impressionist works. The museum is open Tuesdays through Fridays, from 10 a.m. to 5 p.m.; on Saturdays from 10 a.m. to 4 p.m.; and on Sundays from 2–5 p.m. From here it is only a short stroll back to the train station.

Salisbury and Stonehenge

The cathedral city of Salisbury is a relative newcomer as English towns go. It was first settled in 1220 when the local bishop moved his cathedral down from a hilltop stronghold known as *Sarum*. Dating from prehistoric times, this earlier site was of great importance to the Romans, who called it *Sor viodunum*. Later becoming the Saxon settlement of *Searoburh*, it acquired a Norman castle and a cathedral during the 11th century. Frequent clashes between the clergy and the military, as well as harsh conditions imposed by a dry, windswept location, led to the establishment of a new town in the more hospitable meadows along the River Avon, just two miles to the south. After this, Old Sarum gradually died out. Its abandoned cathedral was demolished in 1331 and the stones reused for building a wall around the new town's cathedral close. By the 16th century the site was completely deserted although, as the rottenest of the Rotten Boroughs, it continued to send two members to Parliament until 1832.

The new town of Salisbury has always been a peaceful place that escaped the vicissitudes of history. Since its cathedral was one of the few to be based on a chapter of secular canons rather than a monastery, it quickly became a worldly center with all of the features of a thriving provincial capital. Salisbury today is an extraordinarily beautiful town made all the more fascinating by its proximity to the mysterious Stonehenge, one of England's most popular tourist attractions.

GETTING THERE:
   Trains depart London's Waterloo Station at hourly intervals for the 1½-hour ride to Salisbury, with return service operating until mid-evening. Schedules are somewhat reduced on Sundays and holidays. There is bus service for Stonehenge from Salisbury.
   By car, Salisbury is 91 miles southwest of London via the M-3 and A-30 highways. To get to Stonehenge, take the A-345 north to Amesbury, then the A-303 and A-344 west to the site. Stonehenge is about ten miles from Salisbury. Old Sarum is along the way, about two miles north of Salisbury on the A-345.

WHEN TO GO:

Salisbury may be visited on any day, although some sights are closed on Sundays. Getting to Stonehenge without a car may be difficult in winter or early spring, or on Sundays or holidays. A colorful market is held on Tuesdays and Saturdays.

FOOD AND DRINK:

Salisbury is famous for its ancient pubs. Some of the best of these, and restaurants too, are:

> **Haunch of Venison** (1 Minster St., near St. Thomas' Church) A very famous pub with meals, dating from the 14th century. $$
>
> **Old Mill** (Town Path, Harnham) A delightful old mill by the River Nadder, with a great view and good food. $$
>
> **King's Arms** (9 St. John St., just east of the cathedral) A half-timbered inn with lots of character. $ and $$
>
> **Pheasant Inn** (Salt Lane, north of Market Place) A pub and a restaurant, dating from 1400. $ and $$
>
> **New Inn** (41 New St., near North Gate) A pub with good food in a 15th-century building. $
>
> **Michael Snell** (5 St. Thomas Sq., near St. Thomas' Church) Light meals in a coffeeshop, with homemade sweets. X: Sun. $

TOURIST INFORMATION:

The local tourist office, phone (0722) 33-49-56, is in the Guildhall on the Market Place.

SUGGESTED TOUR:

Depending on your arrival time, it is probably best to head out for Stonehenge immediately, getting there before the crowds get too thick. Buses leave from the train station (1) a few times daily except on Sundays or holidays, from mid-April to mid-December. More frequent service is available from the bus station near the Market Place (9). For more information, check with the tourist office. Those driving their own cars should just follow the directions in "Getting There," above.

Stonehenge (2) is a massive circular group of standing stones, erected in several stages between the Late Neolithic and Middle Bronze ages. It seems to have been a temple of sorts, but anything beyond that is speculation. What is truly marvelous about the place is that you can believe anything you want about it, no matter how outrageous, and no one can prove you wrong. Go right ahead and indulge your imagination. Perhaps Merlin really did build it by magic, or maybe it actually was an astronomical observatory, or even a temple of the Druids. Who knows? One thing is certain, however. What you get out of it is what you put in. To approach this site without preparation is to

Stonehenge

see a pile of rocks and little else. Pamphlets explaining some of the theories are sold near the entrance, although advance homework will make your visit more rewarding.

On the way back you should try to make a stop at the ruins of **Old Sarum**, the original Salisbury, described in the introductory paragraph above. From there return to the train station and begin your exploration of "new" Salisbury.

Leaving the **train station** (1), walk down to the River Nadder and cross it. A footpath from here leads through delightful countryside to the ancient **Harnham Mill** (3), parts of which may date from the 13th century. Now an inn, its bucolic setting is a scene right out of a Constable landscape. All along the way there are wonderful views of the cathedral.

Return to **Queen Elizabeth Gardens** (4) and follow the map across the 15th-century Crane Bridge. Turn right at High Street and stroll through **North Gate** (5), a 14th-century structure that once protected the bishops from rebellious citizens. The **Mompesson House** (6) on Choristers' Green, built in 1701, has an exquisite Queen Anne interior with notable plasterwork. It belongs to the National Trust and is open from the beginning of April to the end of October, Saturdays through Wednesdays, from 12:30–6 p.m.

Salisbury Cathedral (7) was built over a very short time span, from 1220 to 1258, which accounts for its remarkable architectural unity. It

Salisbury Cathedral

is the purest example of the Early English style to be found anywhere in the kingdom. The graceful tower was added a century later and, at 404 feet, is the loftiest medieval spire in the world.

Enter through the north door. The interior is somewhat disappointing for so majestic a structure. This is due to an ill-advised spring housecleaning in the 18th century during which most of the wonderful medieval clutter that makes other churches so fascinating was removed. Despite this, there are still some interesting things to see. The most famous of these is the 14th-century **clock mechanism** at the west end of the north aisle. Still in operating condition, it is thought to be the oldest in England and perhaps the world. The **west window** contains some good 13th-century glass, as does the **Lady Chapel** at the east end. Stroll out into the **Cloisters,** the largest in England, and visit the adjoining **Chapter House**, whose treasures include one of the four existing original copies of the **Magna Carta**, as well as 13th-century sculptures illustrating scenes from the Old Testament.

A walk around Cathedral Close makes a pleasant break before continuing on. The Bishop's Palace, now occupied by the Cathedral School, and the Old Deanery are particularly fine 13th-century buildings within the precincts. Be sure to visit the **Salisbury and South Wiltshire Museum** (8) in the King's House along West Walk. Its displays include models and relics from Stonehenge and Old Sarum, along with items

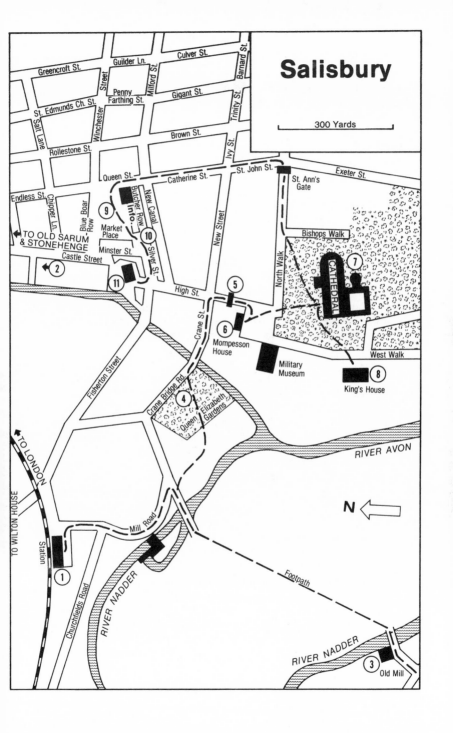

Salisbury

300 Yards

of local history. The museum is open Mondays through Saturdays, from 10 a.m. to 5 p.m., closing at 4 p.m. in winter. During July and August it is also open on Sundays, from 2–5 p.m. You may also be interested in seeing the **Military Museum**, located in another nearby historic house.

Follow North Walk to St. Ann's Gate where, in a room above the gateway, Handel gave his first public concert in England. Pass under this and turn left on St. John's Street. The King's Arms has been an inn since the 15th century. Just beyond it is the White Hart Hotel, an 18th-century coaching inn. Continue on to the **Market Place** (9), where a market has been held twice a week since 1361, a custom that continues today. The Guildhall of 1795 is in the southeast corner and houses the tourist office.

Cut through the market to Silver Street. The beautiful hexagonal **Poultry Cross** (10) was first mentioned in 1335 as the spot where poultry was sold. Around the corner, approached through alleyways, is **St. Thomas' Church** (11), one of the most interesting buildings in Salisbury. Founded in honor of Thomas à Becket about 1220, it was rebuilt in the 15th century and has a marvelous fresco depicting the Last Judgement above its chancel arch. The area immediately surrounding it is the quintessence of a medieval merchants' town and the perfect place to wind up your tour.

Those who have decided not to go to Stonehenge may want to visit **Wilton House** instead. One of England's most attractive stately homes, it is filled with outstanding art and has lovely gardens. You can get a bus there from outside the cinema on New Canal. Wilton House is open from late March through mid-October, Tuesdays through Saturdays from 11 a.m. to 6 p.m.; and on Sundays from 1–6 p.m.

Windsor and Eton

Windsor, like Stratford, Oxford, and the Tower of London, is one of England's greatest tourist attractions. It has just the right combination of elements to make an ideal daytrip destination for first-time visitors and seasoned travelers alike. To begin with, it is very close to the capital and easy to reach. Second, it contains within a small area much of what is considered to be typically English. There is the Royal Castle, still in use after 850 years, a picturesque riverside location on the Thames, a colorful Victorian town, and in Eton one of the great public schools that have molded British character since the Middle Ages. Add these together and you have a carefree and thoroughly delightful day ahead of you.

GETTING THERE:

Trains depart London's Paddington Station at frequent intervals for Slough, where you change to a shuttle train for Windsor and Eton Central. The total journey takes about 30 minutes, with return service operating until late evening. There is also direct service from London's Waterloo Station to Windsor and Eton Riverside, taking about 50 minutes and running about twice an hour. Most travelers will find the route via Paddington to be more convenient.

Coaches operated by the Green Line leave from their terminal at Eccleston Bridge near Victoria Station in London every half-hour or so to Windsor. The trip takes between 50 and 90 minutes and deposits you on High Street.

By car, Windsor is 28 miles from London via the M-4 motorway. Get off at Junction 6.

WHEN TO GO:

The castle grounds are open daily except for special events. The State Apartments are also open daily, with the exception of Sundays in winter, but are closed when the Queen is in residence. Other sights are open most of the time. If in doubt, check with the tourist office in Windsor.

FOOD AND DRINK:

Windsor and Eton both have a very wide selection of pubs and restaurants in all price ranges. Some choices are:

In Windsor:

Wren's Old House (Thames St., near the bridge) Meals at an inn, once the home of Sir Christopher Wren. X: Sat. lunch. $$$

La Taverna (2 River St., near the bridge) Good Italian food in a nice location. X: Sun. $$

Country Kitchen (3 King Edward Court, in the shopping center just south of Central Station) International specialties in a self-service cafeteria. X: Sun. $

Carpenters Arms (Market St., behind the Guildhall) A comfortable pub with lunches. X for meals: Sun. $

In Eton:

Antico (42 High St., near the bridge) Fine dining with an Italian accent. X: Sat. lunch, Sun. $$$

Eton Wine Bar (82 High St., near the bridge) Imaginative cooking with a changing menu. $$

TOURIST INFORMATION:

The local tourist office, phone (0753) 85-20-10, is in the Windsor and Eton Central Station.

SUGGESTED TOUR:

Start your walk at **Windsor and Eton Central Station** (1). Directly adjacent to this is the wonderful **Royalty and Empire** exhibition that re-creates moments of the Victorian era with replicas of old railway equipment, animated figures of Queen Victoria and other notables, and a 15-minute audio-visual extravaganza. This perfect introduction to Windsor, operated by Madame Tussaud's, is open daily from 9:30 a.m. to 5:30 p.m.

Now cross the main street, passing the statue of Queen Victoria, and enter the castle grounds. Begun by William the Conqueror in the 11th century, **Windsor Castle** has been altered by nearly every succeeding monarch. It is the largest inhabited castle in the world and remains a chief residence for the sovereigns of England.

Enter through Henry VIII's Gateway and visit **St. George's Chapel** (2), one of the most beautiful churches in England. Many of the country's kings and queens are buried here. Continue on past the massive **Round Tower** and go out on the North Terrace, which has magnificent views up and down the River Thames. The entrance to the **State Apartments** (3) is nearby. A stroll through them is worthwhile, but don't fret if they are closed because the Queen is here. Much more interesting is **Queen Mary's Dolls' House**, a miniature 20th-century palace in exquisite detail, and the exhibition of **Old Masters Drawings**, both of which are also entered from the North Terrace. They are

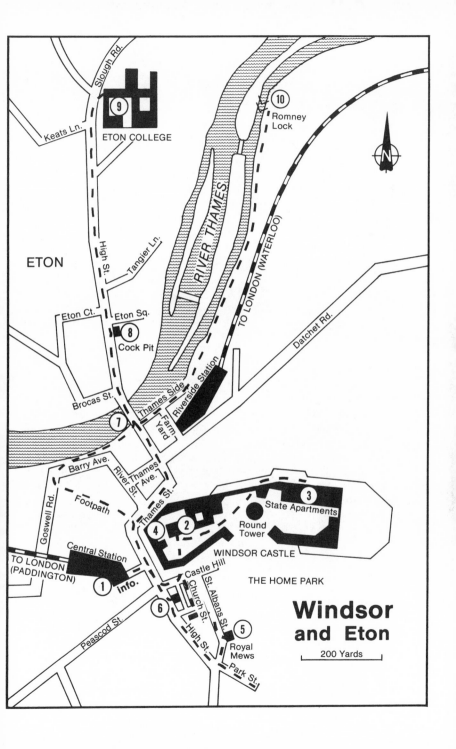

ETON

Slough Rd.

Keats Ln.

⑨
ETON COLLEGE

High St.

Tangier Ln.

Eton Ct. | Eton Sq.
⑧
Cock Pit

Brocas St.

RIVER THAMES

Romney Lock
⑩

TO LONDON (WATERLOO)

Datchet Rd.

N

⑦

Thames Side

Farm Yard

Riverside Station

Barry Ave.

River St.

Thames Ave.

Goswell Rd.

Footpath

Thames St.

③
State Apartments

②
④

Round Tower

WINDSOR CASTLE

THE HOME PARK

Central Station

TO LONDON (PADDINGTON)

①   Info.

⑥

Castle Hill

Church St.

St. Albans St.

High St.

⑤
Royal Mews

Peascod St.

Park St.

Windsor
and Eton

├─── 200 Yards ───┤

A Statue of Queen Victoria Guards the Castle

usually open Mondays through Saturdays, from 10:30 a.m. to 5 p.m.; and on Sundays from 1:30–5 p.m.; closing at 3 p.m. in winter. They are also closed on winter Sundays and on some holidays. The rest of your tour can be spent just poking about any area that is not off limits, and visiting the **Curfew Tower** (4).

Leave the castle and stroll down Church Street, perhaps stopping at the Parish Church and Brass Rubbing Centre. Walk through the graveyard to St. Alban's Street, near the foot of which is the **Royal Mews Exhibition** (5), a display of ceremonial carriages and various gifts received by the Queen. From here you might go down Park Street for a walk in the Home Park.

The elegant **Guildhall** (6) on High Street was completed in 1707 by Sir Christopher Wren. Step onto its porch and note that the center columns do not quite reach the ceiling they allegedly support, a trick played by the architect to prove the soundness of his design. Continue down High Street and Thames Street, making a left on the footpath to the river. Along the way you will pass a bowling green, tennis courts, and a lovely waterside park. **Boat trips**, some as short as 35 minutes, are available here.

The old **cast-iron bridge** (7) to Eton is reserved for pedestrians. Once across it follow High Street past numerous shops and pubs to the **Cock Pit** (8), a 15th-century timbered inn where cockfighting was

Boat Trips on the Thames

once patronized by Charles II, the Merry Monarch. Outside it are the town stocks and a unique Victorian mailbox.

Eton College (9) was founded in 1440 by Henry VI, himself a teenager at the time. It is the most famous of England's public (meaning very private) schools and has educated many of the nation's greatest leaders. As you walk around you will notice the peculiar traditional garb of the students, which makes them look a little like penguins. Parts of the school are open to visitors, including the schoolyard, cloisters, and the chapel. The Upper and Lower schools may also be seen at times. Guided tours, led by senior boys, are available. Be sure to visit the **Museum of Eton Life**, which re-creates life among the students in bygone times. Located in the cellars of the original 15th-century buildings, it is usually open between 2–5 p.m., depending on school activities.

Return to the bridge. If you have any strength or time left you may want to take a pleasant walk along the Thames to the **Romney Lock** (10), or visit a pub before returning to London.

Bath

Legend has it that the hot mineral springs of Bath were discovered about 500 B.C. by Prince Bladud who, suffering from leprosy, was cured and became king. Whatever truth lies behind this story, we do know that the Romans built a settlement there named *Aquae Sulis,* which served as their spa for nearly 400 years.

During the Middle Ages the waters of Bath were well known for their curative properties, but the splendor of the Romans had vanished. The town was renovated for Queen Anne's visit in 1702 and a master of ceremonies appointed to oversee the spa. This post remained after the queen's departure and was filled in 1705 by a bizarre young gambler named Richard "Beau" Nash, who in the next 40 years virtually invented the resort business.

Nash began by persuading the local leaders to invest vast sums into building a town of unmatched elegance. Much of this job fell to one John Wood, an architect with monumental ideas. Under his plan, individual houses were only components of a larger structure behind a common façade. This thinking reached its height in that triumph of the Palladian style, the Royal Crescent, designed by his son in 1767.

Today, Bath remains much the same as it was when the Georgian aristocracy made it their playground. The remains of the Roman era have since been unearthed, adding to its many attractions. What makes Bath such a first-rate daytrip destination is that, despite its stylish refinement, it is really a fun place to visit. Virtually all who visit there thoroughly enjoy themselves.

GETTING THERE:

Trains leave London's Paddington station at least hourly for Bath Spa Station, a ride of about 80 minutes. Return service operates until mid-evening.

Coaches depart London's Victoria Coach Station every two hours for the three-hour ride to Bath.

By car, take the M-4 highway to Junction 18, then drive a few miles south on the A-46. Bath is 119 miles west of London.

WHEN TO GO:

Bath may be visited at any time. Although this walk is short and can be completed in a few hours, try to allow the better part of a leisurely day to enjoy the sights, most of which are open daily.

FOOD AND DRINK:

Bath has an enormous number of restaurants and pubs to suit all tastes and purses. Some particularly fine choices are:

Hole in the Wall (16 George St., 2 blocks south of the Assembly Rooms) World-renowned for its French-inspired cuisine. X: Sun. lunch $$$

Royal Crescent Hotel (16 Royal Crescent) Very fine food with an outstanding wine selection. $$$

Clos du Roy (7 Edgar Buildings, George St., 2 blocks south of the Assembly Rooms) Imaginative French cuisine with good-value lunches. X: Sun., Mon. $$ and $$$

Flowers (27 Monmouth St., west of the Theatre Royal) A delightfully pleasant restaurant offering a reasonably priced lunch menu. X: Sun. $$ and $$$

Moon and Sixpence (6a Broad St., east of the Octagon) Simple lunches and full dinners, with outdoor tables available. $$ and $$$

Woods (9 Alfred St., near the Assembly Rooms) Famous for its good food and Georgian elegance. X: Sun. $$

Rajpoot Tandoori (4 Argyle St., east of the Pulteney Bridge) Try a superb Indian meal for a change. $$

Sweeney Todd's (15 Milsom St., near the Octagon) Pizza, burgers, chili, and the like—in a nice atmosphere. $

Huckleberry's (34 Broad St., east of the Octagon) A fine place for vegetarian meals. X: Sun. $

TOURIST INFORMATION:

The local tourist office is on Abbey Churchyard, by the Abbey and the Roman Baths. You can phone them at (0225) 62-831.

SUGGESTED TOUR:

Leaving **Bath Spa Station** (1), walk straight ahead on Manvers Street past the bus station to **South Parade** (2), part of a group of find Palladian buildings begun by the architect John Wood in 1740. Continue along Pierrepont Street and turn left at North Parade. In one block this becomes a colorful lane called Old Lilliput Alley, lined with some of the oldest houses in Bath. Note in particular **Sally Lunn's House**, built in 1482 on Roman foundations, and famous for its sinfully rich hot Bath buns for as long as anyone can remember. At the end of the passage is Abbey Green, an especially attractive spot.

Turn right on Church Street and follow it for two blocks to the **Abbey** (3). This splendid example of the Perpendicular style was begun in 1499, although it did not gain a roof until the 17th century. Earlier churches existed on the same spot for several hundred years

The Abbey

before a cathedral was built in 1088, a Norman structure that was destroyed by fire in 1137. The present abbey is noted for its enormous clerestory windows that flood the interior with light, and for its vaulted ceiling, planned from the start but not added until 1864.

Walk across the Abbey Churchyard, past the tourist office and through the colonnade, then turn left to the entrance of the **Roman Baths and Pump Room** (4). The tour through this ancient complex begins with a fascinating **museum** of Roman and prehistoric relics, featuring the renowned gilt-bronze head of the goddess Minerva. An overflowing part of the original Roman reservoir is also in this area. Continue on to the **Great Bath**, a marvelously preserved pool that is today open to the sky. The original Roman lead plumbing is still in use, while the columns and statues above are Victorian additions. Another group of small baths and hypocaust rooms lie beyond, as do the King's Bath and the Circular Bath. A few of the ruins were discovered in the 18th century, but it was not until the 19th that the major finds were excavated, with digs still going on. Above all of this is the famous **Pump Room**, an elegant Georgian assembly hall that reflects a gentility long vanished elsewhere. Be sure to see the wonderful equation clock of 1709, as well as the charming prints and 18th-century furniture. There is a fountain where you can drink the rather foul-tasting mineral water, bubbling up hot from the springs below. The entire

The Great Bath

complex is open daily from 9 a.m. to 6 p.m., closing at 5 p.m. in winter. It is also open in the evening from 8:30–10:30 p.m. during August only.

Leave the baths and continue down Bath Street, passing the outdoor mineral-water drinking fountain and the Cross Bath, originally medieval but rebuilt in 1787. A right here leads into St. Michael's Place, from which you follow a narrow passageway called Chandos Buildings to Westgate Buildings. Turn right again and amble up to St. John's Place.

The **Theatre Royal** (5), adjacent to Beau Nash's last home—now a restaurant named after his mistress, Juliana Popjoy—was first erected in 1720 but later rebuilt. Turn right for one block on Upper Borough Walls, the site of a medieval wall, and make a left through an archway named Trim Bridge. Narrow, cobbled Queen Street has a very attractive collection of small houses and shops. Walk along it to Wood Street, turn left, and right again into Queen Square. Queen's Parade lies a block beyond this. Turn left on it, then right onto Royal Avenue. This shady street leads uphill through Royal Victoria Park.

From the gravel walk to the right you have an excellent view of the **Royal Crescent** (6), a magnificent sweep of 30 houses joined together in one continuous façade of 114 Ionic columns. Designed in 1767 by John Wood the Younger, this is regarded as the epitome of the Palla-

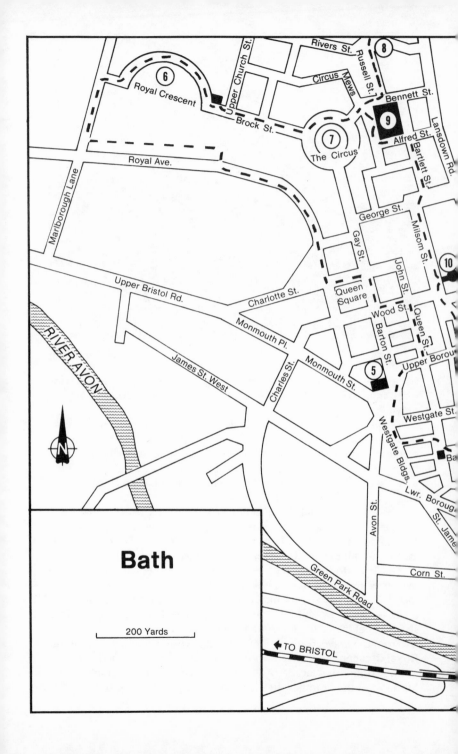

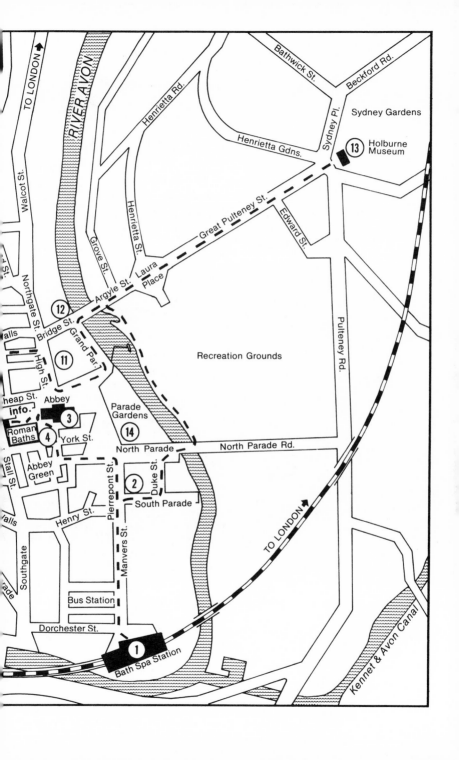

The Royal Crescent

dian style in England. Following the map around the length of the crescent; stop at **Number 1**, whose interior has been restored to its 18th-century splendor. This exquisite house is open to the public from March until mid-December, Tuesdays through Saturdays, from 11 a.m. to 5 p.m., and Sundays from 2–5 p.m. Don't miss it.

Stroll down Brock Street to **The Circus** (7), a circular group of Georgian houses considered to be John Wood's finest work. It is arranged so that no street goes straight through, resulting in a view from every angle. Continue along Bennett Street, from which you can take an interesting little side trip by turning up Russell Street and making a right on Rivers Street to the **Camden Works Museum** (8), just off the map. This Victorian engineering shop, brass foundry, and mineral-water plant is complete with all of its original machinery and related items. An unusually fascinating place to visit, it is open daily from 2–5 p.m., March through November, and on weekends only the rest of the year.

Now retrace your steps to the **Assembly Rooms** (9). Also built by John Wood the Younger, this structure was the center of social activity in Bath, having witnessed many grand balls, banquets, receptions, and the like. The **Museum of Costume** on its lower floor is the largest of its kind in the world. Clothes dating from as far back as the 16th century up to the present are very well displayed, many of them in period room settings. It is open daily, from 9:30 a.m. to 6 p.m., closing at 5 p.m. in winter.

Leaving the museum, turn left on Alfred Street and right on Bartlett. Cross busy George Street and follow Milsom Street, the main shopping thoroughfare. At number 46 you will find the entrance to **The Octagon** (10), an 18th-century hall that now houses the **National Centre of Photography**. This intriguing museum has displays of both contemporary and early camera work as well as an outstanding collection of antique and modern photo equipment, including a vast number of Leicas. It also serves as the headquarters of the Royal Photographic Society, and is open Mondays through Saturdays, from 10 a.m. to 5 p.m.

Continue straight ahead past Upper Borough Walls and turn left into the very charming Northumberland Place. The building on the other side is the **Guildhall** (11), whose banqueting room is one of the finest interiors in Bath. This may be seen Mondays through Fridays, from 8:30 a.m. to 4:30 p.m. Next to it is the Covered Market, which was founded in medieval times and remains very much alive in its 19th-century building.

Turning left around the Orange Grove brings you to Grand Parade. To the left, on Bridge Street, is the **Victoria Art Gallery**, which displays changing exhibitions of interest. It is open Mondays through Fridays, from 10 a.m. to 6 p.m.; and on Saturdays from 10 a.m. to 5 p.m. The **Pulteney Bridge** (12) spanning the Avon is one of the few in Europe to be lined with shops. Built in 1770 with obvious inspiration from the Ponte Vecchio in Florence, it makes a spectacular sight rising above the weir. Once across it, you can either continue straight ahead or stroll down along the river.

Argyle Street and Great Pulteney Street lead to the **Holburne of Menstrie Museum** (13), which specializes in the arts of the Age of Elegance. Silver, porcelains, miniatures, and paintings by Gainsborough and others are among its attractions. Visits may be made Mondays through Saturdays, from 11 a.m. to 5 p.m.; and on Sundays from 2:30–6 p.m. It is closed between mid-December and mid-February, and on Mondays between November and Easter.

Return along Great Pulteney Street almost to the bridge, then go down a flight of steps marked Riverside Walk to the River Avon and stroll past the weir. From the embankment on this side you can take a **boat ride** lasting about one hour. Current information about schedules is available from the tourist office. When you get to the next bridge, climb the stairs and cross it. You are now on North Parade. The **Parade Gardens** (14) on the right are a good place to relax before returning to the station or revisiting your favorite spots in this most enchanting town.

Wells

Completely dominated by its lovely cathedral, the small town of Wells has a timeless beauty that is rare, even in England. Other cathedral towns have grown and become worldly while Wells slept right through the turmoils of history. Its medieval ecclesiastical complex remains complete and untouched, the largest and best preserved in the country. A delight to explore on foot, Wells is the perfect place to become involved with the Middle Ages.

Just two miles away, reached by road or, better still, a tranquil woodland path, is the Wookey Hole, a great cave where early man lived over 2,000 years ago. A tour through its subterranean chambers combined with a visit to Wells makes this a very satisfying daytrip.

GETTING THERE:

Trains depart London's Paddington station at least hourly for the 80-minute ride to Bath Spa, where you change to a bus for Wells. This leaves from the Bath bus station, just one block away. Service to Wells operates hourly (every two hours on Sundays and holidays), taking about 80 minutes to cover the 20-mile distance through lovely villages and down country lanes. Be sure to check the return schedule.

By car, take the M-4 to Junction 18, then head south on the A-46 to Bath. Change here to the A-39 for Wells, which is 132 miles west of London.

WHEN TO GO:

This trip may be made at any time, but note that transportation is reduced on Sundays and holidays. Good weather is essential if you intend to walk to the Wookey Hole. A colorful outdoor market is held in Wells on Wednesdays and Saturdays. Some shops close early on Wednesdays.

FOOD AND DRINK:

There are many old inns and pubs in Wells, mostly in the Market Place and on High and Sadler streets. The town is famous for its cheeses. Out at the Wookey Hole there is a cafeteria, in addition to a nearby pub. Some good places to eat in Wells are:

The Cathedral from St. Andrew's Well

The Swan (11 Sadler St., just west of the cathedral) Fine dining in a 15th-century building, now a small hotel. $$

Crown (Market Place) A 15th-century inn associated with William Penn. $$

Star (14 High St., just west of the Market Place) Bar lunches and full dinners in a 16th-century coaching inn. $ and $$

Red Lion (Market Place) A 15th-century inn with bar snacks at lunch and full dinners in the evening. $ and $$

The Good Earth (4 Priory Rd., south of the bus station) Vegetarian health food in a rustic environment. X: Sun. $

TOURIST INFORMATION:

The local tourist office, phone (0749) 72-552, is in the Town Hall on Market Place. Ask them about getting to the Wookey Hole.

SUGGESTED TOUR:

Leave the **bus station** (1) in Wells and follow the map to the **Market Place** (2), where an outdoor market is held on Wednesdays and Saturdays. The tourist office is nearby.

Penniless Porch, where alms were once distributed, leads to the **Cathedral** (3). A church has stood here since A.D. 704, but the present structure was begun about 1180. Its astonishing **west front** is from the mid-13th century and is decorated with 297 medieval statues, all that remain of the original 400. At one time these were brightly colored, but weather has taken its toll over the centuries. It is still possibly the finest collection of sculpture from the Middle Ages in England.

Enter the nave and examine the remarkable **inverted arch** under the central tower. This was erected in the 14th century to support the newly completed tower, which was already collapsing. Unique in the world of Gothic design, it has done its job well. There is a marvelous clock in the north transept that dates from 1392 and gives an animated performance as it strikes the hour. A spectacular stone staircase nearby leads to the **Chapter House**, one of the finest examples of its style in the country. Continue on through the choir to see the east window, which has some unusual old glass.

A stroll through the 15th-century **cloisters** will bring you to the grounds of the **Bishop's Palace** (4), one of the oldest inhabited houses in England. The strong walls and surrounding moat were added in the 14th century to protect the bishop from rioting townspeople. If you get there on a day when it is open, be sure to cross the drawbridge, visit the palace, and then walk out to the gardens. **St. Andrew's Well** provides the setting for an almost magically serene view of the cathedral. The Bishop's Palace can usually be visited on Thursdays, Sundays, and holiday Mondays from 2–6 p.m., between Easter and late October; or daily during August.

From the south corner of the moat make a right on Silver Street to the early-15th-century **Bishop's Barn** (5). Return along the moat and turn left on Tor Street. Another left at St. Andrew's Street leads to **Vicar's Close** (6), a 14th-century street of immense charm connected to the cathedral by a bridge over the Chain Gate.

Beyond the archway lies the **Wells Museum** (7) on Cathedral Green. Prehistoric artifacts from the Wookey Hole and other nearby caves are featured in its splendid collection, along with natural displays and local bygones. It is open from April through September, daily from 11 a.m. to 5 p.m.; and on Wednesdays, Saturdays, and Sundays during the off-season.

At this point you may be interested in an invigorating hike to the Wookey Hole, two miles away. If your feet are not up to it but you would still like to go, you can take one of the hourly buses from the bus station (1), or a taxi. Those with cars should leave via Wookey Hole Road. On foot you could, of course, follow that same road, but there is a much better scenic route via a series of woodland paths. The map shows how to get out of town, and from there the route is well marked. Half of the distance is uphill, rewarding your efforts with glorious vistas. It may be wise to ask at the tourist office about trail conditions before setting out. The round trip from Wells, including seeing the caves, will take about three hours.

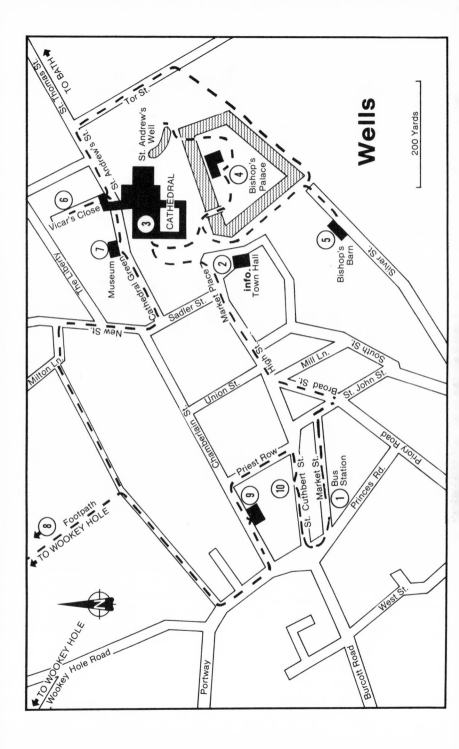

Wells

200 Yards

TO BATH

St. Thomas St.

Tor St.

St. Andrew's St.

St. Andrew's Well

CATHEDRAL

Bishop's Palace ④

Vicar's Close ⑥

Cathedral Green

Museum ⑦

The Liberty

New St.

Milton Ln.

Sadler St.

Market Place

info. Town Hall ②

Bishop's Barn ⑤

Silver St.

High St.

Mill Ln.

South St.

St. John St.

Priory Road

Union St.

Chamberlain St.

Priest Row

Broad St.

St. Cuthbert St.

Market St.

Bus Station ①

Princes Rd.

⑨

⑩

West St.

Burcott Road

Portway

Wookey Hole Road

TO WOOKEY HOLE

Footpath ⑧
TO WOOKEY HOLE

N

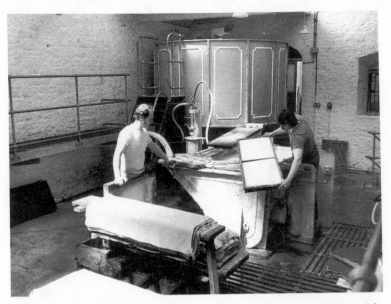

Paper Making at the Wookey Hole

The **Wookey Hole** (8) is operated by Madame Tussaud's of the wax-works fame, so it is somewhat commercialized. This is not a serious detraction from its splendors, and may actually make the visit more fun. You will be taken through the **caves** by an experienced guide who is knowledgeable in their history and legends. Near the exit there is an old **paper mill** that is now a part of the complex. Demonstrations of hand paper-making are given almost continuously. Other parts of the mill are devoted to a fascinating collection of early fairground amusements and **Madame Tussaud's Cabinet of Curiosities**. There is also a small museum and a working waterwheel. The complex is open daily, except around Christmas, from 9:30 a.m. to 5:30 p.m.; closing at 4:30 in winter.

Returning to Wells, there are two more places you may want to visit. The **Almshouses** (9) on Chamberlain Street date from the 15th century. **St. Cuthbert's** (10), one block away, is a parish church from the same era. It has quite an interesting interior and deserves to be seen.

Bristol

Bristol is a delightful city to visit, especially in the summer. Few places combine the serious with the lighthearted quite so well. Where else can you see the sights from a vintage steam train or a tiny ferryboat? Or for that matter, explore the innards of an early-19th-century transatlantic steamship or peer into the cockpit of a Concorde jet? Not many English cities boast as many sidewalk cafés or outstanding restaurants. Culture is not overlooked, either. Bristol has its fair share of medieval buildings, superb museums, churches, two cathedrals, several arts centers, and a world-renowned theater.

A thriving port since Saxon times, Bristol's prosperity was founded on wool, wine, tobacco, and the slave trade. Its enterprising seamen sailed to the far corners of the known world, and in 1497 one of them, John Cabot, first braved the North Atlantic to discover Newfoundland. Its commerce with the New World expanded as did the size of its ships. Eventually the harbor became inadequate and a new one was built at nearby Avonmouth. Heavy bombing during World War II led to extensive reconstruction. Today, the old downtown harbor is used mostly for pleasure, an amenity that makes Bristol an attractive place to visit.

GETTING THERE:

Trains leave London's Paddington Station at least hourly for Bristol's Temple Meads Station, a journey of about 1½ hours. Return trains run until mid-evening. Be certain that the train you board is not just going to Bristol Parkway, which is out in the suburbs. Service is somewhat reduced on Sundays and holidays.

Coaches depart from London's Victoria Coach Station every hour. The trip to Bristol takes about 2½ hours.

By car, head west on the M-4 to the Bristol interchange, then take the M-32 into town. The distance from London is 121 miles.

WHEN TO GO:

Bristol can be visited at any time in good weather. There is more activity, and more fun, on weekends during the summer season. The

Bristol Museum and the Georgian House are closed on Sundays, while the Industrial Museum closes on Thursdays and Fridays.

FOOD AND DRINK:

Bristol has been famous for its wine imports since the 12th century. There are a great many restaurants and pubs all over town, including a few floating in the harbor. Some especially good choices are:

Harvey's (12 Denmark St., between the tourist office and the cathedral) World-renowned for its classical French and English cuisine, in the cellars of the famous wine shipper. There is also a wine museum on the premises. X: Sat. lunch, Sun. $$$

Rajdoot (83 Park St., near the Georgian House) Indian tandoori and curry specialties with a Punjabi origin, set lunches. X: Sun. lunch. $$ and $$$

La Taverna Dell'Arista (33 King St., near the Theatre Royal) Italian-inspired dishes in a charming neighborhood. X: Sun., Mon. $$

Barbizon (43 Corn St., in the medieval heart) French cuisine in the basement of an old building. X: Sat. lunch, Sun., Aug. $$

Arnolfini Gallery (Narrow Quay, at the south end of the quay between the tourist office and the Industrial Museum) Casual meals in an arts center. X: Mon. $

Guild Café (68 Park St., near the Georgian House) Light lunches upstairs in a rather elegant small department store. X: Sun. $

Llandoger Trow (King St., near the Theatre Royal) A centuries-old, highly atmospheric pub with light lunches. $

TOURIST INFORMATION:

The local tourist office is in Colston House on Colston Street, just north of the small harbor. You can phone them at (0272) 29-38-91 or 20-767.

SUGGESTED TOUR:

Leaving **Temple Meads Station** (1), cross the pedestrian bridge over Temple Gate and follow Redcliffe Way to **St. Mary Redcliffe** (2), the massive parish church that Queen Elizabeth I called "the fairest and goodliest" in all the land. Rebuilt in the 14th century, parts of it date from the 12th. If you have time for only one church during your visit, it should be this one.

Continue across Redcliffe Bridge to Queen Square and turn right to King Street. One of the most colorful thoroughfares in town, this cobbled street is lined with old taverns as well as the Theatre Royal, home of the famous Bristol Old Vic repertory company. Now follow

S.S. Great Britain

the map to the **tourist office** (3) at the foot of Colston Street, where you can get current information about what's going on.

Stroll down to Narrow Quay. From here you can either walk to the next destination, or take one of the small open ferries that operate during the warm season. However you get there, the **Industrial Museum** (4) is worth a stop. Its displays cover the full range of Bristol's industries, past and present, including carriages, sports cars, trucks, a steam crane, and a full-scale mock-up of the locally built Concorde. The museum is open on Saturdays through Wednesdays, from 10 a.m. to 1 p.m. and from 2–5 p.m.

Continue on by ferry, on foot, or—when it's running—an ancient steam train, to the **S.S. *Great Britain*** (5). Launched in 1843, it was the first large steamer to be made of iron and the first to be driven by a screw propeller. Used for a while on the transatlantic run to New York, she proved unprofitable and was later put on the Australian service. Finally reduced to hauling coal to San Francisco, she was abandoned in the Falkland Islands after suffering damage during a hurricane in 1886. There she remained until 1937, when the hull was sunk off Port Stanley. In 1970 the S.S. *Great Britain* was refloated and towed all the way back to the very same dry dock in Bristol in which she was built.

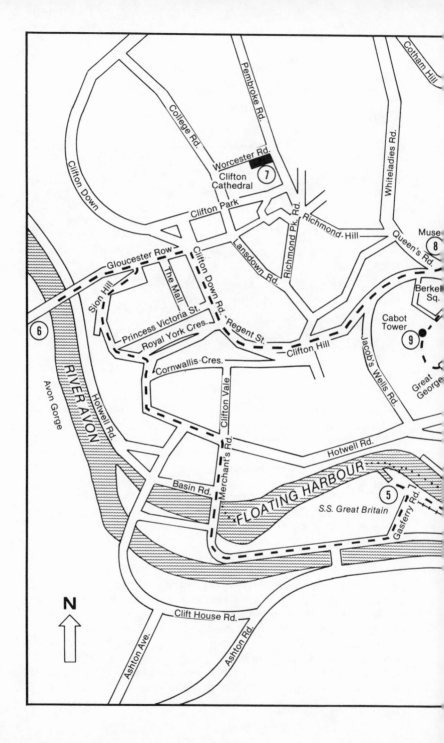

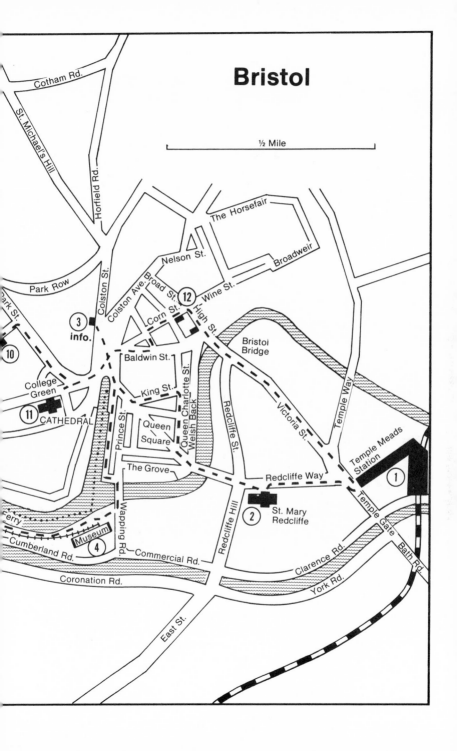

Steam Train Near the Industrial Museum

This indomitable ship, along with other sights in Bristol such as Temple Meads Station and the Clifton Suspension Bridge, were all the work of the great 19th-century engineer, Isambard Kingdom Brunel, who also built the Great Western Railway, the line you traveled over from London if you came by train. Visitors may climb all over the ship, which is currently undergoing painstaking restoration to its original 1843 appearance. It is open daily from 10 a.m. to 6 p.m., closing at 5 p.m. in winter. Enter through the Maritime Heritage Centre and purchase an admission token. Refreshments are available on the site.

From here you can take the ferry back to the town center and then board a bus to Clifton, or you can just walk there. The route shown on the map takes you past the locks of the Floating Harbour, a section of the River Avon in which boats are kept afloat during low tide. From there it is uphill, going by some elegant Georgian houses near the top.

The **Clifton Suspension Bridge** (6), another creation of Brunel's, is among the most outstanding in Britain. Poised high above the Avon Gorge, it offers spectacular views to the pedestrians who cross it. Return and climb the mound to the left for another superb vista.

There is bus service back to town from the corner of Gloucester Row and Clifton Down Road. You may be interested, however, in strolling over a few blocks to see the very contemporary **Clifton Cathedral** (7) on Pembroke Road. Consecrated in 1973, this Roman Catholic cathedral is a striking piece of modern architecture designed to meet the new forms of worship.

By bus or on foot, the next destination is the **City Museum and Art Gallery** (8) on Queen's Road. The collections include items of local archaeology, history, ceramics, and glass, as well as the fine and applied arts. With its unusual mixture of displays, this is really a fun place to visit. It is open Mondays through Saturdays, from 10 a.m. to 5 p.m. Just a short distance away is the **Cabot Tower** (9) on Brandon Hill. There are good views of the city and its harbor from its top. The tower was built in 1897 to commemorate the 400th anniversary of John Cabot's voyage to the New World.

Great George Street is a very pleasant way to return to the town center. Along it is the **Georgian House** (10), an 18th-century merchant's home that has been lovingly restored to its original elegance and is now open to the public as part of the City Museum. Visits may be made Mondays through Saturdays, from 10 a.m. to 1 p.m. and from 2–5 p.m.

Park Street leads to College Green and the **Bristol Cathedral** (11). A mixture of many styles including Norman, Early English, Gothic, and Victorian, its construction spanned a period of over 700 years. The most interesting parts are the choir, which has wonderful misericords, the eastern Lady Chapel, and the Norman Chapter House, dating from 1160.

Continue up Baldwin Street and Corn Street to the intersection with Broad, Wine, and High streets. This was the old **medieval heart** (12) of the city. In front of the Corn Exchange of 1743 are four short pillars of bronze known as "nails," on which merchants completed their cash transactions. From these came the expression "paying on the nail." Make a right on High Street and visit the **St. Nicholas Church Museum**, just before the bridge. The displays include vestments, silver, ecclesiastical art, and an unusual altarpiece by William Hogarth. These can be seen Mondays through Saturdays, from 10 a.m. to 5 p.m. From here cross Bristol Bridge and follow Victoria Street back to Temple Meads Station.

Cardiff
(Caerdydd)

Cardiff. The name alone conjures up visions of a grim industrial port on the south coast of Wales. While this was once true of its dockside areas, the central city is really very appealing. Well laid out with spacious streets and lovely parks, the Welsh capital features superb castles, fine museums, and best of all, a chance to sample a little bit of Wales on an easy daytrip from London.

Both the Romans and the Normans settled here, but the Cardiff of today is largely a creation of Victorian times. The Industrial Revolution and the opening of the Glamorganshire Canal in 1794 paved the way for the building of a vast harbor complex, at one time the world's leader in coal exports. This in turn meant great wealth for its leading citizens, including the Third Marquess of Bute, who just about owned the town in the late 19th century. An extravagant spender, he set an example of civic pride by financing much of Cardiff's beautifully planned expansion. Other tycoons followed his lead, making the city one of the most attractive in Britain.

GETTING THERE:

Trains to Cardiff leave London's Paddington Station at hourly intervals, making the journey in under two hours. Return trains run until early evening. Service is reduced on Sundays and holidays.

By car, take the M-4 all the way. Cardiff is 154 miles west of London.

WHEN TO GO:

The National Museum of Wales is closed on Mondays and some holidays, while the Welsh Folk Museum is closed on a few major holidays. Train service is slower on Sundays and holidays. Fine weather will greatly enhance this trip.

FOOD AND DRINK:

Cardiff has a wide variety of restaurants and pubs in all price ranges. The city is noted for its distinctive local beer, Brain's. A few dining suggestions are:

Cardiff Castle
(Photo courtesy of Welsh Tourist Board)

In the city:

Positano (Church St., just west of St. John's) Traditional Italian cooking in the city center. $$

Riverside Cantonese (44 Tudor St., west of Central station) Authentic Chinese cuisine, a local favorite. $$

The Louis (32 St. Mary St., near the Royal Arcade) One of the oldest restaurants in Cardiff, with an extensive menu. $

Albert (St. Mary St., near the Royal Arcade) A busy pub with lunches and Brain's beer. $

Lexington (Queen St., east of the castle) Burgers and other American fare. $

Out of town:

Boar's Head (Market St., Caerphilly) An old inn near Caerphilly Castle. X for meals: Sun. $

Ystafell Fwyta (in the Welsh Folk Museum at St. Fagan's) Both self-service and waitress service, lunches only. $ and $$

TOURIST INFORMATION:

The local tourist office, phone (0222) 27-281, is at 3–6 Bridge Street, a few blocks northeast of Central Station.

SUGGESTED TOUR:

Leave **Central Station** (1) and follow the map to the **Royal Arcade** (2), one of several charming Victorian ironwork-and-glass-covered walking streets for which Cardiff is noted. Passing a multitude of interesting shops, turn left into The Hayes. In a few steps you will come to St. David's Hall, a magnificent new concert hall next to a modern shopping center. Bear left on the pedestrians-only Trinity Street, which leads past a huge enclosed food market. Just beyond this is **St. John's** (3), a 15th-century parish church noted for its tall tower and fine interior.

Follow Church Street to High Street and turn right. The entrance to **Cardiff Castle** (4) is on Castle Street. Originally a Roman fort dating from about A.D. 75, it was later abandoned and rebuilt by the invading Normans during the 11th century. Their leader, Robert FitzHamon, had a circular moat dug, within what remained of the Roman walls, in the center of which he threw up a mound of earth, called a *motte*, supporting a wooden tower. This was replaced by the present stone keep during the late 12th century. Further additions were made, including the large castle buildings outside the circular moat, with a second moat being dug in the 14th century. The entire castle complex, having been continuously occupied from Norman times to the near present, has never suffered great damage, although it was captured on several occasions.

The real splendor of the castle as it now exists is, however, the result of a wildly romantic reconstruction begun in 1865 to satisfy the strange fantasies of the Third Marquess of Bute. To see this you will have to take a guided tour of the utterly extravagant, dreamlike interior. When the tour is over, visit the original keep in the northwest corner and note the Roman foundations, in lighter-colored stone, of portions of the outer wall. The castle is open daily from 10 a.m. to 12:30 p.m. and from 2–5 p.m., with reduced hours during the off-season.

Now follow Kingsway to the **City Hall** (5), focal point of the elegant Civic Centre, a handsome early-20th-century group of public buildings spaciously spread amid the gardens of Cathays Park. A short stroll behind the City Hall to the War Memorial reveals the careful planning that went into this complex.

Return via Museum Avenue to the **National Museum of Wales** (6). Exhibits here cover just about everything that could possibly pertain to that principality, and much more besides. The most interesting, perhaps, is the industrial section featuring railways, iron-making, manufacturing, and—in the basement—reconstructions of mines. In addition, there are galleries devoted to archaeology, zoology, botany, and geology. Don't miss the fabulous art collection, rich in treasures representing a diversity of European schools from medieval to contemporary. It is especially well endowed with works by Rodin, Renoir, Monet, Cézanne, Rubens, and that great 20th-century Welsh artist,

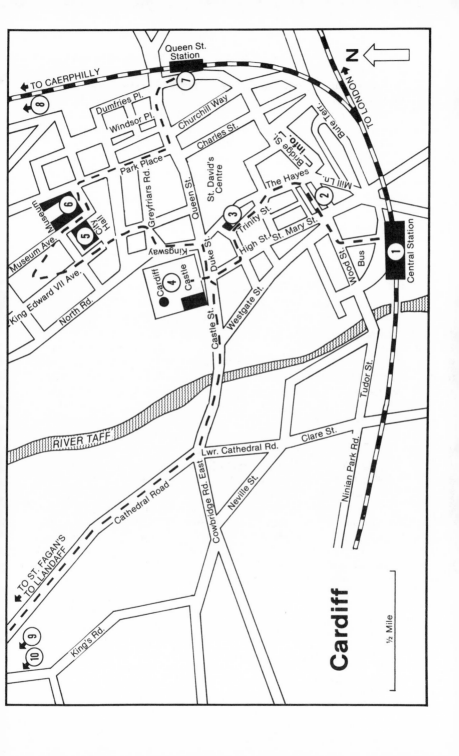

Augustus John. The museum is open Tuesdays through Saturdays, from 10 a.m. to 5 p.m.; and on Sundays from 2:30–5 p.m. It is closed on Mondays and some major holidays. This is a must-see for all visitors to Cardiff.

At this point you will have to decide between going to Caerphilly to see its great castle or making a trip to St. Fagan's and possibly Llandaff for the Welsh Folk Museum and the cathedral. It is virtually impossible to include both in the same day, a good reason for either staying over or coming back another time.

CAERPHILLY:

If you chose Caerphilly, follow Park Place and Queen Street to the **Queen Street Station** (7) and board one of the frequent trains on the Rhymney Valley line for the 15-minute ride to Caerphilly. Those driving should follow North Road and Caerphilly Road (A-469) direct to the castle. There is also hourly bus service from the bus station in front of Central Station. Take bus number 26 or 36 for the 45-minute ride to Caerphilly.

Arriving at Caerphilly, leave the station and turn right on the main street. This goes straight for a few blocks, then bends right to the castle. **Caerphilly Castle** (8), built in the 13th century, is monstrously huge and was once armed to the teeth. It is the second-largest in Europe, exceeded in size only by Windsor. Whereas Cardiff Castle is strangely charming, Caerphilly intimidates and leaves you with a strong impression concerning the savageness of warfare.

As usual, the Romans were here first. Little, however, remains of their fort. The present structure was begun in 1271 by Earl Gilbert de Clare to replace his earlier stronghold of 1268 that was destroyed by the great Welsh patriot, Llywelyn the Last, the first Prince of Wales. No sooner was construction underway than the indefatigable Llywelyn struck again, halted this time by a truce called by Henry III. Clare then recaptured his mighty fortress and went on building. In the end he had an impregnable stronghold, one that was to resist all further sieges. Strangely, it played no part in the conquest of Wales by Edward I, after which its military value declined. Even so, as late as the 17th century it still posed a potential threat, which Oliver Cromwell attempted to eradicate during the Civil War by blowing the place up. Fortunately for us, he did not reckon with the sturdiness of Clare's walls, and the net result of all that gunpowder was one **leaning tower**, which is still there, still leaning wildly out of perpendicular.

A printed guide for exploring the castle on your own is available at the entrance. Follow it and you will gain a good understanding of why this fortress was so difficult to attack. Caerphilly Castle is open daily between mid-March and mid-October, from 9:30 a.m. to 6:30 p.m.

Caerphilly Castle

During the rest of the year it is open Mondays through Saturdays, from 9:30 a.m. to 4 p.m.; and on Sundays from 2–4 p.m. Those returning by rail should continue on to Cardiff Central Station (1), where they can change to an express for London.

ST. FAGAN'S AND LLANDAFF:

If you have decided on seeing St. Fagan's and maybe Llandaff instead of Caerphilly, you should return to the **bus station** in front of Central Station (1). From here you can take bus number 32, which leaves hourly for the four-mile, 20-minute ride to St. Fagan's. You can also drive there via Cathedral Road, following signs for the folk museum.

The **Welsh Folk Museum** (9) at St. Fagan's re-creates rural life in Wales as it was in centuries past. Traditional buildings from all over the principality have been brought to this beautiful 100-acre estate and reassembled for posterity. Here you can watch skilled craftsmen practicing the old trades and visit the Elizabethan mansion, cottages, watermills, smithy, tannery, and many other attractions. There is also a modern exhibition hall housing centuries of bygones along with a restaurant. Be sure to buy a guide booklet so you won't miss anything—some of the best sites are very cleverly hidden. The museum is open Mondays through Saturdays from 10 a.m. to 5 p.m.; and on Sundays from 2:30–5 p.m. It is closed on a few major holidays.

In the Welsh Folk Museum

Time permitting, you may want to continue on to the pretty village of Llandaff. To do this by bus you will first have to take bus number 32 from the folk museum, then transfer to a number 25 or 33 bus en route. Ask the driver about this.

Llandaff Cathedral (10) dates from the 12th century. It was never a great cathedral, and was severely damaged during the Middle Ages, used as a beer hall by Cromwell's troops in the Civil War, and badly bombed during World War II. What makes it worth the trip is the incredible parabolic concrete organ loft bearing a 16-foot-high aluminum Jesus, Jacob Epstein's famous *Christ in Majesty* of 1960. Wander around the lovely grounds by the River Taff and then take bus number 33, running every 30 minutes Mondays through Saturdays and hourly on Sundays, back to Central Station(1). You could also walk the 2½-mile distance via Llandaff Fields and Cathedral Road.

Exeter

There are two excellent reasons that make the rather long journey to Exeter practical as a daytrip from London. The first is its fabulous Maritime Museum and the second is the luxurious high-speed train that gets you there in as little as two hours flat. By car, the trip is better done from a base somewhere in the west country.

Exeter began as a Celtic settlement, being taken over in A.D. 55 by the Romans, who called it *Isca Dumnoniorum* and used it as a frontier outpost. Portions of their stone walls, erected in the early 3rd century, can still be seen. Continuously occupied ever since, it became the *Exanceaster* of the Saxons and was frequently plundered, right down to modern times, when much of it was wiped out by the bombs of World War II. Now a thriving modern city, Exeter still retains many of its medieval treasures as well as reminders that this was once an important seaport.

GETTING THERE:

Trains depart London's Paddington Station several times in the morning for the less-than-2½-hour ride to Exeter. Those going on a Saturday in summer must make reservations. Service on Sundays and holidays is slower. Return trains run until mid-evening. There is another route leaving from London's Waterloo Station and stopping first at Exeter's Central Station, but it is much slower.

By car, Exeter is 172 miles southwest of London via the shortest route, which is the M-3 followed by the A-30 through Salisbury.

WHEN TO GO:

A trip to Exeter requires good weather and an early start. Some of the sights are closed on Sundays and Mondays, but the exciting Maritime Museum is open every day except Christmas and Boxing Day.

FOOD AND DRINK:

Exeter has its fair share of historic inns and pubs, as well as several good restaurants. Some choices are:

Ship Inn (Martin's Lane, just north of the cathedral) An old inn favored by Sir Francis Drake and other sailors, with a pub and an upstairs restaurant. X: Sun. $ and $$

White Hart (66 South St., between the cathedral and the Maritime Museum) An old inn, partly 14th century. Bar lunches and full meals. $ and $$

Turk's Head (High St., near the Guildhall) A pub with traditional English fare. $ and $$

Coolings Wine Bar (11 Gandy St., just southeast of the Royal Albert Museum) A casual and very popular place for traditional dishes and salads. X: Sun. $

Port Royal Inn (The Quay, near the Maritime Museum) A riverside pub with good food. $

TOURIST INFORMATION:

The local tourist office, phone (0392) 72-434, is in the Civic Centre near the Underground Passages.

SUGGESTED TOUR:

Leaving **St. David's Station** (1), you have a choice of walking or taking a bus or taxi to the cathedral, nearly a mile away. Those on foot should follow the route shown on the map.

Exeter Cathedral (2) is famous for its gorgeous interior and the unusual placement of its two Norman towers. Begun in the 12th century on the site of an earlier Saxon church, the cathedral was transformed during the 14th century into the lovely Gothic structure it is today. Its west front is heavily decorated with an amazing array of sculpted figures. "Great Peter," a six-ton bell in the north tower, still tolls the curfew each evening, as it has for nearly 500 years.

Enter the nave and look up at the richly colored roof bosses. The charming **Minstrels' Gallery**, midway down on the left, is used for Christmas carol recitals. In the north transept there is a superb 15th-century wall painting of the Resurrection and an **astronomical clock** from the same era that shows the sun revolving around the earth. The choir has a fabulous 14th-century **Bishop's Throne** and interesting old misericords.

Complete your exploration of the cathedral and stroll out into the close. At the end of Martin's Lane is the small St. Martin's Church. Next to that is **Mol's Coffee Shop** (3), a 16th-century inn now used as a shop. You can enter it and see the room where famous seamen such as Raleigh, Drake, and Hawkins once sipped their brew.

Now follow the map to the **Maritime Museum** (4) on The Quay. Occupying three old warehouses and a canal basin, this is a fun place where visitors are encouraged not only to touch but to climb aboard

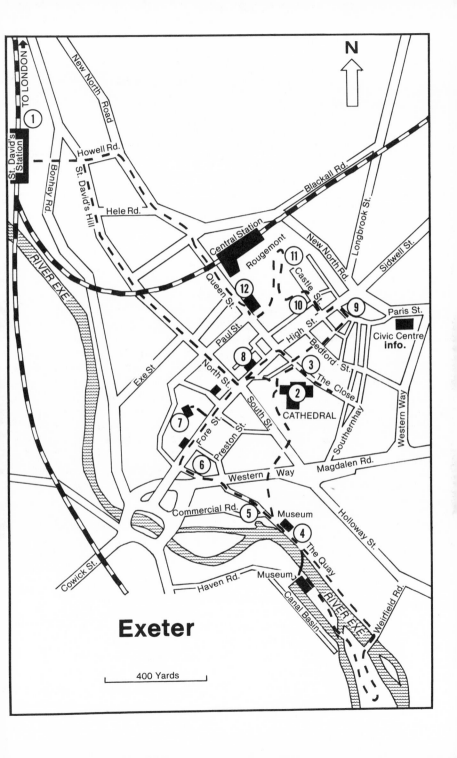

Exeter

N

TO LONDON

St. David's Station

New North Road

Howell Rd.

Bonhay Rd.

St. David's Hill

Hele Rd.

RIVER EXE

Central Station

Rougemont

Blackall Rd.

Longbrook St.

Sidwell St.

New North Rd.

Queen St.

Castle St.

Paris St.

Civic Centre
info.

Paul St.

Exe St.

High St.

Bedford St.

North St.

South St.

The Close

CATHEDRAL

Southernhay

Western Way

Fore St.

Preston St.

Magdalen Rd.

Western Way

Holloway St.

Commercial Rd.

Museum

The Quay

Cowick St.

Haven Rd.

Museum

Canal Basin

RIVER EXE

Weirfield Rd.

400 Yards

① ② ③ ④ ⑤ ⑥ ⑦ ⑧ ⑨ ⑩ ⑪ ⑫

many of the exhibits. Crawl into the engine room of a coal-burning tug, picnic on an exotic Chinese junk, or wear yourself out turning capstans. Well over a hundred boats of all types from all over the world are on display, several of them floating in the basin. Begin your tour with the two warehouses by the quay, then take the hand-operated ferry across the River Exe to the canal basin and a third warehouse. Portuguese rowboats may be rented by the hour, and trips on a steam launch are frequently available. If you love boats at all you will rejoice in this wonderful place. It is open daily, from 10 a.m. to 6 p.m., closing at 5 p.m. in the off-season. There are plans to transfer the entire museum eventually to the canal basin area.

While still in a maritime mood, you can take a short walk along the ancient **canal**, first opened in 1566 and now used for pleasure craft. The route shown on the map is easy to follow and returns you to The Quay. From here walk past the 17th-century **Customs House** (5), built on the site of the Roman quay and now housing an interpretation center. Continue on to West Street and the parish church of **St. Mary Steps** (6), which has a curious 17th-century clock in its bell tower as well as a Norman font and a good rood screen. Opposite it, at number 24, is the **House That Moved**, a timber-framed structure dating from about 1500 that was moved on rollers in 1961 to make way for road construction. Take a look up Stepcote Hill, a medieval street that is little changed.

A right on Fore Street will take you past **Tucker's Hall**, a 15th-century guildhouse that is sometimes open. Turn left on The Mint and visit **St. Nicholas Priory** (7), once a Benedictine monastery founded in 1080 by William the Conqueror. Disbanded in 1536, it is now a museum featuring a fine Norman undercroft, a 15th-century guest hall, an ancient kitchen, and other rooms fitted with period furniture. The garden has a fascinating 7th-century Celtic cross. Visits may be made Tuesdays through Saturdays, from 10 a.m. to 1 p.m. and from 2–5 p.m.

Two other interesting churches in the area are **St. Olave's**, a strange building of the 14th century on Fore Street, and **St. Mary Arches** on Mary Arches Street, a 12th-century parish church with a Norman nave and Jacobean memorials.

Fore Street soon becomes High Street. On your left is the **Guildhall** (8), believed to be the oldest municipal building still in use in Britain. Built in 1330, it has an outstanding 16th-century façade projecting out over the sidewalk. Visitors are welcome Mondays through Saturdays, from 10 a.m. to 5:30 p.m., subject to civic functions.

Continue up High Street and turn right on Martin's Lane for one block, then left on Catherine Street past the ruins of a bombed-out 15th-century almshouse. Princesshay, a modern shopping mall, leads to the entrance of the **Underground Passages** (9). Guided tours are

Exeter Cathedral

run through these medieval water tunnels that date from the 14th century and remained in use until about a hundred years ago. The trip is somewhat spooky and not for the claustrophobic. They can be explored Tuesdays through Saturdays, from 2–4:40 p.m. Nearby are the remains of the ancient town walls and the tourist office in the Civic Centre.

Return to High Street and make a right up Castle Street. To your left are the scanty remains of a Norman gateway and, beyond, a Norman tower. The **Rougemont House Museum** (10) has exhibits of costumes and lace. Stroll through the very pleasant **Rougemont Gardens** (11) and exit onto Queen Street. A right brings you to the **Royal Albert Memorial Museum and Art Gallery** (12), which has something for everyone. There are displays of art, ethnography, exploration, natural history, and many other subjects. It is open Tuesdays through Saturdays, from 10 a.m. to 5 p.m. This is a good place to spend your remaining time before returning to the train station.

Oxford

There is practically nothing you cannot learn at Oxford. Scores of independent schools compete with the 34 colleges that make up the 11,000-student university, each a closed world in itself, barricaded within its separate quandrangle. To this sheltered spot in the very center of England come thousands of visitors curious about English academic life and eager to see the countless treasures accumulated since medieval days.

The town of Oxford is older than the university, which itself dates from the 12th century. As far back as 912, *Oxenford*—the ford for oxen across the Thames—was mentioned in Anglo-Saxon chronicles. In 1071 the conquering Normans built a castle and defensive walls. Always the home of lost causes, Oxford sided with the Royalists during the Civil War of the 17th century and to this day retains a little bit of that sense of privilege largely gone from the rest of Britain. Unlike Cambridge, with which it is inevitably compared, Oxford is also an industrial center, although you would hardly realize this from the old part of town.

There is far more to the town and its university than can possibly be seen in a single day. For this reason, the suggested tour has left out a great deal that is worthwhile and concentrated on a balanced blend of colleges, market-town atmosphere, parks, museums, and notable buildings. As a visitor, you may have to improvise somewhat as public accessibility to some of the places varies at the whim of individual colleges. This will present no problem, since if one quad is closed, another nearby will probably be open. It is always a good idea to ask the porter at each entrance about which specific points of interest are free to public inspection. Please remember that all of the colleges are private and that admission to them is a courtesy, not a right. Magdalen and Christ Church colleges are currently charging a small admission fee.

It is entirely possible to combine this trip with one to Woodstock by leaving London early and cutting short the walk. If you do this, try to visit Woodstock first.

GETTING THERE:

Trains leave London's Paddington Station hourly for the one-hour trip to Oxford, with return service operating until late evening. Service is reduced on Sundays and holidays.

Coaches for Oxford depart from London's Victoria Coach Station at frequent intervals and take less than two hours to get there.

By car, Oxford is 57 miles northwest of London via the A-40 and M-40 highways.

WHEN TO GO:

Oxford can be visited all year round, although it is less hectic and more accessible during the winter months between mid-October and March. The Ashmolean Museum is closed on Mondays and a few holidays, while some of the sights have shorter hours on Sundays.

FOOD AND DRINK:

You can find just about any sort of food you care for in Oxford, from pubs to the fanciest restaurants. A few of the better choices are:

Saraceno (15 Magdalen St., with the Ashmolean Museum) Well hidden in a basement, with superb Italian food. X: Sun., holidays. $$$

Elizabeth (84 St. Aldate's, near Christ Church) Excellent Continental cuisine, with an outstanding wine cellar. X: Mon. $$$

La Sorbonne (130a High St., east of Carfax) A long-established restaurant with classic French cuisine. X: holidays. $$$

Bevers Wholefood Restaurant (36 St. Michael's St., near St. Michael's Church) Organically grown homemade foods. $$

The Nosebag (6 St. Michael's St., near St. Michael's Church) A local favorite for its pleasant atmosphere. $

Brown's (9 Woodstock Rd., west of University Parks) Very popular place serving spaghetti, burgers, salads and the like along with loud music. $

Turf Tavern (4 Bath Place, near the Bridge of Sighs) A pub in a 13th-century building on a small alleyway, with courtyard gardens. Good lunches. $

King's Arms (40 Holywell St. at Parks Rd., near the Bridge of Sighs) A student-hangout pub with meals. $

Bear Inn (Alfred St. at Bear Lane, by Christ Church) A traditional university pub in a 13th-century inn, with light meals. $

TOURIST INFORMATION:

The Oxford Information Centre, phone (0865) 72-68-71, is on St. Aldate's, just south of Carfax. In addition to an incredible variety of booklets and maps, they also offer several excellent guided walking tours covering a broad range of interests, which you might prefer to exploring on your own.

SUGGESTED TOUR:

Leaving the **train station** (1), you have a choice of either walking or taking a bus or taxi to Carfax (2), a bit over a half-mile away. If you choose to walk, follow Park End Street past the **Oxford Canal**. This historic waterway was built in 1790 to provide transportation between London and Birmingham, using the River Thames from here to the capital. Until the development of the railways, it played a very important role in England's Industrial Revolution and is still navigable, being quite popular with pleasure boaters today. Look down it to the right to see the scanty remains of Oxford Castle, which dates from Norman times.

Continue on New Road and Queen Street to **Carfax** (2), whose name derives from the Latin *Quatre Vois*, or four ways. This crossing is the hub of Oxford. The tower in the northwest corner is all that remains of the 14th-century Church of St. Martin, while the helpful tourist information office is just a few steps to the south, on St. Aldate's. Cross the intersection and walk down High Street, known as *The High*. When you get to Catte Street, turn left into Radcliffe Square and enter the **University Church of St. Mary the Virgin** (3). While the main body of the church dates from the 15th century, its tower is late 13th. A relatively easy climb to the top of this will allow you to see in advance the route of the walk to come. The church also contains a brass-rubbing center, where you can make your own souvenir.

Leaving the church, you are now facing the **Radcliffe Camera** (4), a massive domed building from 1737 that serves as a reading room for the Bodleian Library. To the left is Brasenose College, named after the 14th-century "brazen-nosed" doorknocker in its dining hall. Step into its quad for a look around.

At the far end of the square is the **Bodleian Library** (5), the oldest in the world, originally founded in 1450 and entitled by law to a copy of every book published in the United Kingdom. It has millions of them scattered between this and a newer building on Broad Street. Walk through it, stopping to examine some of the unusual exhibits and manuscripts. To one side of its courtyard is the 15th-century **Divinity School**, which has one of the most beautiful stone-vaulted ceilings anywhere. A doorway leads into the **Sheldonian Theatre**, a magnificent auditorium designed by Sir Christopher Wren in 1669 to serve the secular ceremonial needs of the university. You can usually visit this, as well as climb up into its octagonal cupola for a nice view, Mondays through Saturdays, from 10 a.m. to 1 p.m. and from 2–4:45 p.m. (closes at 3:45 p.m. in winter). Adjacent to this is the interesting

The Radcliffe Camera from St. Mary's Church

Museum of the History of Science, open Mondays through Fridays from 10:30 a.m. to 1 p.m. and from 2:30–4 p.m. It is closed on weekends and holidays.

Exit this complex of old buildings and stroll down New College Lane, with its famous **Bridge of Sighs** (6) linking two parts of Hertford College. Pass under it and amble into **New College** (7), which is anything but new. Founded in the late 14th century by William of Wykeham, the bishop of Winchester, it has changed very little in the past 500 years. To the left of its unpretentious entrance are the cloisters, alive with a special feel of the Middle Ages. Just beyond are the gardens, one of the most delightful spots in Oxford. There you will find a well-preserved section of the old city walls that predate the college itself. While at New College, you should also try to see its rather remarkable **chapel**, noted for a strange modern statue of *Lazarus* by Jacob Epstein, a painting of *St. James* by El Greco, and some excellent 14th-century stained glass. New College is usually open to visitors between 2 and 5 p.m. during terms, and from 11 a.m. to 5 p.m. during vacation. It is definitely worth returning for if it hasn't yet opened for the day.

Return to the Bridge of Sighs and walk down Broad Street. To your left is the Clarendon Building which houses university administrative offices, and the Old Ashmolean Building, now used as a natural his-

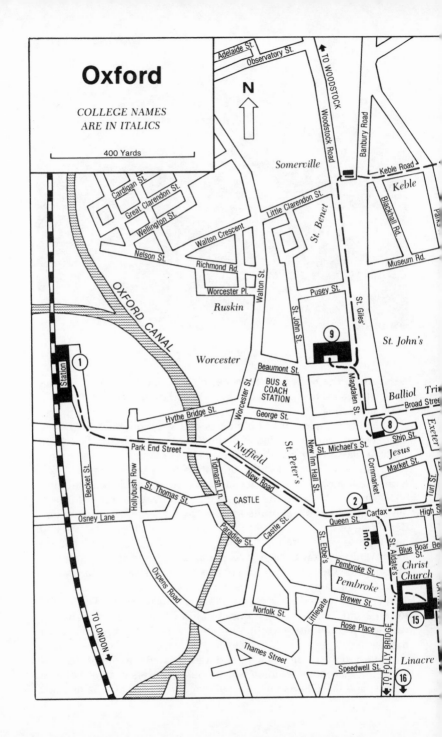

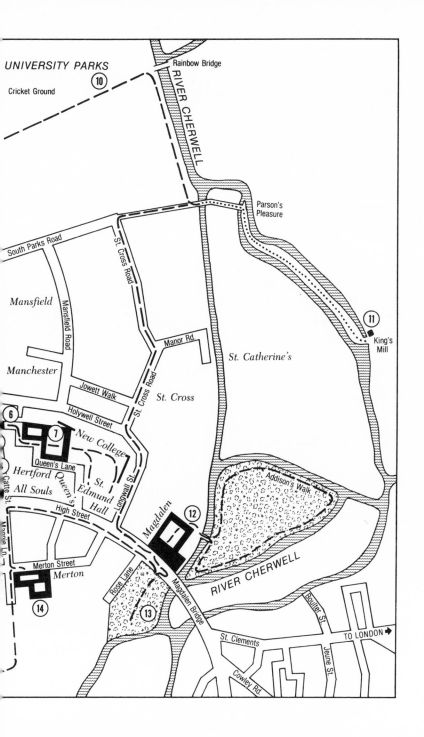

tory museum. Blackwell's Bookshop, across the street, is world famous and makes an interesting stop. Coming to Cornmarket, turn left for a look at **St. Michael's Church** (8), whose tower, dating from before 1050, was once part of the old city walls. You can climb it between 10 a.m. and 5 p.m., but not during services, on Christmas, or after 4:30 p.m. in winter.

Now follow Magdalen Street and make a left on Beaumont Street. Just a few steps down this is the entrance to the renowned **Ashmolean Museum** (9), the oldest public museum in Britain. In 1659 one Elias Ashmole received as a gift "twelve carts of curious things" from an incurable collector named Tradescant. To these he added his own similar collection and offered it all to the university on the condition that it erect a suitable building to house them. Since then, the acquisitions multiplied until they outgrew the Old Ashmolean and were moved in 1845 to the present structure. The collections are eclectic to say the least. Along with the Leonardos, Raphaels, and Michelangelos; the French Impressionists; the Rubens and Rembrandts; the Hogarths and Constables; are displayed all sorts of archaeological and historical curios, including the lantern Guy Fawkes carried when he tried to blow up Parliament in 1605; several mummies, ancient coins, and musical instruments. You will need at least an hour to sample this treasure. The museum is open Tuesdays through Saturdays, from 10 a.m. to 4 p.m.; and on Sundays fro 2–4 p.m. It is closed on Mondays and some major holidays.

At this point you could cut the tour short by returning on Magdalen Street and following Cornmarket and High Street to Magdalen College (12). An enjoyable two-mile walk through lovely parkland awaits those who continue on.

Returning to the corner, make a left up St. Giles' until it becomes Woodstock Road. Cross the street and pass through the yard of the 13th-century St. Giles' Church, then cross Banbury Road and follow straight ahead on Keble Road. On your right is the supremely Victorian Keble College. Enter the **University Parks** (10) and follow the map past the Cricket Grounds where, if you are lucky, a match may be in progress. When you get to the Rainbow Bridge turn right and follow the banks of the River Cherwell. The walk becomes more and more picturesque as you approach Parson's Pleasure. If the weather is fine, you may see students slowly punting along the water, stopping here and there in secluded spots to enjoy a picnic. A delightful side trip can be made by following the path to the ancient **King's Mill** (11). Return to town via St. Cross Road and continue along to the most beautiful college at Oxford.

Magdalen College (12), pronounced *Maudlen*, was built during the 15th century and has long been among the best-endowed at Oxford.

The Bridge of Sighs

Its more than 100 acres include lawns, gardens, water-walks, and a private deer park. There is a small admission charge for entry, which is made from High Street. The adjacent bell tower is perhaps the town's most famous landmark. Be sure to cross the small footbridge for a refreshing stroll along Addison's Walk. Back on High Street, turn left across Magdalen Bridge for a lovely view. If you would like to try your hand at punting, the boats may be rented by the hour at the foot of the bridge. The **Botanic Gardens** (13), opposite, is an inviting place to relax.

Return along High Street to Magpie Lane and turn left. At its end, to the left, is the entrance to **Merton College** (14), generally considered to be the oldest at Oxford, having been transferred here from Sussex in 1274. Its picturesque Mob Quad of 1308, Treasury of 1274, and Chapel of 1294 are the most interesting features.

Now follow straight ahead to the cricket field and turn right to the entrance of Oxford's largest college, **Christ Church** (15). Again, there is a small admission charge. Don't miss the **Dining Hall** with its notable portraits, reached via a staircase. The **Cathedral of Oxford**, one of the smallest in England, is on the east side of the huge Tom Quad. Its age is uncertain, but it predates the entire university. Return to Tom

Punting on the River Cherwell

Quad and take a look at Tom Tower. Every night at five past nine its bell tolls a curfew of 101 strokes, one for each of the original students. But why five past nine? Because Oxford lies 1° 15′ west of the prime meridian, its time is uniquely its own. Christ Church can usually be visited Mondays through Fridays, from 9:30 a.m. to 4:30 p.m.; and on Saturdays from 9:30 a.m. to 12:30 p.m., but these times may vary.

Exit onto St. Aldate's. From here you may want to make a little side trip to nearby **Folly Bridge** (16), off the map. Spanning the River Thames—called the *Isis* in Oxford—this bridge is the starting point for boat trips on the river, and is surrounded by attractive pubs.

Returning up St. Aldate's will take you past the tourist office, where you can get current information about the many other worthwhile sights in Oxford.

Woodstock

Blenheim Palace is the attraction that brings thousands of visitors from all over the globe to the ancient village of Woodstock. One of the greatest of England's stately homes, it was built in the early 18th century as a fitting tribute to John Churchill, the first duke of Marlborough, who routed the French and Bavarians at the Battle of Blenheim in 1704. Before this, the vast property on which it sits was a royal hunting preserve. A manor house existed on the site since at least the time of everyone's favorite Saxon king, Ethelred the Unready. Henry I made great improvements, and his mansion remained a favorite residence of royalty down through Tudor days. By the time Blenheim Palace was built, however, the old structure had almost fallen to ruin and all traces of it were demolished.

Woodstock itself originally grew up to service the royal manor. Several inns were established for this purpose, and today continue to provide hospitality to the many visitors who come to see Blenheim Palace. There is also a fine museum of rural life, an interesting church, and lovely old streets lined with picturesque buildings.

By getting off to an early start it is possible to combine this trip with one to Oxford, which you pass through en route.

GETTING THERE:

Trains depart London's Paddington Station hourly for the one-hour trip to Oxford, where you change to a local bus. These leave at about half-hour intervals from the bus stop on Cornmarket, which can be reached by following the directions to Carfax on the Oxford trip. The ride takes less than 30 minutes. Bus service on Sundays and holidays is reduced, and may have to be taken from the nearby bus station on Beaumont Street instead. Trains return from Oxford to London until late evening.

Coaches leave London's Victoria Coach Station three times a day for the two-hour ride to Blenheim. There is also frequent service to Oxford, requiring a change to the local bus to Woodstock, as above.

By car, Woodstock is 64 miles northwest of London. Take the A-40 and M-40 to Oxford, then continue on the A-34 to Woodstock.

WHEN TO GO:

Blenheim Palace is open daily from the middle of March until the end of October. Fine weather will make this trip much more enjoyable.

FOOD AND DRINK:

The small village of Woodstock has a phenomenal number of inns, pubs, and restaurants—some of them quite ancient. A few choices are:

Feathers (Market St.) Elegant dining in a small hotel. Reservations suggested; phone (0993) 81-22-91. $$$

Bear Hotel (Park St.) Traditional English fare in the pub or dining room of a 16th-century inn. $$ and $$$

Marlborough Arms (Oxford St.) Dining in a small inn. $$

Mawney's Kitchen (52 Oxford St.) Light lunches in a little tea shop. X: Mon., Tues. $

Vanbrughs (16 Oxford St.) Burgers, sandwiches, and light lunches. $

TOURIST INFORMATION:

The local tourist office, phone (0993) 81-10-38, is in the library on Hensington Road.

SUGGESTED TOUR:

Begin your visit at the **bus stop** (1) on Oxford Street opposite the Marlborough Arms Hotel. The **tourist office** (2) is located around the corner on Hensington Road. Follow the map down Market and Park streets to the entrance of the Blenheim Palace grounds. The **Triumphal Arch** (3), designed in 1723 by Nicholas Hawksmoor as a monument to the first duke of Marlborough, is a fitting introduction to so grandiose a place. On your right is a lake created in 1764 by the renowned landscape architect Lancelot "Capability" Brown.

Blenheim Palace (4) has been continuously occupied by the dukes of Marlborough since it was begun by Sir John Vanbrugh in the early 18th century as a gift from Queen Anne. Sir Winston Churchill, grandson of the seventh duke, was born here in 1874 and is buried nearby at Bladon Church. There is an exhibition of his personal belongings in the palace, which remains the home of the present duke. To see its magnificent interior you must take one of the frequent guided tours, lasting about an hour. Blenheim Palace is open daily between mid-March and the end of October, from 10 a.m. to 5:30 p.m.

Be sure to explore at least part of the palace grounds after the tour is finished. Boat rides are usually available on the lake. The **Butterfly and Plant Centre** (5), where exotic tropical butterflies live in a virtually

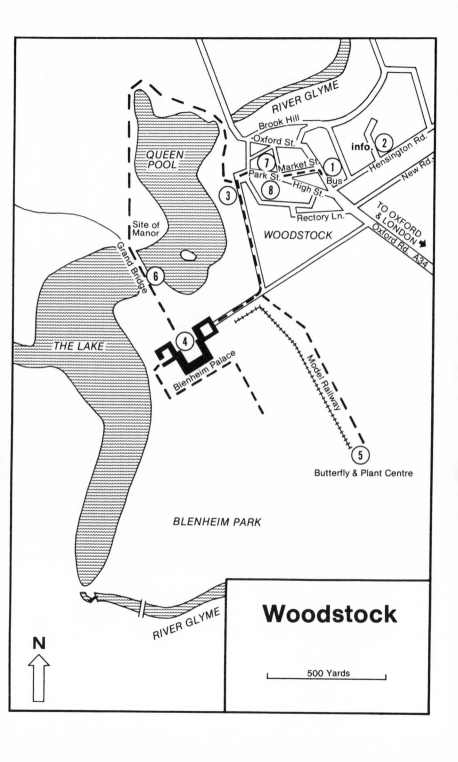

Queen Pool at Blenheim

natural habitat, is an exciting experience as well as a horticulturist's delight. You can get to it by miniature railway or on foot.

A very pleasant way to return to Woodstock is to follow the route on the map. The **Grand Bridge** (6), an extravagant span over what was then only a creek, was part of Vanbrugh's original design. Most of it is now under water. The land just beyond it was the site of the old Woodstock Manor, for centuries a country residence for England's kings and queens.

Back in the village, stroll down Park Street and visit the small but interesting **Oxfordshire County Museum** (7), which features displays on local life through the centuries. It is open Mondays through Fridays, from 10 a.m. to 5 p.m.; on Saturdays from 10 a.m. to 6 p.m; and on Sundays from 2–6 p.m. During the winter it closes earlier. The town stocks, outside the museum, have holes for five legs. Was this a joke or did Woodstock have an unusual number of one-legged culprits? The **Church** (8) is often overlooked but is actually a fascinating study in changing styles, ranging from Norman to Perpendicular. Beyond this, the village offers several interesting shops and some very appealing pubs in which to relax.

Warwick

Many visitors go to see the magnificent castle at Warwick but completely overlook the town itself. That's a pity, because this is surely one of the least spoiled places in England. Small and compact, it has a wonderful blend of Tudor and Georgian architecture, a splendid church, and several fine museums.

Warwick grew up around its castle, whose origins date back to a fortification built here in 914 by Ethelfleda, daughter of Alfred the Great, to protect her kingdom of Mercia. Nothing of this remains, but there are still traces of the motte built by William the Conqueror in 1068. The castle you see today is largely of 14th-century construction with great modifications made down through the years to convert the interior into a luxurious home. Sold to Madame Tussaud's in 1978, it is now a showcase combining medieval elements with those of a more recent stately home and outfitted with the inevitable wax figures.

This trip can be combined with one to nearby Coventry, reached by rail, bus, or road via Leamington Spa. It is also possible to do it in the same day with Stratford-upon-Avon, just eight miles away on the same rail line, although this requires an early start and a lot of rushing.

GETTING THERE:
Trains depart London's Paddington Station several times in the morning for Leamington Spa, where you change to a local for Warwick. The total time is about two hours, with return service operating until mid-evening. Another option is to take the "Shakespeare Connection" train/coach combination from London's Euston Station to Stratford, then a local bus to Warwick. See the Stratford-upon-Avon trip in the next chapter for details.

By car, Warwick is 96 miles northwest of London. Take the M-1 to Junction 17, then the M-45 and A-46 roads.

WHEN TO GO:
The castle is open every day except Christmas, but some of the other sights are closed on Sundays or Mondays. Those coming by train would do well to avoid Sundays or holidays.

FOOD AND DRINK:

Some choice places for lunch include:

Lord Leycester (17 Jury St., east of the tourist office) Dining in a small country hotel. $$

Aylesford (1 High St., near the tourist office) Italian food in the center of town. X: Mon. eve., Sun. $$

Westgate Arms (3 Bowling Green St., near the Lord Leycester Hospital) An English restaurant and a coffeeshop in a small hotel. $$ and $

Zetland Arms (Church St., near St. Mary's) A popular pub with lunches. $

TOURIST INFORMATION:

The local tourist office, phone (0926) 49-22-12, is in the courthouse on Jury Street.

SUGGESTED TOUR:

Leave the **train station** (1) and follow the map to **Warwick Castle** (2). Considered by many to be the finest medieval castle in England, it will easily take two or three hours to explore. Everything is very well marked and explained. The main attractions include the **Barbican and Gatehouse**, a 14th-century complex of some 30 rooms; the **Armoury** with its superb collection of weapons; and the **Dungeon and Torture Chamber**, which has fascinating if grisly displays of medieval torture instruments. Beyond this, **Guy's Tower** may be climbed and the ramparts walked. The **Ghost Tower** is allegedly haunted by a 17th-century apparition. More Victorian in character, the **State Apartments** make a gorgeous show of baronial splendor. Next to them is the **Royal Weekend**, a re-creation of a turn-of-the-century house party enlivened with wax figures of famous nobility.

Beyond the castle are lovely gardens designed by "Capability" Brown in the 18th century. Peacocks roam about the trees, some of which were planted by such luminaries as Queen Victoria and Prince Albert. Cross the bridge over the River Avon to an **island** (3) that has wonderful views of the south face. The **Conservatory** (4) is a fantasy recalling the spirit of Georgian times. Warwick Castle is open every day except Christmas, from 10 a.m. to 5:30 p.m., closing at 4:30 p.m. between November and the end of February.

Leave the castle and return to Castle Hill. A short walk down Mill Street will reward you with splendid views. From here follow the map to **Oken's House** (5), an Elizabethan dwelling that survived the devastating fire of 1694. It now houses an utterly delightful collection of antique and period dolls and toys, which may be seen daily between 10:30 a.m. and 5 p.m.

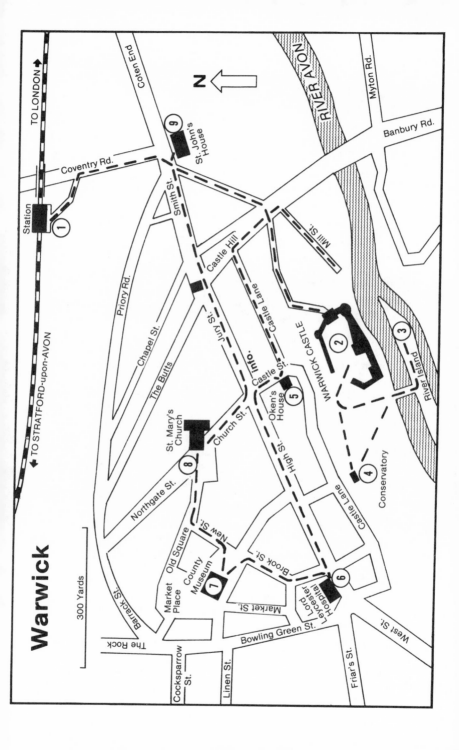

Warwich Castle and the River Avon

Continue up Castle Street to the tourist office in the courthouse at the corner of Jury Street. A left on High Street leads to the **Lord Leycester Hospital** (6), a group of picturesque 14th-century almshouses that have been used since the 16th century as a retirement home for old soldiers. One of these gentlemen will be happy to show you around Mondays through Saturdays, from 10 a.m. to 5:30 p.m., but not after 4 p.m. between October and March.

Walk down Brook Street to the **County Museum** (7) in the Market Place. Displays here cover archaeology, natural history, and local bygones in addition to frequently changing exhibitions. The museum is open Mondays through Saturdays, from 10 a.m. to 5:30 p.m.; and on Sundays between May and September from 2:30–5 p.m.

St. Mary's Church (8), nearby, has parts dating from the 12th century, although it was largely rebuilt after the 1694 fire. Its 15th-century Beauchamp Chapel is incomparable.

Jury Street leads past the East Gate, a relic of the old town wall, and as Smith Street to **St. John's House** (9). This beautiful 17th-century mansion is now a museum of local crafts, costumes, and furniture. There is a regimental military exhibition on the floor above. It is open Tuesdays through Saturdays, from 10 a.m. to 12:30 p.m. and from 1:30–5:30 p.m.; and on Sundays between May and September from 2:30–5 p.m. A short walk in the garden completes your tour before returning to the station, just a few blocks away.

Stratford-upon-Avon

As someone once remarked, there's no business like show business. That, put simply, is what Stratford-upon-Avon is all about. The whole town is one vast theater, entertaining thousands of visitors a day. Despite this, it has miraculously managed to avoid the worst of tourism's trappings and still retains a quite genuine charm. Just about everyone who goes there enjoys the experience.

William Shakespeare was born in Stratford in 1564. This is also where he lived a great deal of his life and where he died in 1616. Many of the buildings associated with the Bard have been lovingly preserved and may be visited. The Royal Shakespeare Theatre, one of the greatest anywhere, is beautifully situated on the banks of the quiet Avon. There are several other attractions, some relating to Shakespeare and others not, but perhaps in the long run it is simply the atmosphere of this delightful old market town that is so memorable.

The best way to savor Stratford is to stay overnight and perhaps take in a performance at the theater. Those with cars will find that it makes an ideal base for exploring the midlands and the Cotswolds. If you can't do this, however, a daytrip from London is still very enjoyable. It is possible, with a lot of rushing, to combine this trip with one to nearby Warwick.

GETTING THERE:
Trains depart London's Paddington station around 7 and 9 a.m. for Leamington Spa, where you change to a local for Stratford-upon-Avon. The total journey takes about 2½ hours, with return trains running until mid-evening. Service is poor on Sundays and holidays.

"**The Shakespeare Connection,**" a **train/coach** combination, leaves London's Euston Station every morning for Coventry, where you change to a special bus. The total ride takes about 2 hours. It is usually possible to make a late-night return on this *on performance days only* if you want to see a performance at the theater and first make a reservation with the coach operator. BritRail Pass users must pay a coach supplement to the driver. Check the schedule in advance or with the coach operator, Guide Friday Ltd., at Stratford, phone (0789) 29-44-66.

Special packages including rail and/or coach transportation, overnight accommodations, theater tickets, and dinner are available through travel agents in London and elsewhere.

By car, take the A-40 and M-40 to Oxford, then the A-34 to Stratford-upon-Avon, which is 96 miles northwest of London.

WHEN TO GO:

The major sights in Stratford are open daily except Christmas and Boxing Day, with generally longer hours from April through September. Some minor attractions close on Sundays between November and March. Performances at the Royal Shakespeare Theater are held from April to November. Try to avoid coming on a weekend, when crowds are at their peak. The colorful outdoor market is held on Fridays.

FOOD AND DRINK:

Stratford has an enormous range of restaurants and pubs in all price categories. Some outstanding choices are:

Da Giovanni (8 Ely St., near Harvard House) Classic Italian cuisine. X: Sun. $$$

Rumours (10 Henley St., near the Birthplace) New-style English cuisine, with vegetarian alternatives. $$$

Shakespeare Hotel (Chapel St., near New Place) An atmospheric 16th-century inn. $$

Box Tree (Waterside, in the theater) Classic food with a wonderful view of the Avon. X for lunch: non-matinee days. $$

Hussain's (6a Chapel St., near New Place) Indian food, with tandoori specialties. $$

Black Swan (Waterside St., near the theater) Also known as the Dirty Duck, very famous with actors. Pub and restaurant. $ and $$

River Terrace (Waterside, in the theater) Self-service cafeteria open to both theatergoers and the public. $

Garrick Inn (High St., near Harvard House) A charming historic pub with lunches. $

Slug and Lettuce (38 Guild St., near the Birthplace) A pub restaurant with garden tables available. $

TOURIST INFORMATION:

The Information Centre is located in Judith Shakespeare's House at 1 High Street. You can phone them at (0789) 29-31-27.

SUGGESTED TOUR:

Leave the **train station** (1) and follow the map to that most logical of beginnings, **Shakespeare's Birthplace** (2). This is actually two houses

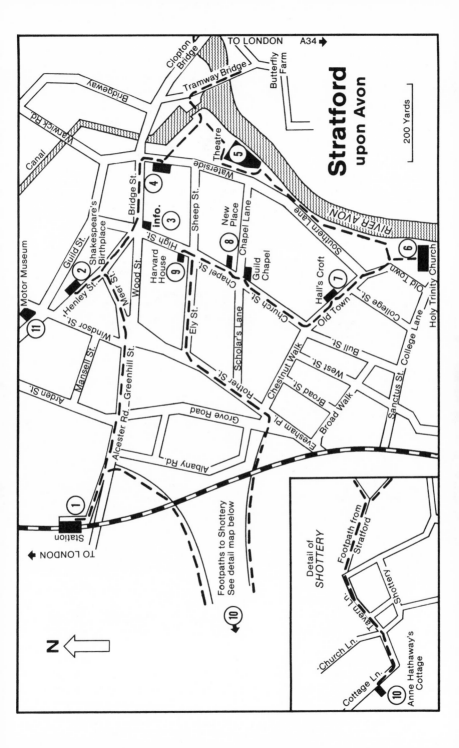

Stratford
upon Avon

200 Yards

TO LONDON   A34 →

Clopton Bridge

Tramway Bridge

Butterfly Farm

RIVER AVON

Theatre ⑤

Waterside

Southern Lane

Bridge St.

info. ③

④

Sheep St.

New Place ⑧

Chapel Lane

⑥ Old Town

Holy Trinity Church

High St.

Guild St.

Shakespeare's Birthplace ②

Henley St.

Wood St.

Meer St.

Harvard House ⑨

Chapel St.

Guild Chapel

Hall's Croft ⑦

Old Town

College St.

College Lane

Sanctus St.

Canal

Warwick Rd.

Bridgeway

Motor Museum

⑪

Windsor St.

Ely St.

Rother St.

Scholar's Lane

Church St.

Bull St.

West St.

Chestnut Walk

Mansell St.

Arden St.

Greenhill St.

Grove Road

Evesham Pl.

Broad St.

Broad Walk

Alcester Rd.

Albany Rd.

① Station

← TO LONDON

Footpaths to Shottery
See detail map below

⑩

N ⇐

Detail of SHOTTERY

Footpath from Stratford

Shottery

Tavern Ln.

Church Ln.

Cottage Ln.

Anne Hathaway's Cottage ⑩

Shakespeare's Birthplace

joined together, the eastern part having been his father's shop and the western half the family residence. To the left of it is the modern Shakespeare Centre, which houses exhibitions, a library, and a study center. Enter this and wander through the delightful garden, complete with flowers, shrubs, and trees mentioned in his plays. The well-marked trail then takes you into the old house itself, where you will visit the bedroom in which Shakespeare was presumably born on or about April 23, 1564. The entire house is furnished as it might have been during his youth, including an interesting period kitchen and an oak-beamed living room. Visits may be made any day except Christmas and Boxing Day. On Mondays through Saturdays it is open from 9 a.m. to 6 p.m., closing at 5 p.m. in October and 4:30 p.m. from November through March. On Sundays from April through October it is open from 10 a.m. to 6 p.m., closing at 5 p.m. in October; and from November through March from 1:30–4:30 p.m. A reduced-price joint ticket covering all of the "Shakespearian Properties" is available.

Return on Henley Street and continue on to the **tourist information office** (3), located in the former home of Shakespeare's daughter, Judith.

Walk down Bridge Street and turn right at Waterside. The *World of Shakespeare* at the **Heritage Theatre** (4) provides a good, if somewhat commercialized, introduction to Elizabethan England. This multime-

The Royal Shakespeare Theatre

dia extravaganza surrounds the audience with 25 stage sets depicting such events as the London plague and Queen Elizabeth I's epic journey to Kenilworth, all brought to life through the clever use of sound, light, and special effects. The show runs continuously every half-hour. It is open daily May through September, from 9:30 a.m. to 10 p.m.; and October through April, from 10 a.m. to 5 p.m.

Stroll through Bancroft Gardens, going past the canal basin and locks. Overlooking this pleasant scene is the **Shakespeare Memorial**, a life-size bronze statue of the Bard with figures of Hamlet, Lady Macbeth, Falstaff, and Prince Hal. Continue on and cross the footbridge over the Avon. This span was formerly used by a horse-drawn tramway that once connected Stratford with Moreton-in-Marsh. From here you will have a beautiful view of the river and the modern Royal Shakespeare Theatre. Just beyond the bridge is the **Butterfly Farm**, where exotic flora and fauna exist in an indoor "natural" setting, the largest of its kind in the world. It is open every day except Christmas. The 15th-century Clopton Bridge with its 14 arches, to the left, still carries heavy traffic.

Return and walk over to the **Royal Shakespeare Theatre** (5). Built in 1932 to replace a smaller 19th-century theater that burned down, its performances of Shakespearian plays are world famous. Although tickets should be booked well in advance, they are frequently available on the day of performance. The attached **RSC Collection** has interesting mementoes of theatrical personalities and other Shakespeariana. You can ask here about **backstage tours** of the theater. Near this is the new **Swan Theatre**, specially designed to present plays by Shakespeare's contemporaries and playwrights influenced by him.

From here, a path leads along the river's edge, passing the Brass Rubbing Centre where you can make your own inexpensive souvenir of Stratford. Continue on to **Holy Trinity Church** (6), the scene of Shakespeare's baptism in 1564 and burial in 1616. Copies of the church registers showing both events are on display. His tomb is inscribed with the famous lines ending in *"and curst be he that moves my bones."* There are a few other interesting items in this 14th-century church, particularly the humorous misericords under the choir seats.

Hall's Croft (7) on Old Town is the next stop. This splendid Tudor house was the home of Shakespeare's eldest daughter, Susanna, and her husband, Dr. John Hall. Its interior is well worth visiting for a glimpse of how a prosperous doctor's family lived in those days. Be sure to see the dispensary with its surgical instruments, herbs, and potions. A stroll through the garden in the rear is a delight. Hall's Croft is open during the same times as the Birthplace (2), except that it is closed on Sundays from November through March.

Turn right on Church Street and pass, on the right, the King Edward VI Grammar School, where the young Shakespeare learned his "small Latin and less Greek." Adjoining this is the 15th-century Guild Chapel with its noted fresco of the Last Judgement above the chancel arch. Just beyond, on Chapel Street, is the site of Shakespeare's own home, **New Place** (8), which he purchased in 1597 and in which he died in 1616. Its last owner demolished it in 1759, and today only the foundations and the garden remain. These can be reached by going through the New Place Museum in the former home of Thomas Nash, who was married to Shakespeare's granddaughter, Elizabeth Hall. It is open during the same times as the Birthplace (2), except on Sundays from November through March.

Harvard House (9) has nothing to do with the Bard, but a lot to do with Harvard University, which owns it. This outstanding example of a half-timbered Elizabethan structure was the home of the mother of John Harvard, whose donations helped found the famous institution in the U.S.A. That is why the Stars and Stripes fly from its flagpole. The richly decorated interior may be visited in season Mondays through Saturdays, from 9 a.m. to 1 p.m. and from 2–6 p.m.; and on Sundays from 2–6 p.m. Adjacent to this are two other buildings of similar style and age, one of them being the well-known Garrick Inn, named for the actor David Garrick who organized the first Shakespeare Festival here in 1769.

Anne Hathaway's Cottage

While in Stratford you will probably want to see **Anne Hathaway's Cottage** (10), certainly one of the prettiest (and most visited) sights in England. The home of Shakespeare's wife before their marriage, this 16th-century thatched-roof farmhouse is set in gorgeous surroundings. The furnishings are fairly authentic as the cottage remained in her family until late Victorian times. Located in the nearby hamlet of Shottery, about one mile from Stratford, it is easily reached by bus from Bridge Street or, better still, on foot via a country path that begins at Evesham Place. The route is well marked and is shown on the map and its insert. The cottage is open during the same times as the Birthplace (2). Return by way of the other path to Alcester Road.

There is one remaining sight in town that might interest you. This is the **Stratford Motor Museum** (11) on Shakespeare Street, near the Birthplace. A sumptuous collection of exotic cars from the 1920s and 1930s, it has no connection with Shakespeare but is still pure theater. It is open daily from 9:30 a.m. to 6 p.m., with shorter hours in winter. From here it is only a short stroll back to the station.

Aylesbury

Truly a town with a split personality, Aylesbury is plunging head-strong into the 21st century while jealously guarding its medieval heart. It is only necessary to take a stroll across the Market Square to see this duality. Tiny alleyways at one end lead past a delightful 15th-century inn to an ancient parish church, while at the other end an aggressively modern office tower pierces the skyline. This would not be uncommon in a large city, but then Aylesbury is only a market town, and a very old one at that. Its recorded history begins with the Anglo-Saxon village of *Aigles Burgh,* which became Buckinghamshire's county town during the reign of Henry VIII. The population has increased ever since and began to soar during the past two decades as new industries were attracted. More than a preserved relic of the past, this is a good place to witness the direction England is moving in. While there, you may want to make an interesting side trip to nearby Waddesdon Manor, one of the country's greatest stately homes.

GETTING THERE:
Trains leave London's Marylebone Station hourly for the one-hour ride to Aylesbury. There is no direct service on Sundays and holidays. Return trains run until mid-evening.

Coaches on the Green Line depart hourly from their terminal at Eccleston Bridge near London's Victoria Station. The journey takes up to 2½ hours.

By car, Aylesbury is 38 miles northwest of London via the A-41 road.

WHEN TO GO:
Aylesbury may be visited in any season. Avoid coming on a Sunday or holiday, when the museum and markets are closed and the train service is poor. Waddesdon Manor is open from mid-March through mid-October, Wednesdays through Sundays.

St. Mary's Church

FOOD AND DRINK:
There are a fair number of pubs and restaurants scattered around the town, some of which serve the excellent local ABC beer. A few choices are:

> **Pebbles** (1 Pebble Lane, near the County Museum) Interesting foods in an attractive, informal environment. X: Sat. lunch, Sun. eve., Mon., Aug. $$$
>
> **King's Head** (in an alleyway off the Market Square) Lunch in an historic 15th-century coaching inn. $$
>
> **Bell Hotel** (Market Square) Pub or restaurant meals in a small country hotel with a relaxed atmosphere. $ and $$
>
> **White Swan** (Walton St., near the County Hall) A popular family-run pub with good meals and traditional beers. $

TOURIST INFORMATION:
The county tourist office, phone (0296) 50-00, is in the County Hall on Walton Street.

SUGGESTED TOUR:
Starting at the **train station** (1), follow the map and pass under Friarage Road and then under a shopping center, going past the bus

station. This route will lead you to the **Market Square** (2). On your right is the Bell Hotel, probably 16th-century but with a later façade, and the Town Hall of 1740. Turn left and pass the Victorian clock tower. An alleyway leads off Market Street to the **King's Head** (3), a 15th-century inn now owned by the National Trust. Both Henry VI and Oliver Cromwell are supposed to have stayed here. You can quench your thirst at the cozy pub in the rear.

Continue on Market Street and look down Silver Street. From Bourbon Street there is an entrance to the huge, modern shopping center, **Friar's Square** (4), in whose center court the open-air market is now held. From here the route on the map follows old medieval streets to **St. Mary's Church** (5), mostly 13th-century but with a Norman font and crypt. In its vestry there is a monument from 1584 to Lady Lee, an ancestor of the Lees of Virginia. Another American connection is made with a monument in the Lady Chapel to Sir Francis Bernard, governor of Massachusetts in the 1760s. The church is beautifully situated in the middle of a spacious, shady square. Stroll around this and look down Pebble Lane.

The **County Museum** (6) on Church Street is housed in a handsome group of Georgian houses. Its collections include local archaeology, natural history, bygones, art, and items pertaining to the history of Aylesbury and Buckinghamshire. The museum is open Mondays through Fridays, from 10 a.m. to 5 p.m.; and on Saturdays from 10 a.m. to 12:30 p.m. and from 1:30–5 p.m.; but closed on some holidays. Pay a visit and then continue following the map. Along the way you will pass the tourist office in the County Hall on Walton Street.

Pass the traffic circle and turn left into the **canal basin** (7), the terminus of the old Aylesbury Arm of the Grand Union Canal. Walk along the towpath, which is usually lined with moored narrowboats. From here, the truly ambitious could take a delightful nine-mile walk beside the canal to Tring, from which there is train service back to London's Euston Station. Those with less stamina should cross the footbridge and follow the map through the old **Cattle Market** (8) and return to the station.

Waddesdon Manor (9), a glorious French-style château filled with priceless art, was once a home of the Rothschilds. It is now open to the public and can be reached by bus from the bus station under Friar's Square, or by car via the A-41. The distance is six miles northwest of Aylesbury. Visits may be made from mid-March until mid-October, Wednesdays through Sundays, from 2–6 p.m., closing at 5 p.m. in March, April, and October. It is closed on Wednesdays following a bank holiday.

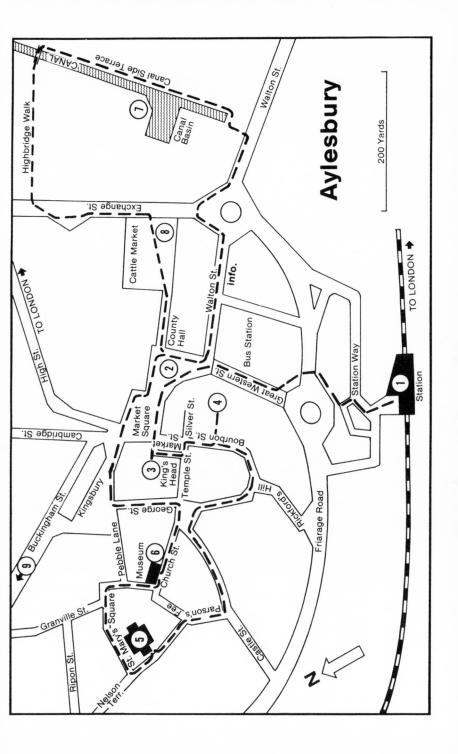

Aylesbury

200 Yards

Coventry

Like the legendary phoenix, Coventry was reborn from the ashes of destruction. On the night of November 14, 1940 it suffered one of the most devastating air raids of World War II, leaving the city's center in rubble, its cathedral a smoldering ruin. Postwar reconstruction followed a radically new plan based on the latest thinking. A stunning new cathedral in contemporary style rose alongside the shards of the old, which remain as mute testimony to the futility of war. Coventry today is a thoroughly modern city, and one that is well worth visiting.

Although its origins may date from a 7th-century convent, the history of Coventry really begins in 1043 with the foundation of a Benedictine abbey by Leofric, Earl of Mercia, and his wife Godgyfu. Known to the world as Lady Godiva, she is reputed to have ridden through the town naked, or at least stripped of her jewelry, to win tax relief for its citizens. By the 14th century Coventry was already an important mercantile center, expanding rapidly in the late 19th century with such new industries as sewing machines, bicycles, and the first English motorcar, a Daimler, in 1896. The city's contribution to the motor industry is beautifully told in its fascinating Museum of British Road Transport, which alone is worth the trip.

This daytrip can be combined with one to Warwick, easily reached by bus or car, or by rail via Leamington Spa.

GETTING THERE:

Trains from London's Euston Station leave twice an hour for the 75-minute journey to Coventry, with reduced service on weekends and holidays. Return trains operate until late evening.

Coaches depart Victoria Coach Station in London every two or three hours, making the ride to Coventry in 2¼ hours.

By car, take the M-1 to Junction 17, then the M-45/A-45 into Coventry, nearly 100 miles northwest of London.

WHEN TO GO:

Being a business city, Coventry is best visited on a working day when its pace is going full strength. The Museum of British Road Transport is open daily from Easter through September, and on Fridays through Sundays only during the rest of the year.

Coventry Cathedral

FOOD AND DRINK:

Restaurants in Coventry, with the exception of a multitude of fast-food outlets, are geared to the business trade. Some choices are:

Leofric Hotel (Broadgate, by The Precinct) A modern business hotel with two restaurants. $$

DeVere Hotel (Cathedral Square, just behind the cathedral) A large, modern hotel with several restaurants. $$

Waters (High St., near Broadgate) A wine bar serving lunches. $

TOURIST INFORMATION:

The local tourist office, phone (0203) 20-084, is in the public library near the north end of The Precinct.

SUGGESTED TOUR:

Leaving the **train station** (1), you have a choice of getting downtown by bus, taxi, or on foot. The very pleasant walk is a little under one mile and completely avoids traffic all the way. It is this separation of pedestrians from cars that makes Coventry such a special place. The path goes through parks, passes under and over busy thoroughfares, and winds up in a modern shopping mall.

Broadgate (2), a large open square, is the heart of the city. Lady Godiva, or at least a statue of her, rides naked astride her horse in the center. The famous scene, complete with a naughty Peeping Tom, is reenacted hourly by animated figures under the clock on the south side.

Stroll over to the ruins of the **Old Cathedral** (3), all that remained following the terrible incendiary bombing of World War II. Miraculously, its 14th-century tower survived and may be climbed for a wonderful view of the city. At the far end there is a crude altar with a cross made of two charred roof timbers. Behind this, a broken wall bears the touching inscription "Father Forgive." Few people can look at this without feeling a lump in the throat.

The magnificent new **Coventry Cathedral**, rising next to the shell of the old, was consecrated in 1962. A storm of controversy raged over the unorthodox design by Sir Basil Spence, but this has died down as its true splendor became apparent to all but the most die-hard of traditionalists.

Enter the nave and examine the **Baptistry** on the right. The stunning window of abstract stained glass is the largest made in this century. In front of it a three-ton boulder, taken from a hillside near Bethlehem, serves as a font. Beyond the original charred cross at the high altar hangs Graham Sutherland's *Christ in Glory* tapestry, the largest in the world. All around you are wonderful examples of modern design. The entire cathedral evokes a strong feeling of contemporary faith, more so perhaps than even the most splendid of Gothic structures. Its **Visitors Centre**, downstairs, presents an exciting audiovisual show dramatizing Coventry's history, along with three-dimensional holograms depicting the Stations of the Cross. Before leaving the cathedral, be sure to visit the **Chapel of Unity**, which is set aside for use by all Christian denominations. Outside, on the east wall near the entrance, there is a great bronze sculpture of *St. Michael and the Devil,* the last major work by Sir Jacob Epstein.

Exit through the Old Cathedral onto Bayley Lane. The **Guildhall of St. Mary** (4) is one of the few medieval buildings to have escaped destruction. Built in the 14th century, it is still used for civic functions and is definitely worth a visit. The same narrow street leads to the **Herbert Art Gallery and Museum** (5), just a block away. In addition to an excellent collection of modern art, the museum has interesting displays of local manufactures, history, bygones, and archaeology. It is open Mondays through Saturdays, from 10 a.m. to 5:30 p.m.; and on Sundays from 2–5 p.m.

Return to Broadgate and make a stop at **Holy Trinity Church** (6), an attractive mixture of 13th- to 17th-century styles. Take a look down Priory Row and then follow the map to the wonderful **Museum of British Road Transport** (7) on Cook Street. At one time Coventry had over one hundred automobile manufacturers. Many of these are rep-

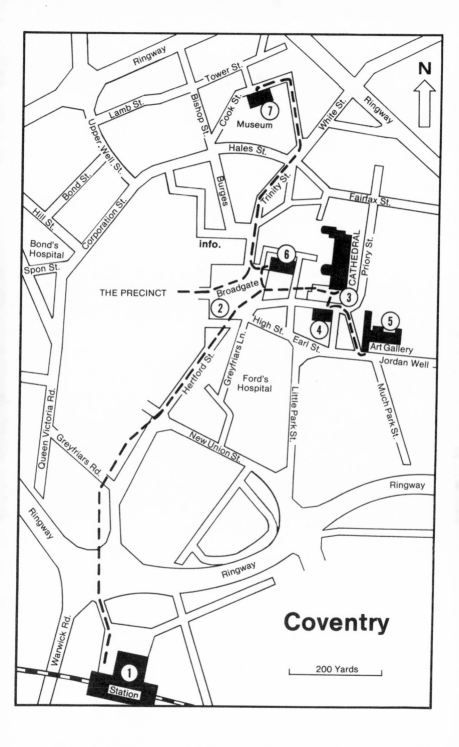

N

Ringway
Tower St.
Lamb St.
Bishop St.
Cook St.
Museum (7)
Upper Well St.
Bond St.
Corporation St.
Hales St.
Burges
Trinity St.
White St.
Ringway
Fairfax St.
Hill St.
Bond's Hospital
Spon St.
info.
THE PRECINCT
Broadgate (2)
(6)
CATHEDRAL
Priory St.
(3)
(4)
(5)
Art Gallery
High St. Earl St.
Jordan Well
Hertford St.
Greyfriars Ln.
Ford's Hospital
Little Park St.
Much Park St.
Queen Victoria Rd.
Greyfriars Rd.
New Union St.
Ringway
Warwick Rd.
Ringway
Ringway

Coventry

200 Yards

(1)
Station

In the Museum of British Road Transport

resented in the immense collection of cars dating from as far back as 1897. There are also trucks, buses, bicycles, motorcycles, and other specialized vehicles from the earliest days right up to the present. Among the most fascinating is Montgomery's staff car, used on the battlefields of World War II. The museum is open daily from Easter through September, Mondays through Fridays, from 10 a.m. to 4 p.m., and on Saturdays and Sundays from 10 a.m. to 5:30 p.m. During the rest of the year it is open on Fridays from 9:30 a.m. to 4 p.m., and on Saturdays and Sundays from 10 a.m. to 5 p.m. Don't miss this treat.

Before returning to the train station, you should take a stroll through the modern shopping precincts off Broadgate. Beyond these, past Corporation Street, there are a few other remnants of the Middle Ages. These include Spon Street, where ancient houses from other parts of town have been relocated. Bond's Hospital, a Tudor almshouse, and St. John's, a restored 14th-century church, are both nearby on Hill Street. Closer to the station is Ford's Hospital on Greyfriars Lane, an exceptional almshouse from 1509.

Ironbridge Gorge

Coalbrookdale is quiet now, but at one time it was the cradle of the Industrial Revolution, a phenomenon that forever changed the face of civilization. It was there, in 1709, that Abraham Darby first smelted iron using abundant coke as a fuel rather than scarce charcoal. This single event made possible the large-scale development of industry in the surrounding Ironbridge Gorge, which eventually spread throughout much of Britain, Europe, and the New World.

In 1779, Darby's grandson, Abraham Darby III, spanned the River Severn with the world's first iron bridge, a direct result of the new technology, at a point near the original furnace. Known as the Iron Bridge, it has since lent its name to the entire area. By the end of the 19th century, however, the iron industry began moving elsewhere as local mines played out, and the Ironbridge region fell into obscurity.

Our early industrial heritage remained almost forgotten in a tangle of weeds until 1968, when a trust was formed to restore and reactivate the surviving relics. Its mission, still under way, has had remarkable success in providing the public with an understanding of one of history's most crucial turning points. A walk along the furnaces, mills, mines, canals, shops, and workers' homes is truly a fascinating adventure.

Ironbridge Gorge may be visited as a rather long but highly worthwhile daytrip out of London or, more easily, as a simple excursion from such Midland centers as Birmingham or Shrewsbury.

GETTING THERE:

Trains depart London's Euston Station in the morning for Telford Central, a new station between Birmingham and Shrewsbury. The fastest of these take about 2½ hours for the trip, while on others it is necessary to change to a local train at Birmingham or Wolverhampton. Return service from Telford Central operates until mid-evening. Once at Telford Central station, it is an easy walk to Telford Town Centre, where you can get a bus for the four-mile ride to Ironbridge, getting off in front of the Tontine Hotel, next to the Iron Bridge. Note that service is reduced on Sundays and holidays.

A more convenient plan is to take the train to Shrewsbury or Wolverhampton and rent a car for the day. The mileage is not great and you would have more freedom, more time, and much less walking.

Travel **by car** is much easier on this trip and has the advantage of eliminating several miles of walking between the sites, except during the peak summer season when a free shuttle bus connects them. From London take the M-1 northwest to Rugby, then the M-6 west to Wolverhampton, and the M-54 to Telford. From there it is only four miles on local roads to Ironbridge. The total distance from London is 140 miles.

WHEN TO GO:

Most of the museum sights are open every day except Christmas. Those that might be closed during the winter are the Blists Hill complex and the Coalbrookdale Museum of Iron. Much of this trip is outdoors, making decent weather important. Try to allow five hours to tour the major sites. If this is not possible and you must eliminate some, remember that Blists Hill, Coalport, and the Iron Bridge are probably the most interesting.

FOOD AND DRINK:

There are quite a few eating and drinking establishments near the Iron Bridge, along with a Victorian pub and a tea room within the Blists Hill site. Some choices are:

> **Tontine Hotel** (The Square, by the Iron Bridge) An old country inn from 1806, with a pub and a restaurant. $ and $$
>
> **Malthouse** (The Wharfage, between the Iron Bridge and the Museum Visitor Centre) Meals in a riverside pub with outdoor tables available. $
>
> **Boat Inn** (in Jackfield, near the footbridge from Coalport) A delightful pub with meals, on the banks of the Severn. $

TOURIST INFORMATION:

The local tourist office, phone (0952) 88-27-53, is in the toll house by the Iron Bridge.

SUGGESTED TOUR:

Begin at the **Iron Bridge** (1). Built in 1779, this was the forerunner of all metal bridges in the world and represented the height of metalworking technology in its day. Stroll across the bridge to the **information office**, where you can ask about the latest developments in this long-term restoration project. During July and August a free bus service operates between all of the sites, otherwise you will either have to walk or drive.

Outside the Pub at Blists Hill
(Photo courtesy of Ironbridge Gorge Museum Trust)

Returning to the Tontine Hotel, turn right and follow High Street and Waterloo Street to the **Bedlam Furnaces** (2), built in 1757. Continuing on for about a mile to a fork in the road, make a left uphill to the entrance of the **Blists Hill Open Air Museum** (3). Detailed brochures are available here that describe the history and workings of each attraction.

Here a working **industrial village** (4) is being re-created from buildings once located elsewhere in the region. Included in this group is a sawmill, a printer's, a candlemaker's, a cobbler's, a baker's, a doctor's, a bank, and other similar shops. In keeping with the atmosphere, all of the staff wear 19th-century costumes. Nearby are some railway sidings with an old locomotive and several freight cars.

In a few steps you will come to the **Shropshire Canal** (5), opened in 1793. This once linked the River Severn with factories and mines in the interior. By its side is the **Blists Hill Mine**, dug in the 18th century, which reached a depth of 600 feet before being abandoned in 1941. The headgear and winding house are exact replicas of the originals. Walk along the canal past stop locks and turn right to examine the upper parts of a blast furnace.

At the end of the canal is the **Hay Inclined Plane** (6), dating from 1793, on which canal boats were raised and lowered 207 vertical feet between the canal and the River Severn below by being placed on

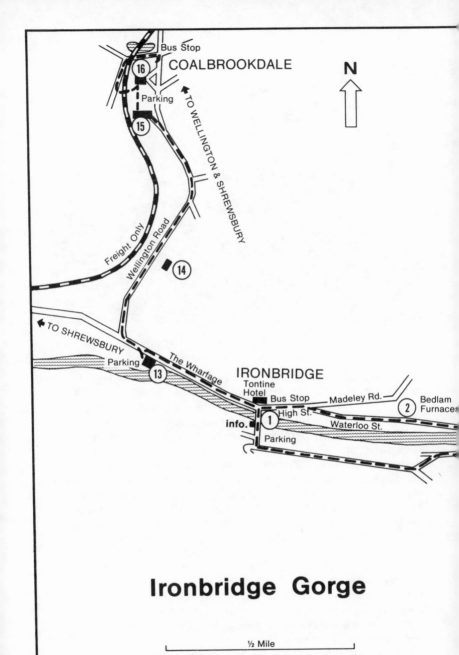

Ironbridge Gorge

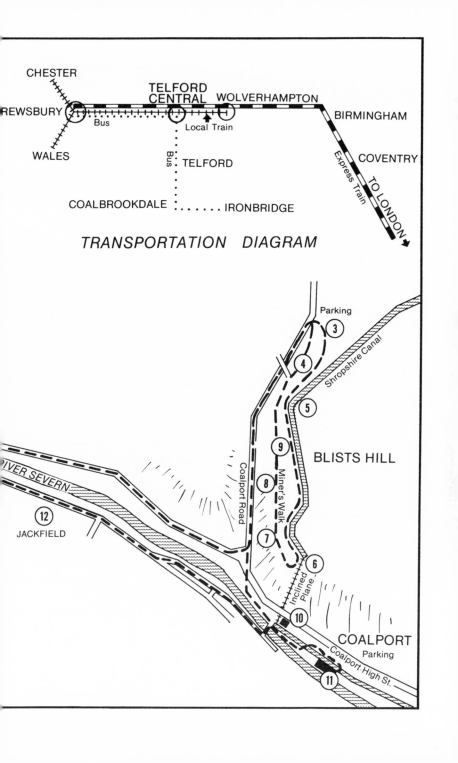

cradles that ran over rails, the down boat pulling the up boat with help from a stationary steam engine. Continue down the hill along the tracks until you get to a path on the right.

Stroll along the **Miners' Walk** past the Adit (a hillside mine entrance) and several types of mine headgear (7) to St. Chad's Mission Church, a simple corrugated iron structure in which miners once worshipped. Just beyond is the **Shelton Tollhouse** (8), originally built in 1830 near Shrewsbury and moved here to avoid demolition. To the left is a reconstructed **squatter's cottage**, complete with a combination pig-sty and outhouse.

Continue on to the **Blast Furnaces** (9), constructed between 1832 and 1844 and used to produce pig iron until 1912. Adjacent to this is the **Wrought Ironworks**, where restoration of an early puddling furnace, steam hammer, and rolling mill is underway. From here walk back through the industrial village to the museum entrance.

Leaving the museum, go down Coalport Road until you come to the intersection. If you are driving, turn left to the parking lot on the map. Otherwise, cross Coalport High Street and turn left on the path along the river's edge. This leads to a footbridge over the Severn. Immediately to the left of this is the entrance to the **Tar Tunnel** (10), located at the base of a house. The tunnel, which can be visited, extends at least a thousand yards under Blists Hill and was dug in 1787, probably in search of coal. What they found was running natural tar. At one time the yield was over a thousand gallons a week, and the sticky stuff still oozes out. Across the road is the bottom of the Hay Inclined Plane.

Continuing along the path, which twice crosses a canal, you will reach the **Coalport China Museum** (11), where exquisite porcelain was once made. Inside, there are many interesting displays as well as workshops where all of the stages in the manufacture of china can be seen.

Those driving should now return to the Iron Bridge (1). If you are on foot, the best route is to return to the footbridge opposite the tar tunnel and cross it. To your right a series of roads and paths lead to the village of **Jackfield** (12), home of the **Tile Museum**, housed in a former factory. Follow the map back to the Iron Bridge (1) and recross the Severn. You are now back where you started. At this point you could either call it quits and take a bus to Telford Central, or continue on to two more major sights.

From the Iron Bridge make a left and go down Tontine Hill to the **Museum Visitor Centre** (13). This former warehouse now contains an exhibition depicting the history of Ironbridge Gorge. There is an audiovisual presentation at frequent intervals that is particularly fascinating. When you are finished, continue along to an intersection and turn

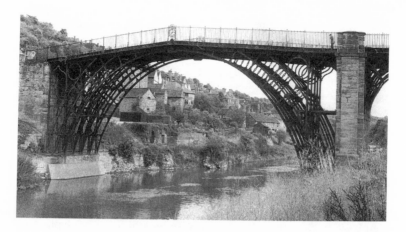

The Iron Bridge

right up Dale Road, which soon becomes Wellington Road. On the right you will pass the **Rose Cottages** (14), built in 1636 as homes for early iron founders. They are now restored and partly used as a workshop for handmade furniture.

Continue along Wellington Road, passing a modern foundry, and turn left into the **Coalbrookdale Museum of Iron** and **Furnace Site** (15). The Great Warehouse, built in 1838 when the local ironworks were perhaps the largest in the world, has been converted into a large museum of the history of iron and steel. Beyond the parking lot, by the railway viaduct, is the **Old Furnace** (16) where Abraham Darby changed the course of history by smelting iron with coke in 1709. It was probably built in 1638 and later enlarged by Abraham Darby III to allow for the huge castings needed for the Iron Bridge. The furnace was retired in 1818 and forgotten about until 1959, when it was uncovered during demolition of several workshops. It is now enclosed and has a sound-and-light display.

Your tour is now complete. All of the sites are open daily except on Christmas, from 10 a.m. to 6 p.m. in summer and from 10 a.m. to 5 p.m. in winter. The Blists Hill complex and the Coalbrookdale Museum of Iron may be closed between early November and early March.

Shrewsbury

Nearly encircled by the River Severn, the ancient market town of Shrewsbury has preserved its medieval past without denying the present. Picturesque timbered buildings coexist with later structures on streets bearing such quaint names as Grope Lane, Gullet Passage, Seventy Steps, Shoplatch, and Dog Pole. A 16th-century map could still be used to negotiate the winding, hilly lanes that lead upwards from the river to the old market place.

Shrewsbury is the county town of Shropshire, otherwise known as Salop. It was first settled in the 5th century when inhabitants of the nearby Roman town of *Virconium* were looking for a safer place to live in those uneasy years following the fall of the empire. The town's name, originally *Scrobesbyrig*, dates from the 8th century when it was part of the Kingdom of Mercia.

Prosperity came during Tudor times after the town became an important market place, a role it plays to this day. Although much of the Industrial Revolution began nearby, Shrewsbury was spared its effects and evolved into an intellectual center with the founding of the Shrewsbury School in 1552 by Edward VI.

Shrewsbury is unexcelled as a base for exploring the Midlands and Central Wales. Its rail and road facilities are first rate, as are the many old inns that have catered to travelers since the Middle Ages.

GETTING THERE:

Trains leave about hourly from London's Euston Station. Some go direct to Shrewsbury while others require a change at Birmingham New Street or Wolverhampton. The journey takes nearly three hours, with returns operating until mid-evening.

By car, take the M-1 to Rugby, then the M-6 past Birmingham and the M-54 and A-5 into Shrewsbury, which is 157 miles northwest of London.

WHEN TO GO:

Saturdays, when the market is busiest, are probably the best days to visit Shrewsbury. Markets are also held on Wednesdays and Fridays. Avoid coming on a Sunday, when most of the sights are closed.

A Narrow Lane in Shrewsbury

FOOD AND DRINK:

Shrewsbury has a nice assortment of restaurants and pubs, some good choices being:

Prince Rupert Hotel (Butcher Row, near St. Mary's) Dining in a delightful old hotel with 3 restaurants. $$

Lion Hotel (Wyle Cop, near the English Bridge) An ancient coaching inn with a Victorian-style restaurant. $$

Old Police House (Castle Court, Castle St., near the castle) Traditional foods in a cozy atmosphere. X: Sat. lunch, Sun. $$

Antonio's (Victorian Arcade, Hills Lane, near the Welsh Bridge) International cuisine in an elegant setting. X: Sun. eve., Mon. lunch $$

Castle Vaults (Castle Gates, near the castle) A pub specializing in Mexican food. $

TOURIST INFORMATION:

The local tourist office, phone (0743) 50-761, is in the Music Hall on The Square.

SUGGESTED TOUR:

Leaving the **train station** (1), walk straight ahead up Castle Gates and turn left into the **Castle** (2), which has undergone many changes since it was first built in the 11th century. The last of these was in 1790 when the noted engineer Thomas Telford rebuilt it as a private mansion. The castle now houses the **Shropshire Regimental Museum**, whose interesting displays proudly recall over 300 years of military glory. It is open daily from 10 a.m. to 5 p.m., except between October and Easter, when it closes at 4 p.m., and all day on Sundays.

Across the street are the old 17th-century buildings of the Shrewsbury School, which has since moved to another part of town. The statue in front of them is of Charles Darwin, Shrewsbury's most famous son. Continuing up Castle Street you will pass, on the left, the half-timbered **Council House Gateway** (3) of 1620. The building it leads to was erected in 1502 as the meeting place of the Council of the Marches, and was later used by Charles I and James II. Beyond this, opposite the post office, is the modern High Cross on the site where the rebellious Harry Hotspur was drawn and quartered in 1403 following the Battle of Shrewsbury.

Make a left on St. Mary's Street and follow it to **St. Mary's Church** (4), the most beautiful in town. Built around 1200, it has a wealth of gorgeous stained glass, including an enormous Jesse window at the east end that dates from 1350.

Leaving the church, you will pass the half-timbered **Draper's Hall** on the left and, as the street name changes to Dog Pole, the 17th-century **Guildhall**, also on the left. At the end of the street bear left and stroll down the curiously named Wyle Cop. The **Lion Hotel** on the right is quite old and was once the setting for performances by such musical luminaries as Paganini and Jenny Lind. The many guests who have stayed here include Dickens and Disraeli.

At the bottom of the hill make a hard right on Beeches Lane and follow Town Walls. Continue past an old 15th-century watchtower on the left and walk down Murivance to **New St. Chad's** (5), a strange circular church built in 1792 by Telford. Below it lies an open park of some 25 acres known as **The Quarry** (6). Stroll down a path to The Dingle, a splendid garden with a pond its center. Continue on the path to the river, across which you can see the new Shrewsbury School of 1882, and turn right to the Welsh Bridge. Across this, on The Mount, is the house where Charles Darwin was born in 1809.

Make a right onto Bridge Street and bear left on Barker Street to **Rowley's House** (7), a half-timbered structure from 1618 which now houses the outstanding **Virconium Museum of Roman Artifacts** from nearby Wroxeter. The museum is open daily except Sundays, from 10 a.m. to 5 p.m.

Follow Bellstone to Shoplatch and turn left. On the corner is the modern General Market, just beyond which is Mardol, a street with many delightful old buildings. Take a look down this and then con-

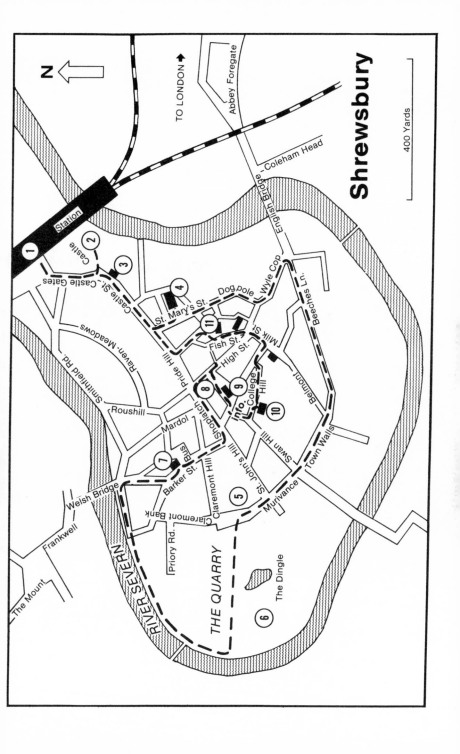

Shrewsbury

N ←

TO LONDON ↑

400 Yards

Abbey Foregate

Coleham Head

English Bridge

Station

Castle

Castle Gates

Castle St.

St. Mary's St.

Dog Pole

Wyle Cop

Beeches Ln.

Raven Meadows

Fish St.

High St.

Milk St.

Pride Hill

College Hill

Info.

Belmont

Smithfield Rd.

Roushill

Mardol

Shoplatch

Town Walls

Swan Hill

St. John's Hill

Murivance

Claremont Hill

Barker St.

Bus

Welsh Bridge

Claremont Bank

Priory Rd.

RIVER SEVERN

Frankwell

The Mount

THE QUARRY

The Dingle

1 2 3 4 5 6 7 8 9 10 11

The Bear Steps

tinue on Pride Hill to High Street. Make a right here and pass **Ireland's Mansion** (8), an elegant timbered house from the 16th century. Opposite, on the left, is **Owen's Mansion**, which is almost as old. Just down the street, the extremely narrow Grope Lane leads off to the left, a passageway that has hardly changed since the days of Elizabeth I. Turn into The Square, with its 16th-century **Old Market Hall** (9).

A right on Market Street, followed by an immediate left on Swan Hill, leads to College Hill. Turn left here and walk down to **Clive House** (10), once the residence of Lord Clive of India and now a museum of early Shropshire industries. It is open Mondays through Saturdays, from 10 a.m. to 5 p.m.

Continue down College Hill and turn right into Princess Street. At the foot of this are the remains of **Old St. Chad's**, a 14th-century church. Making a left on Milk Street, stroll up Fish Street and pass St. Julian's Church, which has an early-13th-century west tower. Just beyond is St. Alkmund's, also with an old tower. A fascinating group of medieval cottages called the **Bear Steps** (11) is adjacent to this. Be sure to step up into the courtyard for a better look. From here it is only a few yards down picturesque Butcher Row to Pride Hill, which leads back to the station.

North Wales
Rail Excursion

Rail fans will really enjoy this long but easy daytrip through the majestic natural splendors of northern Wales. The entire day is spent riding a succession of connecting trains ranging from sleek InterCity expresses to the latest Sprinter railcars to a 19th-century narrow-gauge steam train. A complete loop through Mid and North Wales, leaving England near Shrewsbury and returning via Chester, takes you through a wide variety of spectacular scenery encompassing both mountain wilderness and rugged seacoasts.

The highlight of the trip is a ride on the famous Ffestiniog Link, one of the delightful "Great Little Trains of Wales," a narrow-gauge mountain steam line that joins together British Rail's Mid and North Wales routes.

For BritRail Pass holders, this is also a very economical day's outing. Their only expense, aside from meals and refreshments, will be the very reasonable fare on the private Ffestiniog Railway. Although it was designed to be taken from London, this trip can also be made from Shrewsbury or Chester, both excellent bases for exploring the Midlands as well as northern Wales.

GETTING THERE:

You will have to check the **train schedules** very carefully before setting out on this adventure, as there are days when the connections are impossible. The best place to do this is at the information counter in London's Euston Station, or by phoning (01) 387–7070. This trip should not be made on a Sunday or holiday. Basically, you must take an early morning train, around 7:30 a.m., from London's Euston Station to Shrewsbury, where you change to a local for Porthmadog, possibly again changing at Machynlleth en route. On Saturdays there is a special express called the Snowdonian that goes all the way from London's Euston Station to Porthmadog and beyond—making life a lot easier.

Change to the steam train at either Porthmadog or Minffordd and ride it to the end of the line, Blaenau Ffestiniog, where there is an easy connection to Llandudno Junction. From here you will have a choice of trains via Chester and Crewe back to Euston, arriving around 9 p.m. At least one of these trains is direct. Note that the private Ffestiniog steam railway does not accept the BritRail Pass, but their fares are very reasonable.

WHEN TO GO:

The best time to make this trip will be determined by the train schedules. The all-important steam train link operates hourly every day in summer, but infrequently during winter. Sundays and holidays are virtually impossible. Saturdays are excellent and weekdays almost as good.

FOOD AND DRINK:

There is no opportunity for restaurant dining on this trip, although there is a good, inexpensive cafeteria and pub at the Porthmadog steam train station. Snacks, light meals and/or dining-car meals are available on the trains to and from London. You could, of course, bring along your own sandwiches to eat en route. Snacks and drinks are sold on the steam train.

TOURIST INFORMATION:

Travel information for the entire route is available at any British Rail station by calling (01) 387–7070, or by contacting the Ffestiniog Railway in Wales at (0766) 2340 or 2384.

SUGGESTED TOUR:

Depart London's **Euston Station** (1) around 7:30 a.m. on a modern InterCity express to Shrewsbury. On Saturdays there is a direct express, marked for Pwllheli, that takes you all the way to Porthmadog without a change. Along the way there are ever-changing views as you pass Rugby, Coventry, Birmingham, and Wolverhampton.

Arriving at **Shrewsbury** (2) around 10:30 a.m., change to one of the comfortable new Sprinter railcars for the journey across Mid Wales, going by way of Welshpool. If the train you are on is marked for Aberystwyth, it will be necessary to change at **Machynlleth** (3) to another Sprinter marked for Pwllheli. On Saturdays, of course, none of these changes are needed. By now you are aware of the impossibly tounge-twisting names many of these Welsh towns have, so just look out for the signs. The really spectacular scenery begins at Dovey Junction and continues all the way north. Be sure to sit on the left side for the best views.

It is possible to change to the Ffestiniog steam railway at either **Minffordd** (4) or **Porthmadog** (5). At Minffordd the connection is much easier as both railways use adjoining stations. Making the change at Porthmadog involves a half-mile walk down High Street from the British Rail station to the **Ffestiniog Railway Harbour Station** (6) (see map insert). This is more than compensated for, however, by the cafeteria, pub, and small railway museum at the Harbour station. The choice is up to you.

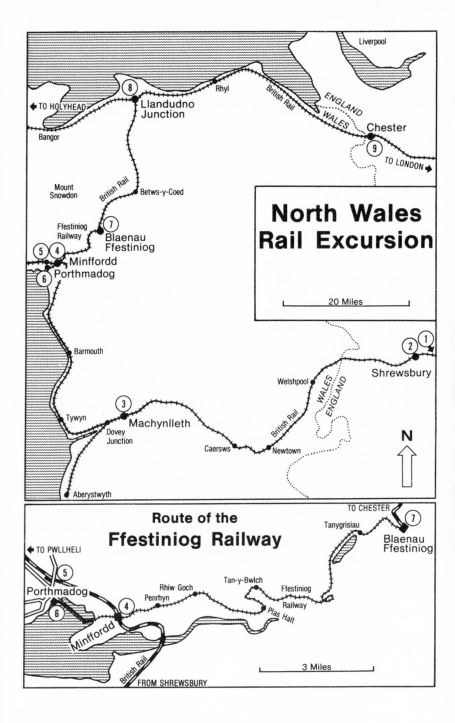

North Wales
Rail Excursion

20 Miles

N

TO HOLYHEAD
Bangor
Llandudno Junction ⑧
Rhyl
British Rail
Liverpool
ENGLAND
WALES
Chester
⑨ TO LONDON

Mount Snowdon
British Rail
Betws-y-Coed
Ffestiniog Railway ⑦
Blaenau Ffestiniog
⑤ ④ Minffordd
⑥ Porthmadog

Barmouth
② ①
Shrewsbury
Welshpool
WALES
ENGLAND
③ Machynlleth
Tywyn
Dovey Junction
Caersws
Newtown
British Rail
Aberystwyth

Route of the
Ffestiniog Railway

TO CHESTER
⑦
Tanygrisiau
Blaenau Ffestiniog

TO PWLLHELI
⑤
Porthmadog
Rhiw Goch
Penrhyn
Tan-y-Bwlch
Ffestiniog Railway
Plas Halt
⑥ ④ Minffordd
British Rail
FROM SHREWSBURY

3 Miles

Along the Ffestiniog Railway

The **Ffestiniog Railway** was built in the 1830s to haul slate from the quarries of Blaenau Ffestiniog to the harbor at Porthmadog, where it was loaded onto ships. Originally using horse traction uphill and gravity down, the line developed suitable steam engines in 1863 and began passenger service in 1865. As the slate industry declined after the turn of the century, the line turned increasingly to the tourist trade for survival. This lasted until the beginning of World War II, after which the railway was abandoned. In 1954 it was taken over by a dedicated group of voluntary preservationists, who began a short passenger service in 1956, only to be frustrated by the construction of a pumped-storage hydroelectric facility that put part of the line under water. This setback was overcome by a spectacular detour, adding greatly to the railway's scenic beauty. Reliance on volunteer labor and a chronic lack of funds delayed completion, but in 1982 the railway was totally restored all the way to Blaenau Ffestiniog, where it again links up with the British Rail system.

From Porthmadog to Blaenau Ffestiniog, a distance of 13½ miles, the railway twists and climbs its way through the foothills of **Snowdonia National Park**, climbing over 700 feet and doubling around itself in a great horseshoe bend. The one-hour journey passes pastures and forests, lakes and waterfalls, always providing breathtaking vistas along the way.

In an Observation Car of the Ffestiniog Railway

The Ffestiniog Railway offers two classes of service, Third and First. The first-class observation car, at the rear of the train, affords the best views and the most comfortable seats. Snacks and drinks are always available in both classes.

Purchase a one-way (single) ticket to Blaenau Ffestiniog and board the train. With luck, you may be hauled by *Prince,* one of the original 1863 locomotives; or by *Merddin Emrys,* an 1879 Double Fairlie. Most of the other steam locomotives date from the late 19th century, although there are some recent replicas in use. A look at the builder's plate tells all. There are also a few diesel engines, but these are only used during off-peak hours.

Arriving at **Blaenau Ffestiniog** (7) an hour later, you make an immediate connection in the same station to a British Rail Sprinter train bound for Llandudno on the north coast of Wales. This is another exceptionally lovely ride, lasting about 55 minutes. Get off at **Llandudno Junction** (8) and change to a main line express for London. A further transfer at **Chester** (9) or Crewe may be necessary, depending on the connection time, but in any case you should arrive back in London's Euston Station around 9 p.m.

Chester

Of all the ancient towns in England, Chester stands out as perhaps the best preserved. Its medieval walls remain intact, still surrounding the picturesque streets lined with half-timbered houses. The scene today, except for the traffic, is right out of an old engraving.

Originally known as *Deva*, Chester was founded about A.D. 60 as the headquarters camp of the Roman XX Legion, one of the three that guarded Britain. After their departure around A.D. 380, the town became an obscure settlement until the 10th century, when it was enlarged by Ethelred of Mercia. During the Norman Conquest of 1066 it held out against William the Conqueror longer than any other English town, but in 1070 the inevitable happened and Chester was made an earldom, granted by William to his nephew, Hugh of Avrances. The town prospered in its role as a port, with ships from all over Europe entering the harbor.

By the end of the Middle Ages, however, the gradual silting of the River Dee made shipping unprofitable. In the Civil War of the 17th century, Chester supported Charles I, but was badly defeated in 1645. The building of the Shropshire Union Canal in the late 18th century and the development of railways shortly afterwards brought back the prosperity that today makes Chester such a beautiful and thriving city.

GETTING THERE:

Trains leave London's Euston Station several times in the morning for the nearly three-hour journey to Chester. Some of these require a change at Crewe, and service is poor on Sundays and holidays. Return trains operate until early evening.

By car, Chester is about 200 miles northwest of London. The fastest route is via the M-1 to Rugby, then the M-6 north to the M-56. Head west on this and take the A-56 into Chester.

WHEN TO GO:

Chester can be visited any day of the week, although on Sunday some of the sights have reduced hours and rail service is not good.

At The Cross

FOOD AND DRINK:

For a town its size, Chester is blessed with an exceptionally good range of restaurants and pubs. Some choices, more or less in walking tour sequence, are:

Grosvenor Hotel (Eastgate St., near the Eastgate) The main restaurant features classic French cuisine in elegant surroundings, with a good wine selection. $$$

Olde Custom House (Watergate St., near the Stanley Palace) Pub lunches in an historic timbered building. $

Ye Olde King's Head (48 Lower Bridge St., near the Heritage Centre) An old half-timbered inn with a good restaurant. $$

Claverton's Wine Bar (Lower Bridge St., near the Heritage Centre) Daily specials of English and vegetarian food, with wine by the glass. $$

Aphrodite (Lower Bridge St., near the Heritage Centre) Greek cuisine in an historic house, both a restaurant and a taverna. X: Sun. $ and $$

Bear and Billet (Lower Bridge St., near the Heritage Centre) A 17th-century timbered pub with food. $

Albion (Park St., near Newgate) Good lunches in an attractive Edwardian pub. $

The Courtyard (13 St. Werburgh St., near the cathedral) Crêpes, salads, fondues, and the like, with larger dinners. X: Sun. $ and $$

Sidoli (25 Northgate, near the cathedral) A pizzeria, with Italian meals served upstairs) X: Sun. $

TOURIST INFORMATION:

The main tourist office is located in the Town Hall on Northgate Street. You can phone them at (0244) 40–144, extension 2111 or 2250. There is a branch in the Visitor Centre on Vicar's Lane and another in the Grosvenor Precinct shopping center.

SUGGESTED TOUR:

The **train station** (1) is a little over a half-mile from Eastgate, where the Old Town begins. You can cover this rather uninteresting distance by bus, taxi, or on foot. If you decide to walk, just follow the map.

Eastgate (2) is the main entrance to the city. The present structure was built in 1769, replacing medieval and Roman predecessors. Above the arch is an ornamental clock tower commemorating Queen Victoria's Diamond Jubilee. A climb up the steps will put you atop the ancient **City Walls** that still completely encircle the town. Follow the walkway to the right, passing the medieval cathedral and its modern detached bell tower. In a short while you will come to **King Charles' Tower** (3). According to legend, it was from here that Charles I witnessed the defeat of his Loyalist forces against Parliamentary troops in 1645. The tower now contains a small but interesting museum of the Civil War. Be sure to see the relics on the upper floor.

At this point the walls follow the Shropshire Union Canal, built over the old town moat. Beyond Northgate there are excellent views of the Welsh hills in the distance. Soon you will cross a busy expressway on the modern St. Martin's Gate. Go down the steps on the far side to the **canal locks** (4) where, if your timing is right, you will see narrowboats passing through on their way to the basin below. This operation is fascinating to watch. Some of the colorful boats, now used for pleasure, are still drawn by horses. Walk downhill past the locks and under the railway viaduct, then bear right and visit the **canal basin** where many of the water people tie up their boats. Rides are often available from here. Retrace your steps past the locks and climb back to the city walls.

Continuing your circuit of the walls, you will pass the Goblin Tower and then Bonewaldesthorne's Tower. From here a spur wall leads to the **Water Tower** (5), built in 1322 and at one time surrounded by the River Dee. The walls now descend to street level at the **Watergate** (6), once the main gate leading to the port.

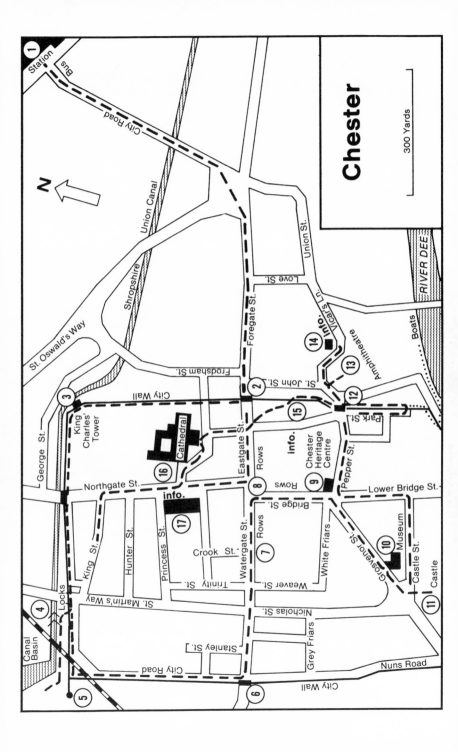

Chester

N

300 Yards

RIVER DEE

Station
Bus
City Road
Union Canal
Shropshire
St. Oswald's Way
George St.
King Charles' Tower
City Wall
Northgate St.
Frodsham St.
Foregate St.
Love St.
Union St.
Vicar's Ln.
info.
Amphitheatre
Boats
St. John St.
Park St.
Eastgate St.
Rows
Rows
info.
Chester Heritage Centre
Pepper St.
Lower Bridge St.
Cathedral
info.
King St.
Hunter St.
Princess St.
St. Martin's Way
Crook St.
Trinity St.
Watergate St.
Rows
Weaver St.
White Friars
Bridge St.
Grosvenor St.
Museum
Castle St.
Castle
Nicholas St.
Grey Friars
Nuns Road
City Wall
Stanley St.
City Road
Canal Basin
Locks

Canal Locks at Chester

Turn left on Watergate Street, the *Via Principalis*, or main street, of Roman Deva. On the right is the **Stanley Palace**, a residence dating from 1591 that is now occupied by the English Speaking Union. It may be visited at set times. Beyond Nicholas Street you will pass Trinity Church on the left, and at Weaver Street encounter the first of the famous **Rows**, an architectural feature unique to Chester. These consist of galleries that form a continuous protected walkway through the buildings of the main streets. One story above street level, they shield pedestrians from both weather and traffic. The origins of this strange but very practical building style are clouded in the mysteries of the Middle Ages. One particularly romantic theory has it that when the Rows were first built, probably in the 13th century, the streets were so cluttered with Roman ruins that passage at street level was difficult. Whatever their original purpose, they remain an attractive way to stroll about the town.

Climb the steps on the right side of Watergate Street and walk along the Row to number 51, **Bishop Lloyd's House** (7), the richest example of carved timberwork in Chester. A better view of it can be had from across the street. Other outstanding houses along this Row are the Leche House at number 21; the Crypt, now used for wine storage, at number 11; and God's Providence House at number 9, near the end. Some of these may be visited by entering the shops and

Along the Rows

asking permission to look around.

The intersection at Bridge Street is known as **The Cross** (8), after the stone High Cross that stands in front of St. Peter's Church. The **Chester Town Crier** shouts his proclamations here, complete with commercials, at 12 noon and 3 p.m., daily from Tuesdays through Saturdays. Continue to the Row on the opposite side and follow Bridge Street to the right. There was once a Roman bath on this site, remains of which still exist in the crypts below. In two blocks you will reach the former St. Michael's Church, now the **Chester Heritage Centre** (9). Here, in addition to interesting artifacts, you can see an audiovisual presentation of the city's history. There is a well-stocked bookstall with local publications as well. The center is open between April and September, on Mondays, Tuesdays, and Thursdays through Saturdays, from 10 a.m. to 5 p.m.; and on Sundays from 2–5 p.m. Between October and March the hours are from 1:30–4:30 p.m.

Stroll down Grosvenor Street to the **Grosvenor Museum** (10), which has an excellent exhibition of Roman life in Chester. Attached to it is an interesting 18th-century house with room settings and costumes of bygone times. The museum is open Mondays through Saturdays, from 10:30 a.m. to 5 p.m.; and on Sundays from 2–5 p.m. Admission is free.

Chester Castle (11) is nearby. Construction on this began about

1070, but most of it was torn down during the 19th century to make way for government buildings. The only ancient structure still standing is the 13th-century Agricola Tower, which houses an old chapel. Close to it is the Cheshire Military Museum, which may be visited.

From here, Castle Street will take you to Lower Bridge Street, on which you make a left. At the corner of Pepper Street turn right and go through Newgate to the **Roman Gardens** (12), a collection of old ruins from other parts of town that have been relocated here. Continue on St. John's Street to the **Roman Amphitheatre** (13), of which only vestiges exist. Dating from about A.D. 100, this is the largest Roman structure of its type yet discovered in Britain.

Across the street is the **Chester Visitor Centre** (14) on Vicar's Lane. A tourist information office is located here, along with a variety of crafts shops and an audio-visual show of life in Chester's Rows.

Return through Newgate and turn left on Park Street, passing an unusually attractive row of 17th-century timber-framed houses. At the end of the block climb the steps onto the **City Walls**. From here you can make a little side trip down to the River Dee, where boat trips are offered.

Back on the walls, continue over Newgate and the ancient Wolfe Gate to a modern pedestrian ramp on the left that leads to an indoor shopping center, the **Grosvenor Precinct** (15). Here, in familiar surroundings, you can see the logical extension of the ideas incorporated in the medieval Rows adapted to contemporary use. Follow through the building and exit onto Eastgate Street.

St. Werburgh Street leads from here to the **Cathedral** (16). Begun as a Benedictine abbey in 1093 on the site of an earlier church, it was converted into a cathedral during the Reformation. Reflecting many centuries of change, its architectural styles range all the way from early Norman to late Perpendicular. Although not large, it is among the most interesting cathedrals in England. Be sure to see the **choir**, noted for its outstanding misericords, as well as the **cloister** and adjoining chapter house and refectory.

Leaving the cathedral, stroll up Northgate Street and walk a short distance down King Street for some pleasant views of Georgian houses. Returning on Northgate Street will bring you to the **Town Hall** (17), a Victorian Gothic structure that houses the main tourist office. From here you can walk back to the train station.

St. Albans

The first Christian martyr in Britain was a Roman soldier named Alban, who was beheaded for embracing the faith and sheltering a persecuted priest. The spot where this happened is now the town of St. Albans, which overlooks the site of the important Roman city of *Verulamium*. An abbey in his memory was erected during the 8th century by King Offa II of Mercia. Following the Norman Conquest this was rebuilt and eventually became the great cathedral that it is today.

Verulamium itself died out after the fall of the empire and slowly fell to ruin. Many of its stones were used to build the cathedral, but a surprising amount still remain in what is now parkland. There is a Roman theater, the only one of its kind in Britain, a well-preserved hypocaust, and large sections of the original walls. A splendid collection of archaeological finds is displayed in the Verulamium Museum. The town of St. Albans, on the other side of the River Ver, has a long and colorful history. Its medieval streets are lined with ancient structures which, added to the cathedral and remains of the Roman city, make this a fascinating destination for an easily accomplished daytrip.

GETTING THERE:

Trains leave London's St. Pancras Station frequently for the 20-minute run to St. Albans. Service is reduced on Sundays and holidays. Return trains run until late evening. There is also frequent service from London's Moorgate, Barbican, and some other small stations.

Coaches operated by the Green Line depart hourly from their terminal at Eccleston Bridge near Victoria Station in London. The journey takes about 70 minutes.

By car, St. Albans is 20 miles north of London via the M-1 highway to Junction 6.

WHEN TO GO:

Most of the sights are open daily throughout the year, with some closing or having reduced hours on Sundays. Visitors to the cathedral should avoid coming during Sunday services. Open-air markets are held in St. Peter's Street on Wednesdays and Saturdays.

FOOD AND DRINK:

St. Albans has no shortage of pubs and restaurants. A few choices are:

Langtry's (London Rd., a bit east of the cathedral) Makes a speciality of seafood. X: Mon. lunch, Sun. $$$

La Province (13 George St., by the cathedral) Noted for its fine French cuisine. X: Sun., Mon. $$

Koh-I-Noor (8 George St., by the cathedral) Both Indian and English food. $

Ye Olde Fighting Cocks (Abbey Mill Lane, by the river near Verulamium) A very ancient inn with pub lunches. $

TOURIST INFORMATION:

The local tourist office, phone (0727) 64–511, is at 37 Chequer Street, near the Market Place.

SUGGESTED TOUR:

Leave the **train station** (1) and follow Victoria Street to Chequer Street. This half-mile walk can be avoided by taking a bus. Once there, cut through a passageway to the Market Place and turn left. French Row maintains much of its medieval appearance, including the 14th-century Fleur de Lys Inn where King John II of France was imprisoned following the Battle of Poitiers in 1356. Just beyond this is the **Clock Tower** (2), a flint-and-rubble structure of 1412, which is one of the few remaining curfew towers in the country. It is sometimes open and may be climbed.

Cross High Street and pass through the rebuilt Waxhouse Gateway, where pilgrims going to the shrine of St. Alban once bought their candles. From here a path leads to the west front of the **Cathedral** (3), one of the largest in Britain. An abbey church dedicated to St. Alban stood here since Saxon times, but the present structure was begun in the 11th century by the Normans and incorporates many later additions. It did not become a cathedral until 1877, when a new diocese was created. The interior is rather plain but graceful. A good deal of the original **wall paintings**, once whitewashed by the Puritans, have been restored to their former splendor. Be sure to see **St. Alban's Shrine** in the chapel behind the altar screen. Dating from the 14th century, this was later destroyed and was rebuilt in 1872, when over 2,000 of its broken fragments were carefully pieced together.

Leave the cathedral and stroll past the **Abbey Gateway** of 1361, at one time the town jail and now occupied by St. Albans School, founded in the 10th century. Abbey Mill Lane leads to the site of Roman Verulamium. The Fighting Cocks Inn, by the river, was a notorious center of cockfighting and claims to be one of the oldest pubs in England.

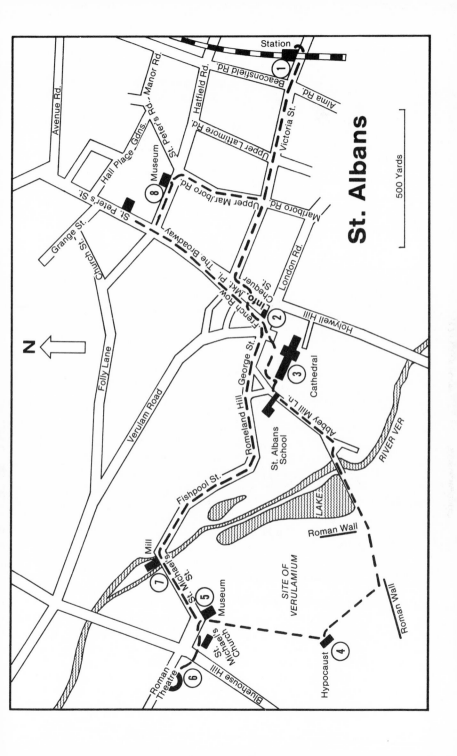

St. Albans

N

500 Yards

Station

Beaconsfield Rd.
Alma Rd.
Avenue Rd.
Manor Rd.
St. Peter's Rd.
Hall Place Gdns.
Hatfield Rd.
Upper Lattimore Rd.
Victoria St.
Museum
St. Peter's St.
Grange St.
Church St.
Upper Marlboro Rd.
Marlboro Rd.
The Broadway
London Rd.
Chequer St.
Info. Mkt. Pl.
French Row
Folly Lane
Verulam Road
Holywell Hill
Cathedral
George St.
Romeland Hill
Abbey Mill Ln.
St. Albans School
Fishpool St.
RIVER VER
LAKE
SITE OF VERULAMIUM
Roman Wall
Roman Wall
Mill
St. Michael's St.
Museum
Hypocaust
Roman Theatre
Bluehouse Hill
St. Michael's Church

Ruins of the Roman Theatre

Cross the bridge and explore the remains of ancient **Verulamium**. The importance of this city is made obvious by the fact that it was the only town in Britain to be declared a *municipum*, a status that conferred Roman citizenship on its inhabitants. Founded shortly after the conquest of A.D. 43 and sacked by Boadicea in A.D. 61, it rose to become the third-largest city, after London and Colchester, in Roman Britain. The town flourished until about A.D. 410, when it fell into decay and what was left after the stones were salvaged was slowly covered by earth.

Continue on past remains of the Roman walls to the **Hypocaust** (4), a preserved mosaic floor and heating system of a large house, now protected *in situ* by a modern structure. A path leads to the **Verulamium Museum** (5), which displays some of the greatest treasures of Roman Britain. These include jewelry, household utensils, pottery, wall paintings, a bronze figure, and many other fascinating objects discovered during the excavations. The museum is open Mondays through Saturdays, from 10 a.m. to 5:30 p.m.; and on Sundays from 2–5:30 p.m.; with shorter hours in winter.

St. Michael's Church, near the museum entrance, was begun in 948 and still retains considerable traces of its original Saxon work. Inside, there is a monument to Sir Francis Bacon, who is buried there.

St. Albans Cathedral

Walk across the road to the **Roman Theatre** (6), built to accommodate a crowd of 1,600 spectators. Semicircular in shape, it is the only one of its type in Britain. Although only the lower walls remain, visualizing what it must have looked like is not too difficult. It is open daily from 10 a.m. to 5 p.m.

Return to St. Michael's Street and turn left. At the River Ver is the **Kingsbury Water Mill** (7), which operated until 1936. There was a mill on this site since Saxon times and the present one, restored in 1970, is now a delightful museum and tea room. Visits may be made Wednesdays through Sundays, from 11 a.m. to 6 p.m., opening at noon on Sundays and closing at 5 p.m. in winter.

Follow the map past wonderful old houses on Fishpool Street, Romeland Hill, and George Street. Turn left on French Row and continue up St. Peter's Street to St. Peter's Church. A right on Hatfield Road leads to the **City Museum** (8), whose exhibits concentrate on local crafts and industries, bygones, natural history, and regional archaelogy. It is open Mondays through Saturdays, from 10 a.m. to 5 p.m., and admission is free. From here it is only a short walk back to the station.

Nottingham

Nottingham is a good introduction to the industrial Midlands, a part of England too often overlooked by visitors. This sprawling, vigorous, surprisingly attractive city has superb museums, excellent shopping facilities, and some of the most interesting pubs in the country.

Best known for the legendary Robin Hood, Nottingham dates back to the Anglo-Saxon village of *Snotingaham*, which was captured by the Danes in A.D. 868. William the Conqueror built a massive castle there in 1068, which became a stronghold of bad King John in the 13th century. The Civil War began nearby when Charles I unfurled his banner in defiance of Parliament during the mid-17th century. It was the Industrial Revolution, however, that really molded the city's character and made it the thriving giant it is today.

GETTING THERE:

Trains depart London's St. Pancras Station several times in the morning for Nottingham, a direct ride of under two hours. Service is reduced on Saturdays and poor on Sundays and holidays. Return trains operate until mid-evening. There is also service from London's King's Cross Station, requiring a change at Grantham.

By car, Nottingham is 123 miles northwest of London via the M-1.

WHEN TO GO:

The best time to come to Nottingham is on a working day, when the city bustles with activity. Most of the museums are open daily, except the Canal Museum.

FOOD AND DRINK:

Pub lovers should be sure to visit the venerable **Trip to Jerusalem** in Brewhouse Yard and the **Salutation Inn** on Hounds Gate. For regular meals, some choice dining spots along the walking route are:

> **Pagoda** (31 Greyfriar Gate, near the Canal Museum) A popular Chinese restaurant with both dim sum and full meals. $ and $$
>
> **Trattoria Conti** (14–16 Wheeler Gate, near the Old Market Square) An Italian restaurant in the heart of town. X: Sun., Aug. $$
>
> **Café Punchinello** (35 Forman St., just west of Victoria Centre) Light home-cooked foods. $

The Trip to Jerusalem in Brewhouse Yard

Chand (26 Mansfield Rd., at the north end of Victoria Centre)
  Good Indian cuisine. $
Castle (202 Lower Parliament St., near Victoria Centre) A town
  pub with meals. $
Le Têtard (10 Pilcher Gate, in the Lace Market just north of High
  Pavement) Classic French cuisine with good wines. X: Sun. $$

TOURIST INFORMATION:
  The local tourist office, phone (0602) 47–06–61, is at 18 Milton Street
in the Victoria Shopping Centre. There is a seasonal branch in the
castle gatehouse, near the Robin Hood statue.

SUGGESTED TOUR:
  Leaving the **train station** (1), turn right on Carrington Street and
left on Canal Street. The **Canal Museum** (2) is housed in an old ware-
house with its own wharf, sheds, and crane. Exhibitions here cover
the fascinating history of local canals and their economic importance
in the past. There are several narrowboats on display, including one
floating in a section of the canal that runs inside the museum. Be sure
to go outside on the dock. The museum is open between Easter and
October, Wednesdays through Saturdays, from 10 a.m. to noon and

from 1–5:45 p.m.; and on Sundays from 1–5:45 p.m. During the rest of the year it is open similar hours, but closed on Fridays. Admission is free.

From here follow the map to **Brewhouse Yard** (3), a group of 17th-century houses huddled against a cliff under the castle's ancient walls. Man-made caves lead from inside these to rooms carved from solid rock. The first building is the famous **Ye Olde Trip to Jerusalem**, which claims to be the oldest inn in England and one frequented by crusaders on their way to the Holy Land. It bears the date 1189, though this must refer to the underground portions only. In any case it is a wonderful place to stop for a drink. The other houses now form an intriguing **museum of domestic life** in old Nottingham, one that should definitely not be missed. It is open daily from 10 a.m. to noon and from 1–5 p.m., and admission is free.

Continue up Castle Road. Just beyond the statue of Robin Hood is the entrance to **Nottingham Castle** (4). The original Norman fortress was torn down in 1651 following the Civil War and replaced by a ducal palace, which became the city's major museum in 1878. It has an outstanding collection of fine and applied arts, antiquities, Nottingham's famous alabaster sculptures, and various displays of historic and archaeological interest. Tours through the subterranean passages, including the curious **Mortimer's Hole**, are conducted at regular intervals. Visits may be made daily from 10 a.m. to 5:45 p.m (until 4:45 p.m. in winter), and admission is free except on Sundays and bank holidays.

Stroll over to Castle Gate and visit the **Museum of Costumes and Textiles** (5), which presents superb examples of the products for which Nottingham has long been noted. It is open daily from 10 a.m. to 5 p.m., admission free. From here walk across busy Maid Marian Way and turn left on Spaniel Row. The Salutation Inn at Hounds Gate is another famous medieval pub.

Now follow the map to **Old Market Square** (6), an elegant open area next to the imposing Council House. An ancient passageway called Hurts Yard leads to Upper Parliament Street. Turn right and stroll over to the **Victoria Shopping Centre** (7). The tourist office is located on the Milton Street side of this huge modern complex. Wander inside for a good look at today's Britain and then follow the route to the 11th-century **St. Peter's Church** (8). Although modified in later years, its interior is still fascinating.

Low Pavement is reached via Church Walk. From here an interesting side trip could be made to the Lace Market district, just north of High Pavement, about two blocks off the map. The **Broad Marsh Centre** (9), another recent addition to the city's great shopping facilities, completes the tour.

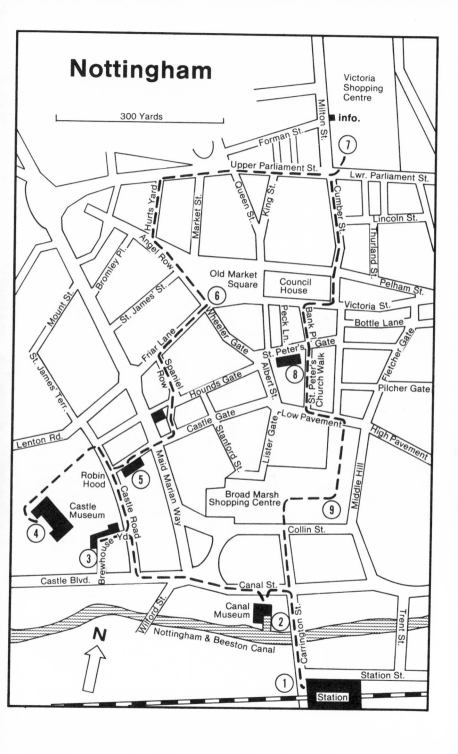

Stamford

One of the most beautiful towns in England, Stamford has changed little since its period of prosperity during Georgian times. Its narrow streets are lined with mellowed stone houses, and its many church spires look down on the peaceful River Welland. This is a delightful place to explore on foot, a tranquil town whose roots are planted firmly in the past. Nearby Burghley House is considered to be Britain's finest stately home of the Elizabethan era and is worth the trip in itself. Also of paramount interest is the Stamford Brewery Museum, an old-fashioned Victorian brew house where the ancient art of beermaking is on display.

GETTING THERE:

Trains depart London's King's Cross Station several times in the morning for Peterborough, where there is a connecting local to Stamford. The total journey takes about 1½ hours, with return trains until late evening. Service is not good on Sundays or holidays.

By car, Stamford is 91 miles north of London via the A-1 highway.

WHERE TO GO:

Burghley House is open daily from Easter through September, while the Brewery Museum operates from April through September, Wednesdays through Sundays. On bank holiday weeks it is open on Mondays instead of Wednesdays.

FOOD AND DRINK:

Stamford has a good selection of restaurants and pubs, of which some choices are:

Inside the Stamford Brewery Museum

The George of Stamford (71 St. Martin's High St., near the Town Bridge) An historic 17th-century inn with a noted restaurant. $$

Lady Anne's Hotel (37 St. Martin's High St., near St. Martin's Church) Good food in a pleasant old country hotel. $$

The Courtyard (18a Maiden Lane, near St. George's Church) A popular place in the town center. X: Sun. eve., Mon. $$

Green Man (29 Scotgate, near the Brewery Museum) Lunch in a cozy pub. X for food: Sun. $

TOURIST INFORMATION:

The local tourist office, phone (0780) 55–611, is in the Stamford Museum on Broad Street.

SUGGESTED TOUR:

Leave the **train station** (1) and follow the map across the Town Bridge to the Town Hall. Just beyond this is **St. Mary's Church** (2), built in the 13th century with an enormous spire added a century later. Inside, there is a wonderful chapel near the choir with a beautifully painted ceiling.

Turn right on St. Mary's Street and pass the Old Theatre, opened in 1768. Around the corner is St. George's Square with its elegant Assembly Room of 1727. Both this and the theater have been restored as an arts complex. **St. George's Church** (3) has some interesting medieval stained glass dating to a reconstruction of 1449.

Maiden Lane leads to High Street. The Public Library, a classical structure of 1804, was originally a meat market. Bear right and follow St. Paul's Street to the Stamford School, founded in 1532 with an earlier 12th-century chapel. Opposite this, incorporated in the school wall, is the ancient **gateway** (4) of Brasenose College, built for students who had fled Oxford in the 1330s, but demolished some 300 years later.

Retrace your steps and make a right up Star Lane. Broad Street has been a market since the earliest times. **Stamford Museum** (5) features a small but rather interesting collection of local history and archaeology, and also houses the tourist office.

A little farther on is **Browne's Hospital** (6), one of England's most outstanding medieval almshouses. Founded in the 15th century, it has an attractive chapel and cloisters, which may be visited. From here continue on to Red Lion Square. All Saints' Church dominates the scene with its towering spire; inside there are some fine old brasses. A stroll up Barn Hill will reward you with some particularly nice Queen Anne and Georgian houses. King Charles I spent one of his last nights as a free man at Stukeley House, number 9, in 1646, before being betrayed.

The **Stamford Brewery Museum** (7) on All Saints' Street is a delightful step into the Victorian age. An old-fashioned country brew house that ceased operations in 1974, it is now a re-creation of the wonderful days when brewing beer was an art. Drafts of real ale from the wood are available during pub hours. The museum is open between April and September, Wednesdays through Sundays, from 10 a.m. to 4 p.m. On bank holiday weeks it is open on Mondays instead of Wednesdays.

Follow the map down winding passageways to the ancient **King's Mill** (8) on the River Welland. Mentioned in the Domesday Book of 1086, it is now a home for retarded children. A path leads through a charming park to Station Road.

From here you can walk to **Burghley House** (9), about a mile away. Built in the 16th century, this is probably the finest Elizabethan mansion in all England. It is located in an enormous park designed in the 18th century by the famous landscape architect "Capability" Brown. The superb art collection must be the envy of many a major museum. Be sure to allow more than an hour to take it in before returning to the train station. Burghley House is open from Easter through September, Mondays through Saturdays, from 11 a.m. to 5 p.m.; and on Sundays from 2–5 p.m.

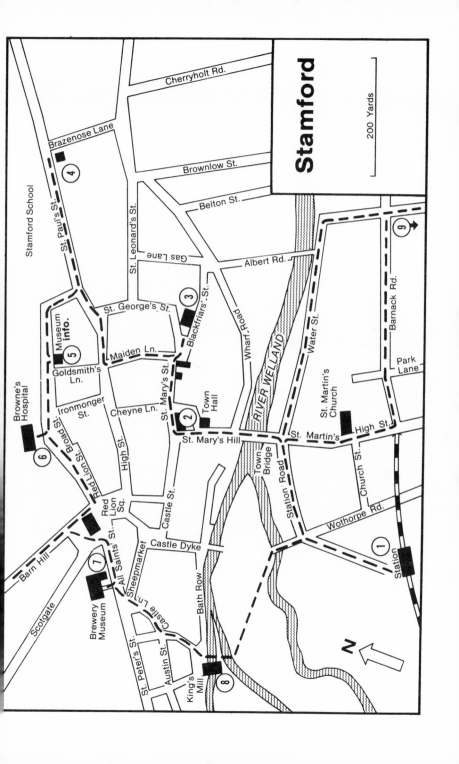

Stamford

200 Yards

Lincoln

There are really two Lincolns, one a hundred feet above the other. What is probably the finest cathedral in England dominates the countryside from its lofty perch in the upper town. It was here, on the site of a Celtic settlement, that the Romans built their fortress of *Lindum Colonia* in A.D. 47, one of the greatest colonies in Britain. As this grew, it descended the hill to the River Witham, and was taken over first by the Saxons and later by the Danes. William the Conqueror also knew a good location when he saw one. Parts of his castle, erected atop the hill in 1068, still stand among the later additions.

Lincoln is particularly rich in structures from Roman and early medieval times. Its wealth was based on the wool trade, which declined in the 14th century as business moved to larger ports on the seacoast. The plague of 1349 decimated its population and by the 18th century Lincoln was almost a ghost town. Revival started with the coming of the railways a hundred years later. Today it is the lower town that grows and prospers as a regional shopping center with engineering and high-tech industries, while the beautifully preserved ancient quarter on the hill attracts visitors by the thousands.

GETTING THERE:

Trains leave King's Cross Station in London several times in the morning for Newark North Gate, where they connect with locals for Lincoln. The total journey takes about two hours, with return trains until mid-evening. Service is poor on Sundays and holidays.

By car, Lincoln is 133 miles north of London. Take the A-1 highway to Newark and then change to the A-46.

WHEN TO GO:

Lincoln may be visited just about any time, as most of the sights are open daily. Train service is poor on Sundays and holidays.

FOOD AND DRINK:

There are a great many restaurants and pubs in all price ranges along most of the walking route. Some particularly fine choices, in tour sequence, are:

The Jew's House

Whites (15 The Strait) Imaginative food in the historic 12th-century Jew's House. X: Sun., Mon. lunch $$$

Wig and Mitre (29 Steep Hill, below the cathedral) A traditional pub with tasty food served all day long. $

Spinning Wheel (39 Steep Hill, below the cathedral) Light meals and pastries. $

Harveys (1 Exchequer Gate, by the cathedral) Excellent lunches and fancier evening meals. X: Sun. lunch $$ and $$$

White Hart (Bailgate, near the cathedral) A 15th-century inn with light lunches and elegant dinners. $$ and $$$

Blandings (339 High St., near Central Station) A combination pub and restaurant known for good food. $ and $$

TOURIST INFORMATION:

The local tourist office, phone (0522) 29–828, is at 9 Castle Hill, near the cathedral. There is a branch just off High Street, north of Central Station.

SUGGESTED TOUR:

Begin at **Central Station** (1) and turn right on High Street. At this point you will have to decide whether or not to make the climb on foot. The section between The Strait and the cathedral is very steep and closed to traffic, but includes some of the most picturesque sights in town. An alternative is to take a bus or taxi to the cathedral and re-route the walk accordingly.

Those walking should continue on High Street to the **High Bridge** (2), originally built by the Normans in the 12th century. This is one of the few bridges in England still to carry a house, in this case a 16th-century half-timbered structure. Beyond this is the **Stonebow** (3), a 15th-century town gate on the site of an earlier Roman gateway. The Guildhall, sometimes open to visitors, is built above the arch. Pass under it and continue on High Street to The Strait, the heart of medieval Lincoln, where the real climb begins. The famous early-12th-century **Jew's House** (4), now a restaurant, is among the oldest domestic buildings in England.

Steep Hill, an apt name, leads past several other ancient houses to Castle Hill. The tourist office is on the corner. Turn right and pass through the 14th-century Exchequer Gate to the **Cathedral** (5), considered by many to be the finest in England. Its fabric contains a mixture of every architectural style from early Norman to Victorian Gothic, but it is basically a product of the 12th and 13th centuries. The splendid west front, facing you, incorporates parts of an earlier cathedral completed in 1092.

Enter the nave and stroll up to the south transept, which has a lovely rose window known as the **Bishop's Eye**. Opposite this is the **Dean's Eye** in the north transept, a similar window of 13th-century stained glass. The **choir** was begun in 1192 and is noted for its elaborately carved stalls, whose misericords are among the best in the country. Behind the high altar is the renowned **Angel Choir**, a supreme achievement in beauty. The famous carving of the Lincoln Imp can be seen atop the northeast column. At the rear of the cathedral is the great east window, the best of its period.

Walk out into the **Cloisters** and visit the **Library**, designed by Sir Christopher Wren in 1674. A vault here contains one of the four existing copies of the **Magna Carta**, which can be examined. Next to this is the graceful 13th-century **Chapter House** where some of the first meetings of Parliament took place. Leave the cathedral and stroll around its close, known as Minster Yard, for a good look at some interesting medieval structures.

Return to Castle Hill and enter the **Castle** (6), begun in 1068 by William the Conqueror himself. Little remains of the original structure besides portions of the wall, but there is still enough here to make a visit worthwhile. The castle was greatly modified over the centuries, used as a prison from 1787 to 1878, and currently houses courts and archives. Be sure to see the 13th-century **Cobb Hall** in the northeast corner, an eerie place of confinement and public execution until 1868. The **Observatory Tower** in the southeast corner can be climbed for

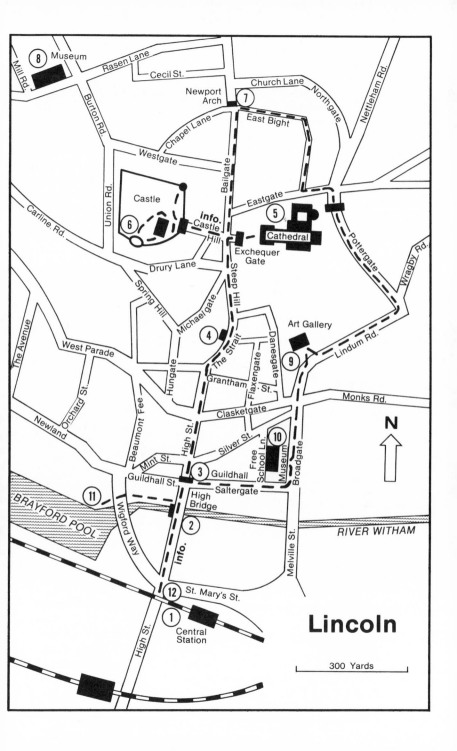

Lincoln

300 Yards

an excellent view. The keep, or **Lucy Tower**, is probably of 12th-century origin and contains the graves of some criminals hanged in the 19th century. In the Old Gaol you can see a very strange **chapel** with coffinlike pews. The castle is open between April and October, Mondays through Saturdays, from 10 a.m. to 6 p.m.; and on Sundays from 11 a.m. to 6 p.m. During the rest of the year it closes at 4 p.m. and is closed all day on Sundays.

Leaving this powerfully evocative spot, turn left on Bailgate and follow it to **Newport Arch** (7). Dating from the 2nd century A.D., this is the only remaining Roman gateway in Britain that still spans a road. From here you can make a side trip to the nearby **Museum of Lincolnshire Life** (8) by following the map. Displaying social, domestic, agricultural, and commercial life in the country over the past centuries, the museum is open Mondays through Saturdays, from 10 a.m. to 5:30 p.m.; and on Sundays from 2–5:30 p.m.

Return to the town via East Bight. Along the way you will pass remains of the Roman wall, then emerge at Eastgate. Pottergate and Lindum Road lead to the **Usher Gallery** (9), a splendid collection of art, ancient relics, antique timepieces, porcelains, and other beautiful objects. The opening times are the same as those of the Lincolnshire Life museum above.

Just beyond, on Broadgate, is the **City and County Museum** (10), housing local archaeological finds, historical items, and armor in the former 13th-century Grey Friars Priory. Again, the times are the same as those of the Lincolnshire Life museum above.

Follow the map back to High Bridge. A path to the right of its half-timbered house leads to **Brayford Pool** (11), the city's port on the River Witham since Roman times. It is still used as a marina. You may want to stop in at the nearby **National Cycle Museum**, an exhibition of bicycles and related objects from 1820 to the present. Between Easter and October it is open daily from 10 a.m. to 5 p.m.; the rest of the year on Fridays through Sundays only.

Return to High Street and turn right. The ancient **Church of St. Mary-le-Wigford** (12) has a Saxon tower with a curious Roman tombstone used as a dedication stone. From here it is only steps to the train station.

York

Layer upon layer, the passing centuries since the time of the Romans have all left their mark on York, that delightful city in the north of England that has preserved more of its heritage than just about any other European town. Its narrow medieval streets still wind their way among more ancient ruins, while all around are reminders of other eras—Elizabethan, Jacobean, Georgian, and Victorian. Amid this throbs the heart of a modern city, and an attractive one at that. Although situated about 200 miles north of London, transportation to York is so good that a daytrip there is entirely practical. It also makes a wonderful overnight stop for those going to or from Scotland.

The ancient Britons called it *Caer Ebrauc*, but York was really established in A.D. 71 by the Romans. Their fortress, known as *Eboracum*, became the headquarters of the Sixth Legion. The emperor Hadrian visited in A.D. 121, and Constantine the Great was proclaimed Emperor of Rome there in 306. After the fall of the empire and a dark era of destruction, York reemerged as the Saxon town of *Eoforwic*, playing a prominent part in the spread of Christianity and learning. In 867 it fell to the Vikings and acquired the name *Jorvik*, which lasted until 944 when it became part of the Anglo-Saxon kingdom of England.

Following the Norman Conquest of 1066, the north rebelled, and William the Conqueror marched to York to put down the revolt, scorching the earth all about him. The stone walls and gates were erected in the 13th century when the city prospered as a commercial and religious center. After Henry VIII put an end to the Church's power in the 16th century, York entered an age of decline. The Industrial Revolution had little effect on it before the 1830s, when the coming of the railways brought the city back to life. As a major communications center, York has prospered greatly ever since. Its chief attraction for visitors, however, is its past, those ancient stones weathered by the passing centuries that make up the whole of England's history.

There is much more to York than can possibly be seen in one day, so you will have to choose your attractions carefully. Better still, stay for a while and really enjoy the city.

GETTING THERE:

Trains depart King's Cross Station in London at least hourly for the 2¼-hour ride to York aboard an InterCity 125 express. Return trains operate until mid-evening; service is poor on Sundays and holidays. BritRail Pass holders will really get their money's worth on this trip.

By car, York is about 200 miles north of London. Take the M-1 to the vicinity of Sheffield, then the M-18 to Doncaster. From there follow the A-1 (M) and the A-64 into York. This is better done as part of a trip to Scotland.

WHEN TO GO:

Most of the attractions in York are open daily throughout the year, but some close or have shorter hours on Sundays and/or holidays.

FOOD AND DRINK:

Those traveling by train may want to take advantage of British Rail's famous breakfasts in the dining car, which really eliminate the need to have lunch. In the city, you will find a great many restaurants and pubs. Some outstanding choices, in walking tour sequence, are:

Thomas' Wine Bar (3 Museum St., near the Museum Gardens) Both a wine bar and a bistro. $ and $$

Ye Olde Starre Inn (40 Stonegate, 2 blocks southwest of the cathedral) Traditional pub food in a Victorian atmosphere, with an outdoor beer garden. $

Betty's (6 St. Helens Sq., 3 blocks southwest of the cathedral) A tea room with good meals. $

St. William's Restaurant (College St., by St. William's College) Light lunches in a medieval courtyard. $

Bari (15 The Shambles) Pizza and other Italian dishes. $

Lew's Place (King's Staith, by the River Ouse) Home-style cooking. X: Sun. $$

Tony's (39 Tanner Row, near Micklegate and the station) Greek and English food. X: Sat. lunch, Sun. $$

York Wholefood (98 Micklegate) Natural vegetarian dishes. X: Sun. $

TOURIST INFORMATION:

The main tourist office, phone (0904) 21–756, is in DeGrey House on Exhibition Square near Bootham Bar. There is also a handy branch in the train station, phone (0904) 643–700. Either can help you get accommodations should you decide to stay overnight.

SUGGESTED TOUR:

Leaving the **train station** (1), follow the map to the nearby **National**

In the National Railway Museum

Railway Museum (2). Located in a refurbished engine shed, this is the largest of its kind in Britain and one of the best in the world. Anyone who loves old trains will be absolutely mesmerized by the range of displays. The museum is open Mondays through Saturdays, from 10 a.m. to 6 p.m.; and on Sundays from 2:30–6 p.m. It is closed on major holidays. Don't miss it.

Return via Leeman Road and, passing through the city walls, turn left on Station Road. Cross the River Ouse on Lendal Bridge, then make a left into Museum Gardens, which you may want to visit. On your right is the **Multangular Tower** (3), a corner of the original Roman walls. Its lower 19 feet date from about A.D. 300, while the upper parts are medieval. A path to the left leads to the **Hospitum** (4), a 16th-century guest house of St. Mary's Abbey. Extensive archaeological collections are displayed on its two floors. Continuing along the path, you will soon come to the ruins of the **Abbey** (5) itself, once the most important Benedictine monastery in the north of England. Next to this is the **Yorkshire Museum** (6), featuring splendid galleries of Anglo-Saxon and Viking life along with other ancient diggings. It is open Mondays through Saturdays, from 10 a.m. to 5 p.m.; and on Sundays from 1–5 p.m.

Leave the gardens by the same gate and turn left on Museum Street. Another left at St. Leonard's takes you past the tourist office and the **City Art Gallery** on Exhibition Square. Facing this is **Bootham Bar** (7), a defensive bastion dating from early Norman times. Cross the inter-

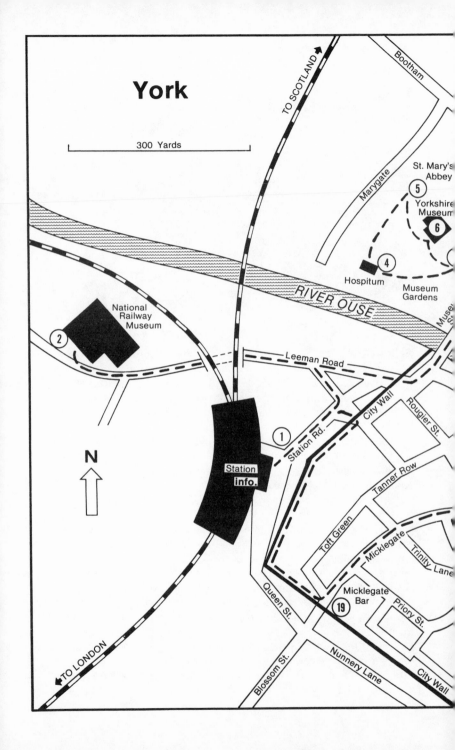

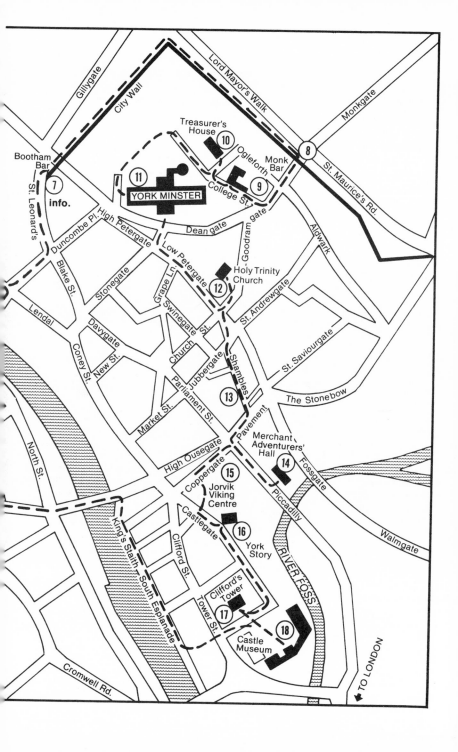

section and climb the steps to the top of the **City Walls**. From here the walk reveals wonderful glimpses of the Minster (11) and its gardens. Descend at the next gate, medieval **Monk Bar** (8), and stroll down busy Goodramgate. The ending -*gate*, incidentally, is an old Viking word for street.

A right on College Street takes you past **St. William's College** (9), built in 1453 as a lodging for the Minster's chantry priests. It now serves as a general meeting place. Step through the doorway and enter the picturesque quadrangle, then continue on to the **Treasurer's House** (10). This 17th-century mansion, once the home of the Minster's treasurer, is well worth a visit for its gorgeous interior. It is open daily April through October, from 10:30 a.m. to 5 p.m.

A pathway through Dean's Park leads to the front entrance of **York Minster** (11), the Cathedral Church of St. Peter. Both a cathedral and a minster, this is the largest Gothic church in Britain. It stands on the site of the Roman military headquarters and of several earlier churches. The present structure was begun in 1220, requiring some 250 years to build. As you stroll around its spacious interior, be sure to see the **Chapter House** just off the north transept, a wonder of medieval architecture whose conical roof spans a great distance without central support. Also in the north transept is the famous **Five Sisters Window**—five giant lancets of 13th-century grisaille glass—and an astronomical clock of recent date. Beyond the choir are several interesting chapels and the monumental **Great East Window** that celebrates the beginning and end of time in over 2,000 square feet of medieval stained glass.

While in the cathedral, you may want to climb the central tower for a bird's-eye view of the city. Another fascinating sight is the **Undercroft**, a spin-off of restoration work on the cathedral's foundations. Enter it by way of a staircase in the south transept. Here you can walk among the remains of the earlier churches and the Roman headquarters as well as see many of the Minster's treasures.

Leaving the Minster through the south doorway, make a left on Low Petergate, the *Via Principalis* of Roman York. At Goodramgate, turn left for a few yards and visit **Holy Trinity Church** (12), a small and extremely picturesque 14th-century church, now seldom used. Its box pews and Jacobean altar are quite interesting. Then cross King's Square and enter the **Shambles** (13), one of the best-preserved medieval streets in Europe. Once the street of butchers, its overhanging, timbered buildings now house antique shops, booksellers, and similar enterprises.

At the end turn right onto Pavement, then make a left on Piccadilly, which leads to the **Merchant Adventurers' Hall** (14), built in the 14th century by the city's wealthiest trade guild. Visit the Great Hall and

In the Shambles

the Undercroft, where guild pensioners lived in cubicles as late as the 19th century.

Return on Piccadilly, turning left onto Coppergate, and visit the **Jorvik Viking Centre** (15). Excavations here in recent years have unearthed the original Viking city of Jorvik, dating from the 10th century. Many of its buildings, now located beneath a modern shopping center, have been faithfully re-created. Together with Viking figures, sound effects, and even smells, these offer an opportunity to experience a glimpse of life in an age long past, although some may find the method of presentation a bit too theatrical. Between April and October it is open daily from 9 a.m. to 7 p.m.; closing at 5:30 p.m. the rest of the year.

From here stroll down to the **York Story** (16), an exhibition of the city's heritage housed in the former St. Mary's Church. Two thousand years of history are made clear by the clever use of models and audiovisual presentations. The York Story is open Mondays through Saturdays, from 10 a.m. to 5 p.m.; and on Sundays from 1–5 p.m.

Continue on to **Clifford's Tower** (17), a defensive fortification built in the 13th century to replace an earlier one erected by William the Conqueror. In 1684 an explosion blew the roof off, and it remains in that condition today. You can climb to the top for a nice view.

Just across the square is the **Castle Museum** (18), among the most extraordinary folk museums in the world and a must for every visitor

In the Jorvik Viking Centre
(Photo courtesy of the Viking Centre)

to York. Allow plenty of time to see it, even at the expense of skipping other sights. Housed in two former prisons, the musuem displays a nearly endless succession of rooms, buildings, and even entire streets of bygone eras, each stuffed to overflowing with just about every item imaginable. A working outdoor watermill on the River Foss is part of it, as is the untouched condemned cell of the old prison. The route through the museum is very well laid out—just follow it and you won't miss a thing. It is open daily until 6:30 p.m., closing at 5 p.m. in the winter. Last admission is one hour before closing time. Don't miss this special treat.

Beyond this, stroll over to the River Ouse and follow its banks to the Ouse Bridge, which you cross. Micklegate leads to **Micklegate Bar** (19), a Norman archway from which the heads of traitors were once displayed. A walk from here along the top of the city walls will return you to the train station.

Cambridge

Cambridge, one of the most beautiful towns in Europe, has long been a favorite daytrip destination. For nearly 700 years its colleges have vied with one another for architectural as well as academic excellence. Taking full advantage of its delightful riverside location, it has developed an ambiance that sets it apart from any other college town in England. Inevitably a comparison with Oxford must be made, but they are actually two very different places. Cambridge is serene, dreamy in character; while its older and larger rival is more intense, more worldly. Given the chance, you should really see both.

The site of Cambridge was important in ancient times, being the only practical place to cross the River Cam for miles around. In the century preceding the Roman conquest, a Celtic settlement was established just north of the river. This was taken over by the Romans and enlarged, spreading south after their departure. When the Normans came, they built a castle, long vanished, on the site of the Roman camp. By the time of the Domesday Book, 1086, the town had some 400 houses and was already a trading center. From Cambridge northwards the River Cam, then called the Granta, was navigable all the way to the North Sea, a factor of vital importance in a time of poor land communications.

Scholars began to gather here about 1209 after being run out of Oxford by angry townspeople. Some of them stayed on and by 1284 the first proper college, Peterhouse, was founded. This was quickly followed by others; a university evolved, and the town flourished. New colleges are still being added, with a present total of 35 not including those independent of the university.

It is impossible to see all of Cambridge in a single day. The suggested tour was designed to include only the most notable highlights of the colleges, some of the town, a few museums, gardens, and the famous Backs along the river. Please remember that all of the colleges are private, and that admission to them is a courtesy, not a right.

GETTING THERE:
Trains leave London's Liverpool Street Station hourly for the one-hour ride to Cambridge. There are also locals taking 1½ hours. Return trains run until mid-evening, and service is somewhat reduced on Sundays and holidays.

Coaches depart London's Victoria Coach Station for the two-hour ride to Cambridge about once an hour.

By car, Cambridge is 55 miles north of London via the M-11.

WHEN TO GO:

Cambridge may be visited in any season, although most of the colleges are closed to the public while student exams take place between May and mid-June. The museums are closed on Mondays.

FOOD AND DRINK:

You can find just about any sort of food in Cambridge, from pubs to fancy restaurants. Some good choices are:

Jean Louis (15 Magdalene St., near the bridge) A pleasant French restaurant with luncheon specials. X: Mon. $$ and $$$

Shades (1 King's Parade, by King's College) Both a wine bar and a restaurant. Bar X: Sun; Restaurant X: Sun., Mon. $$ and $$$

Charlie Chan (14 Regent St., near Emmanuel College) A modern Chinese restaurant with good cooking. $$

Angeline (8 Market Passage, near Market Square) An upstairs restaurant with a French flair; good-value set lunches. X: Sun. $ and $$

Varsity (35 St. Andrew's St., near Emmanuel College) Greek cuisine with English influence. $

Nettles (5 St. Edward's Passage, near King's College) A small vegetarian health-food place. X: Sun. $

Eagle (Bene't St., near King's College) An historic 17th-century pub with good meals. $

Anchor Pub (Silver St., by the Mill Pond) Downstairs pub and upstairs restaurant. $ and $$

Fitzwilliam Museum Café (in the museum) An unusually good museum cafeteria. X: Sun., Mon. $

TOURIST INFORMATION:

The local tourist office, phone (0223) 32-26-40, is on Wheeler Street just south of the Market Square.

SUGGESTED TOUR:

Leaving the **train station** (1), you can either walk or take a bus or taxi to **Market Square** (2), a distance of about a mile. If you walk, just follow the map up Regent and St. Andrew's streets, then make a left on Petty Curry to the square. An outdoor market is held here from Mondays through Saturdays. The tourist office is nearby on Wheeler Street.

Great St. Mary's Church, next to the square, is the University

King's College Chapel

Church. Enter it and climb to the top of the tower for an excellent view of the entire town.

Make a left onto King's Parade and enter the Great Court of **King's College** (3). Founded by Henry VI in 1441, the school originally occupied a site directly to the north. Henry's ambitions grew, however, and what was then the center of medieval Cambridge was ruthlessly torn down to make way for a monumental college. At that point the War of the Roses intervened and Henry was deposed, leaving only part of the chapel finished and the rest an open field. It was another 280 years before any new buildings were erected. In the meantime, the chapel was completed during the reign of Henry VIII. This is, quite simply, the finest building in Cambridge and possibly the greatest Gothic structure in England.

Enter the **Chapel** and look up at the miraculous fan vaulting on the ceiling, then at the dark wooden choir screen, and finally at the sheer expanse of glass. The total effect is breathtaking. Stroll through the choir and examine the *Adoration of the Magi* by Rubens that hangs behind the altar. An experience never to be forgotten is to return in the late afternoon for Evensong, a service held daily during terms, except on Mondays.

Leaving the chapel, walk straight ahead past the Fellows' Building of 1724 and turn right into the **Backs**, those idyllic gardens and mead-

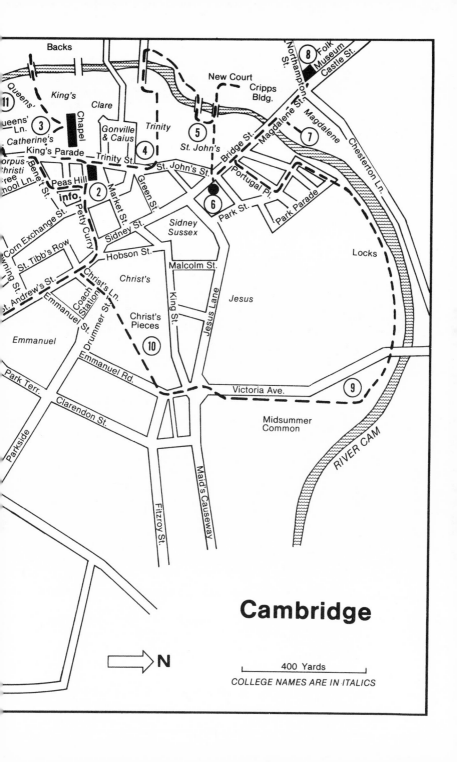

The Market Square and Great St. Mary's Church

ows along the River Cam that give Cambridge its special character. Cross the bridge for your first sight of this, then return to King's Parade and turn left. Passing the Senate House and Gonville & Caius College, continue up Trinity Street to Trinity College.

With over 800 students, **Trinity** (4) is the largest college in Cambridge. It was founded by Henry VIII in 1546 and has long had connections with royalty. The Great Gate leads into the **Great Court**, so vast that the lack of symmetry along its sides is hardly noticeable. An extremely different ambiance permeates the cloistered Nevil's Court, reached by passing through the hall at the west end. The magnificent **Library**, built by Sir Christopher Wren in 1676, completes the west façade of the cloister. This may be visited from noon until 2 p.m., Mondays through Fridays, and is well worth returning for. Continue through a third court, turn right to the Backs, and cross a footbridge over the Cam.

Follow the map and cross another bridge into **St. John's College** (5). To your left is the famous Bridge of Sighs that connects two halves of the college. Continue to the first courtyard and cross the bridge into New Court, a Victorian Gothic structure of 1831. Beyond this lies the contemporary Cripps Building, which makes good use of the river. Return over the Bridge of Sighs and stroll through two more courts to

Punting on the Cam

the main entrance at the junction of Bridge Street and St. John's Street.

The fascinating **Round Church** (6) of 1130 was inspired by the Holy Sepulchre in Jerusalem. It is one of the very few medieval circular churches surviving in England. Restored during the 19th century, it still conveys the character of early Norman architecture.

Now follow Bridge Street across the Cam and turn right into **Magdalene College** (7). Pronounced *Maudlen,* it was founded in 1542, using the buildings of a former Benedictine monks' hostel. Samuel Pepys was a student here from 1650 to 1653 and left behind his collection of books, including an original manuscript of his immortal diary. These can be seen, kept in Pepys' unique bookshelves, in the library facing the second court on weekdays from 11:30 a.m. to 12:30 p.m. and from 2:30–3:30 p.m., with shorter hours off-season.

Magdalene Street is lined with restored 16th- and 17th-century houses. Turn right and follow it to the **Folk Museum** (8), which features re-created room settings of bygone years as well as other memorabilia relating to Cambridge's past. It is open Tuesdays through Saturdays, from 10:30 a.m. to 5 p.m.; and on Sundays from 2:30–4:30 p.m. While there, you may want to stop in at the famous **Kettle's Yard**, an important collection of modern art in a nearby house on Northampton Street.

At this point you can skip ahead to Queens' College (11) by following the map, or continue on for a lovely walk along the river and through a park. To do this, turn left into Portugal Place, make another left at New Park Street, and a right on Thompson's Lane.

Stroll along the picturesque footpath by the river's edge. Once beyond Victoria Avenue turn right through **Midsummer Common** (9). Crossing the Four Lamps intersection, walk down Short Street and into a pleasant park called **Christ's Pieces** (10). Arriving at Drummer Street, continue on Christ's Lane, then turn right to Petty Curry and return to Market Square (2). A left here leads down Peas Hill to Bene't Street. Make a right and then a left onto Trumpington Street. In another block turn right and pass through St. Catherine's College.

Across Queens' Lane is the imposing entrance to **Queens' College** (11), often regarded as the most charming in Cambridge. Little changed over the centuries, Queens' appears today much as it did in the 15th century when it was founded by two separate queens. Enter the medieval Old Court, built in 1449, and pass through the Cloister Court of 1495. From here cross the so-called Mathematical Bridge, a curious wooden span over the Cam, first erected in 1749. The present bridge is a faithful copy from this century. Turn right and stroll down along the river to the Grove, a garden with lovely views. Returning to the Cloister Court, walk through the Walnut Tree Court and the Old Court, then exit onto Queens' Lane. If you have had enough walking by now you can go direct to the Fitzwilliam Museum (13) or return to Market Square (2) and take a bus or taxi to the station.

If you choose to carry on, make a right on Silver Street and a left at Laundress Lane. This leads to the **Mill Pond** (12), where boats may be rented. Walk along the path, crossing a footbridge to the left, and turn right to the Fen Causeway. Follow this to Trumpington Street. To the left is the **Fitzwilliam Museum** (13), one of the most important art museums in England. Its collection ranges from ancient Egyptian to Impressionist art and includes, besides paintings, drawings, and sculpture, a vast assortment of armor, silver, porcelains, and manuscripts. You can easily spend the better part of a day here, but a quick tour can be done in an hour or so. The museum is open Tuesdays through Saturdays, from 10 a.m. to 5 p.m.; and on Sundays from 2:15–5 p.m. Not all of the galleries are open at the same time.

Now follow Trumpington Street to Bateman Street and turn left. To your right is the entrance of the **University Botanic Gardens** (14), a delightfully varied area devoted to research but open to the public Mondays through Saturdays, from 8 a.m. to 6:30 p.m. or dusk, whichever is earlier; and on summer Sundays from 2:30–6:30 p.m. Stroll through it and exit onto Hills Road. A left here followed by a right on Station Road will return you to the train station.

Ely

The origins of Ely are shrouded in Anglo-Saxon folklore; fascinating to read but far too complex to go into here. At one time this was virtually an island, surrounded by the marshy Fens that for centuries had defied all attempts at drainage. Great quantities of eels lived in these swampy waters, accounting for the old name of *Elig*, or eel island, later corrupted to Ely.

In A.D. 673 an abbey for both monks and nuns was founded here by St. Etheldreda, which eventually led to the construction of Ely Cathedral. The town was sacked by the Danes in 870, and a hundred years later the King's School was established. Hereward the Wake, the "last of the English," defended the island against William the Conqueror until 1071, when the Anglo-Saxons finally succumbed to Norman supremacy. Ely remained an isolated place until the Fens were drained during the 17th century. Since then it has become a prosperous market town whose charming atmosphere, majestic cathedral, and lovely old buildings attract visitors from all over.

This trip can be combined in the same day with one to Ipswich, Bury St. Edmunds, or King's Lynn. Cambridge is temptingly close but really requires an entire day by itself.

GETTING THERE:

Trains depart London's Liverpool Street Station at about two-hour intervals for Ely, or hourly by changing at Cambridge. The journey takes about 1½ hours, with return trains operating until mid-evening. Service is greatly reduced on Sundays and holidays.

By car, Ely is 71 miles north of London. Take the M-11 to Cambridge, then change to the A-10.

WHEN TO GO:

Avoid coming on a Sunday, when much of the town is closed, the cathedral busy, and train service poor. The colorful outdoor market is held on Thursdays and most of the shops close early on Tuesdays.

FOOD AND DRINK:

Ely has a surprising number of good restaurants and pubs. A few choices are:

> **Old Fire Engine House** (25 St. Mary's St., near St. Mary's Church) English fare from mostly local ingredients, very popular. X: Sun. eve. $$

> **Peking Duck** (26 Fore Hill, near the Market Place) Noted for its fine Chinese cuisine. X: Tues. lunch, Mon. $$

> **Barton Restaurant in Lamb Hotel** (2 Lynn Rd., near the cathedral) Lunch in a cozy country hotel. $$

> **Pilgrims Parlour** (54 St. Mary's St., near St. Mary's Church) Light meals. X: Tues. $

> **Royal Standard** (24 Fore Hill, near the Market Place) A popular place for pub lunches. X: Sun. $

TOURIST INFORMATION:

The local tourist office, phone (0353) 20-62, is in the library on Palace Green, just in front of the cathedral.

SUGGESTED TOUR:

Leaving the **train station** (1), turn left on Station Road and then right on Annesdale. This leads to a delightful walk along the River Great Ouse, complete with pleasure craft and a waterside pub. From here follow the map to St. Mary's Street. Oliver Cromwell lived in the **timbered house** (2) next to the church between 1636 and 1647, two years before he became England's only dictator. The house is now the vicarage of **St. Mary's Church** (3), which dates from 1215. Step inside for a good look at an unusually attractive parish church.

Stroll across Palace Green to the splendid west front of **Ely Cathedral** (4), begun in 1083 on the site of St. Etheldreda's 7th-century abbey. The castellated west tower rises to a height of 217 feet. To the right of this is an unusual southwest transept. This was once balanced on the left by another transept that collapsed in the 15th century and was never replaced.

Enter through the magnificent **Galilee Porch** and look down the entire length of the nave, then up at the beautifully painted wooden ceiling. The **central octagon** under the crossing was a daring and ingenious solution to the problem of a heavy Norman tower that collapsed in 1322. Extending the full width of the nave, it is considered to be one of the highlights of English architecture. Beyond the screen are some nicely carved stalls. Walk over to the north transept and visit the huge and elaborately decorated 14th-century **Lady Chapel**, which served as a parish church from Elizabethan times until 1938. Don't miss the very interesting **Stained Glass Museum** with its well-lit col-

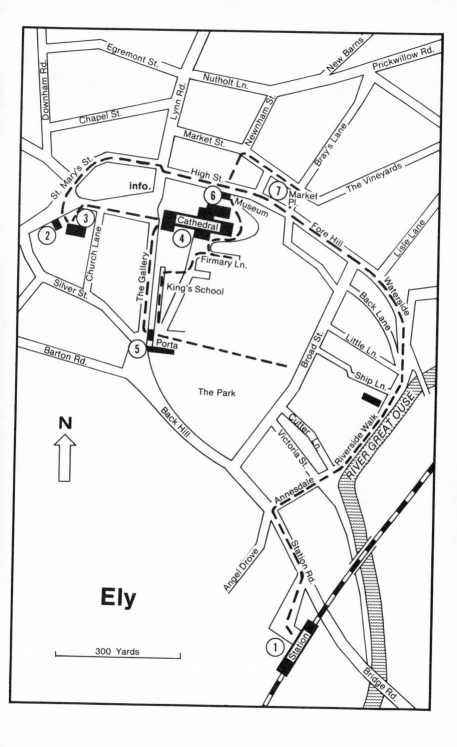

Ely

300 Yards

N

Ely Cathedral

lection of stained glass from medieval to modern times, rescued from redundant churches and secular buildings. Located in the north triforium, it is open daily from March through October. There is also a brass rubbing center.

Leave the cathedral and stroll down The Gallery to **Ely Porta** (5), built in the 14th century as an entrance to the former monastery. It is now part of the King's School, one of the oldest public schools in the country. Pass through it and examine the Monks' Granary to the right, now used as a dining hall by the school. The earthen mound just beyond this is all that remains of a 12th-century Norman castle.

From here take a walk down the pathway for some wonderfully bucolic views of the cathedral, then return and make a right past more medieval buildings used by the school. Some of these, including the chapel, may be visited at certain times. Closer to the cathedral is Firmary Lane, a delightful little street.

Walk around the rear of the cathedral and come out on High Street. **Ely Museum** (6), in the Sacrist's Gate, has a fine collection of local bygones, toys, and historical items. It is open on Saturday and Sunday afternoons, and also on Thursday afternoons from June through September. Complete your tour by meandering through some of the back streets to the **Market Place** (7), where an outdoor market is held on Thursdays.

King's Lynn

Steeped in atmosphere and haunted by its past, King's Lynn is neither quaint nor picturesque. What makes it appealing, though, is the sharply medieval aura of its narrow streets and ancient buildings. Once an outpost of the Hanseatic League, its older sections are more reminiscent of northern Germany or the Low Countries than of England. Like many great places, Lynn reveals itself slowly and with reluctance. Much of it is mundane. Yet, to stroll its quays and half-forgotten alleyways is to awaken memories of a world long vanished.

It was the River Great Ouse that brought early prosperity to Lynn. Connecting the seaport with the rich hinterlands of England, the Ouse provided a watery route for commerce to follow. And follow it did. By the end of the 12th century, Lynn was the fifth-largest port in England and the center of trade with the frozen north. Then known as Bishop's Lynn, the town had expanded rapidly during the 11th century and began its Hanseatic association in the 13th. When exports declined in the 14th century, the port turned to coastal shipping and fishing. Henry VIII knew a good thing and made the place his own in 1537, changing the name to King's Lynn. Prosperity continued through the 18th century, when the coming of the railways rendered the inland waterways and coastal shipping obsolete, making Lynn the backwater port and market town that it is today.

GETTING THERE:

Trains for King's Lynn leave at two-hour intervals from London's Liverpool Street Station. The journey takes two hours with return trains operating until early evening. You can also get there by taking an InterCity 125 train from London's King's Cross Station to Peterborough, then a connecting bus to King's Lynn—a total of 2½ hours. Service on Sundays and holidays is very poor.

By car, follow the M-11 to Cambridge and switch to the A-10. King's Lynn is 103 miles north of London.

WHEN TO GO:

This trip can be taken in any season, but avoid coming on a Sunday, when most of the sights are closed. The colorful outdoor market is held every Tuesday and Saturday.

FOOD AND DRINK:

You will find pubs and restaurants all along the walking route. Some choices are:

Duke's Head (Tuesday Market Place) Good food in an historic country hotel $$

Tudor Rose (St. Nicholas St., off Tuesday Market Place) A 15th-century inn with a restaurant. $$

Antonio's Wine Bar (Baxter's Plain, by the Lynn Museum) Italian specialties in a popular wine bar. X: Sun., Mon. $

Wenns Hotel (Saturday Market Place, near the Town Hall) Good food in a busy pub. $

TOURIST INFORMATION:

The local tourist office, phone (0553) 76-30-44, is in the Town Hall on Saturday Market Place.

SUGGESTED TOUR:

Leaving the **train station** (1), follow the map to the **Tuesday Market Place** (2), an attractive open square where a colorful outdoor market is held each Tuesday. At its far end turn right on St. Nicholas Street and stroll over to **St. Nicholas' Chapel** (3), founded in 1145 to handle the overflow from St. Margaret's Church, which by the 12th century had already become too small for the growing population. The present structure dates from 1419 and is well worth seeing.

Return to the Market Place, noticing the fine old houses on its north side, and make a left. At the far corner of Water Lane is the Corn Exchange, an exuberant Victorian building of 1854, now used for entertainment. Turn right on Ferry Street and walk out to the quay for some good views of the old harbor. There is a tiny ferry from here to West Lynn.

Fermoy Centre (4) is an arts complex fronting on King Street. It occupies the former Guildhall of St. George, the oldest and largest medieval merchants' guild building in England. Built about 1410, this is the only building still standing in England in which Shakespeare probably performed in one of his own plays. Again used as a theater, it is the center of the annual King's Lynn Festival held in late July. It may be visited Mondays through Fridays. The adjoining structures, all beautifully restored, now house an art gallery and a restaurant. Close by is the **Museum of Social History**, featuring displays of domestic life in bygone times, which is open Tuesdays through Saturdays, from 10 a.m. to 5 p.m.

King Street has hardly changed through the centuries. Wealthy merchants once lived in the homes along its west side, behind which stand ancient warehouses and private wharfs. Here and there, narrow

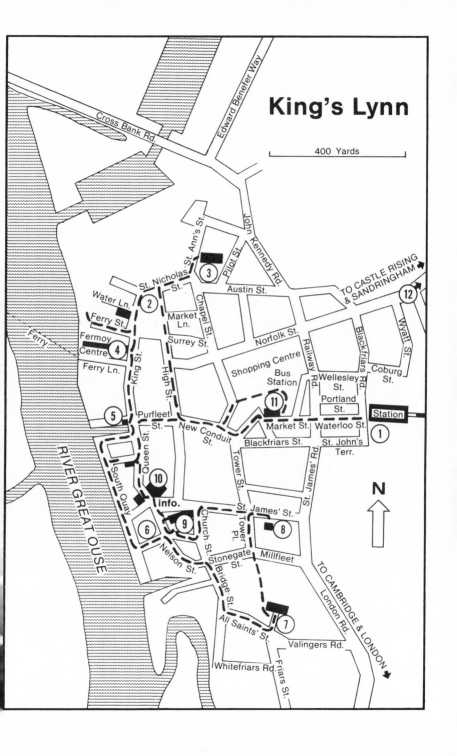

The Harbor at Low Tide

alleyways lead to the river. The same pattern of residences and adjoining warehouses repeats itself on Queen Street and other streets parallel to the Ouse. At the corner of Purfleet Street, once a *fleet*, or creek, is located the most notable structure in Lynn, the **Custom House** (5). Built in 1683 as a merchants' exchange, it was designed in the Palladian style by the town's mayor, Henry Bell, who was also an accomplished architect. The niche over its entrance contains a statue of Charles II.

Turn right into King Staithe Square. A *staithe* is a waterside depot equipped for loading boats. The Bank House on its south side has historic significance as it was from here that the explorer Samuel Cresswell successfully set out in 1850 to discover a northwest passage to India. Note the statue of Charles I above the doorway.

Passing the grain silos, turn left and follow South Quay. King Staithe Lane, to the left, is a delightful remnant of the past. Continue along the quay and make a left into St. Margaret's Lane. The **Hanseatic Warehouses** (6), now restored and used as offices, were built in 1428 by the Hansa merchants as their local depot. Opposite them is Hampton Court, a great block of merchants' homes, countinghouses, warehouses, and apprentices' quarters, begun before 1200 but considerably altered later.

Turn right on Nelson Street, which has some very attractive old

The Guildhall of the Holy Trinity

façades. Follow Bridge Street to All Saints' Street. Along the way you will pass the timber-framed Greenland Fishery of 1605. In the 18th century it became a pub frequented by whalers, hence its name. It is now used for offices. Making a left up Church Lane, stop at **All Saints' Church** (7), built in the 14th century over Norman foundations. The painted rood screen is about 600 years old. Continue through the churchyard to Tower Place and turn right down St. James' Street to the **Greyfriars Tower** (8). Dating from the 15th century, this is all that remains of the old Greyfriars monastery that was disbanded by Henry VIII.

Return to St. James' Street and turn left, then make another left on Church Street. A right on Priory Lane leads to the Priory Cottages. In the courtyard, reached through an archway, stand some magnificently preserved old homes, once part of a Benedictine priory established about 1100. Go around the corner and visit **St. Margaret's Church** (9), one of the few parish churches to have two towers. A mixture of styles ranging from Norman to Victorian, the huge church was founded about 1100 and is noted for its two great Flemish brasses, each nearly ten feet long. Don't miss the flood marks by the entrance; the latest, and highest, being dated 1978. They tell a lot about the hazards of living in Lynn.

Cross the Saturday Market Place to the 15th-century **Guildhall of the Holy Trinity**, now part of the **Town Hall** (10). Inside this is displayed an astonishing collection of regalia, including the famous so-called "King John Cup," dating from the 14th century and possibly the finest in England. Also to be seen is the "King John Sword," probably of 16th-century origin but having nothing to do with the tyrant who, however, did grant the royal charter of 1204. Among the borough archives is the Red Register of 1300, one of the oldest paper books in the world. These may be seen Mondays through Fridays, and on Saturdays between April and October. The Town Hall also houses the tourist office.

Thoresby College, opposite the Guildhall on Queen Street, was built about 1500 and is now a youth hostel. Farther along, at the corner of King Staithe Lane, you will come to the Clifton House, parts of which are from the 14th century. The crypt and Elizabethan watchtower, with views of the harbor, may be visited Mondays through Fridays.

Turn right on Purfleet Street and follow the map through a modern shopping center. From the bus station there you can get a ride to nearby Castle Rising or Sandringham. The **Lynn Museum** (11) on Market Street has good displays of local history. It is open Mondays through Saturdays, from 10 a.m. to 5 p.m. From here it is only a short walk back to the train station.

NEARBY SIGHTS:

Castle Rising (12), built in 1138, is one of the best Norman castles still standing in England. It can be reached by taking the bus marked for Hunstanton, which runs every half-hour. Ask the driver to let you off at the right place and be sure to inquire about the return schedule before leaving Lynn. The ride takes only 20 minutes. **Sandringham**, a home of the Royal Family, lies just beyond this on the same bus route. It is open to the public on certain days during the summer. Check the current schedule with the King's Lynn tourist office. Those with cars should follow the A-149 north in the direction of Hunstanton.

Bury St. Edmunds

Bury St. Edmunds has been called the nicest town in the world. An exaggeration perhaps, but this really is a delightful place to explore. The ruins of its great abbey are wonderfully picturesque and Bury itself, spared the effects of industry, is an elegant reminder of what prosperous country towns were once like.

Its history began during the late 9th century when Edmund, the last king of the East Angles, was defeated by marauding Danes, shot full of arrows, and beheaded. Later made a saint, the martyr's bones were buried at *Beodricesworth*, today's Bury St. Edmunds. An abbey was founded there in A.D. 945 and rebuilt by King Canute in 1021. For centuries this remained a place of holy pilgrimage. It was there that the English barons met in 1214 to demand that King John ratify the Magna Carta. In 1539, the great abbey was disbanded by Henry VIII and gradually fell into the romantic ruin that it is today.

This trip can be combined in the same day with one to Ely or Ipswich. Those traveling by train will have to check the schedules carefully to do this.

GETTING THERE:

Trains depart London's Liverpool Street Station several times in the morning for Cambridge, where they connect with a local for Bury St. Edmunds. The total journey takes about two hours, with return trains operating until early evening. It is also possible to go by way of Ipswich. Service is greatly reduced on Sundays and holidays.

By car, Bury is 75 miles northeast of London. Take the M-11 and A-11 to Newmarket, then the A-45 into Bury.

WHEN TO GO:

Avoid coming to Bury on a Sunday, when the museums are closed. Outdoor markets are held on Wednesdays and Saturdays, and some shops close early on Thursdays.

FOOD AND DRINK:

Bury is noted for its Greene King ales, especially their Abbot Ale. These are served, among many other places, at **The Nutshell** on The Traverse, which claims to be England's smallest pub. Some good places to eat are:

Angel Hotel (3 Angel Hill, by the Abbey Gate) A 15th-century inn with two fine restaurants. $$

Suffolk Hotel (38 The Buttermarket, near Moyse's Hall) Lunch in a former coaching inn. $$

Beaumonts (6 Brentgovel St., near Moyse's Hall) A vegetarian restaurant and coffeeshop. X: Sun. $

Masons Arms (Whiting St., near the Guildhall) A favorite old pub with meals. $

TOURIST INFORMATION:

The local tourist office, phone (0284) 64-667, is inside the Abbey Gate during the summer; and across the street in winter, phone (0284) 63-233.

SUGGESTED TOUR:

Leave the **train station** (1) and follow the map down Northgate Street to the **Abbey Gate** (2), erected in 1327 following an uprising of the townspeople. Stroll through the lovely Abbey Gardens to the 13th-century **Abbot's Bridge**, then walk along the River Lark to the ruins of the **Abbey** (3). A plaque marks the location of the high altar where in 1214 the barons swore they would compel King John to grant them their rights. The largest surviving part of the 11th-century abbey is its **west front**, now incorporated into a very strange row of houses. Walk over to the ruined **Charnel House**, then leave the abbey grounds.

The **Cathedral Church of St. James** (4) dates from the early 16th century, but did not become the seat of a bishop until 1914. Since then, major modifications have been made to render it more suitable as a cathedral. The 12th-century **Norman Tower**, opposite, serves as its bell tower.

Turn left on Crown Street and visit **St. Mary's Church** (5), one of the finest in the region. Built in the 15th century, it houses the tomb of Mary Tudor, sister of Henry VIII. The church is famous for its magnificently painted ceiling.

Continue up Crown Street to the **Theatre Royal** (6), a Regency structure restored by the National Trust. You may visit the interior when it is not in use. From here follow the map past the medieval Guildhall on Guildhall Street, and the Victorian Corn Exchange on Cornhill. The Traverse is a delightful lane featuring the smallest pub in England and a fine 17th-century inn, the Cupola House.

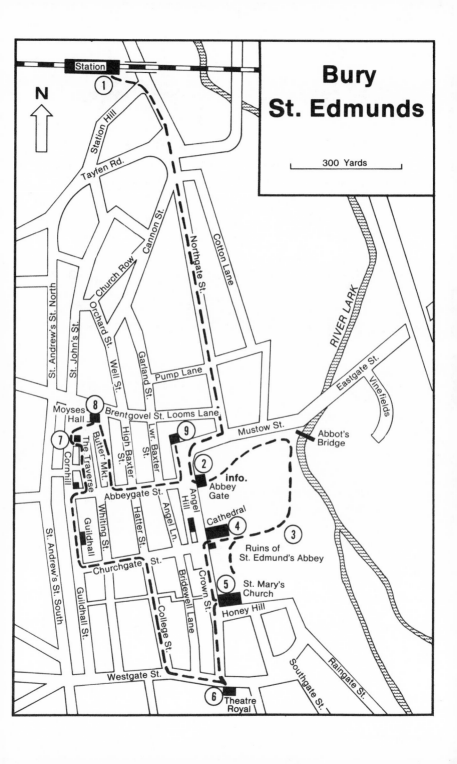

Ruins of the Abbey

The **Market Cross Art Gallery** (7) is a good museum that should not be missed. Cross the open square of the 12th-century **Moyse's Hall** (8), one of the oldest domestic buildings in England. This is now an interesting museum of local history, bygones, and archaeological finds. It is open Mondays through Saturdays, from 10 a.m. to 1 p.m. and from 2–5 p.m., closing at 4 p.m. in winter.

Return via Butter Market and Abbeygate Street to Angel Hill. On your right is the Athenaeum, a Regency social center where Charles Dickens once gave readings. He immortalized the nearby Angel Hotel in his *Pickwick Papers*. Beyond this is **Angel Corner** (9), a Queen Anne house owned by the National Trust that houses the splendid **Gershom Parkington Collection of Clocks and Watches,** one of the finest museums of its kind in the country. It is open Mondays through Saturdays, from 10 a.m. to 1 p.m. and from 2–5 p.m., closing at 4 p.m. in winter. From here it is only a short walk back to the station.

Colchester

No other town in England has a recorded history quite as old as Colchester's. Beginning as a small settlement in the Bronze Age, it had already become an important place by the first century A.D. when Cunobelin, Shakespeare's "Cymbeline," made it his capital. This was captured by the Romans in A.D. 44 and became their first colony in Britain, *Colonia Camulodunum*. After the fall of the empire, the town was taken over by the Anglo-Saxons, who called it *Colneceaster*. William the Conqueror built a mighty castle there, and all through the Middle Ages the town thrived on its cloth trade.

Colchester is still a flourishing place, and a very attractive one at that. Its handsome streets are lined with an absorbing mixture of the old and the new, including Roman walls, a surprisingly well-preserved Norman castle keep, many medieval houses, and structures of every age since. There is enough here to keep you busy all day, but those in a hurry may want to combine their visit with one to nearby Ipswich, easily reached by train or car.

GETTING THERE:

Trains leave frequently from London's Liverpool Street Station for the one-hour trip to Colchester, with return trains operating until late evening. Service is slightly reduced on Sundays and holidays.

Coaches depart London's Victoria Coach Station several times in the morning for the two-hour ride to Colchester.

By car, Colchester is 56 miles northeast of London via the A-12.

WHEN TO GO:

Several of the attractions in Colchester are closed on Sundays, while the colorful outdoor market is held on Saturdays.

FOOD AND DRINK:

Colchester has been noted for its oysters since Roman times. Some good places to eat are:

Red Lion Hotel (High St., near the castle) Lunch in an old half-timbered inn. $$

George Hotel (116 High St., near the castle) A longtime favorite with travelers. $$

Bistro 9 (9 North Hill, north of High St.) Imaginative cooking, with vegetarian alternatives. X: Sun., Mon. $$

Rose and Crown (East Hill, beyond the river) A 15th-century inn with a fine restaurant. $$

Norfolk (North Station Rd., on the way to the station) A popular pub with meals. $

TOURIST INFORMATION:

The local tourist office, phone (0206) 71-22-33, is at 1 Queen Street, opposite the Holly Trees Museum.

SUGGESTED TOUR:

The **train station** (1) is nearly a mile from High Street, where the sights begin. You can cover this partly uphill distance by bus, taxi, or on foot. Once there, turn left past the wonderfully Victorian Town Hall and left again on West Stockwell Street.

This quiet and charming old area is known as the Dutch Quarter, where refugee Flemish weavers settled in the 17th and 18th centuries. **St. Martin's Church** (2) has an interesting 12th-century tower. Turn right through the churchyard and follow East Stockwell Street and St. Helen's Lane, passing several fine old houses, to the 13th-century St. Helen's Chapel. A left on Maidenburgh Street leads to the remains of the ancient **Roman walls**. Stroll along these, and then make a right to the castle.

The only part of **Colchester Castle** (3) that survives today is its enormous keep, the largest in England. Built by the Normans about 1085 on the foundations of a Roman temple, it now houses the fabulous **Colchester and Essex Museum** of late Celtic and Roman antiquities. Visits may be made Mondays through Saturdays from 10 a.m. to 5 p.m.; and on Sundays between April and September from 2:30–5 p.m. Don't miss seeing this one.

Walk over to the **Holly Trees** (4), a Georgian mansion dating from 1718. This is now occupied by a splendid museum of 18th- and 19th-century bygones, costumes, and military objects. It is open Mondays through Saturdays, from 10 a.m. to 1 p.m. and from 2–5 p.m. Two other nearby museums are the **Natural History**, housed in the former All Saints' Church and having the same hours as the Holly Trees above; and the **Minories Art Gallery**, open Tuesdays through Saturdays from 11 a.m. to 5 p.m., and on Sundays from 2–6 p.m.

Continue down High Street to the 15th-century St. James' Church

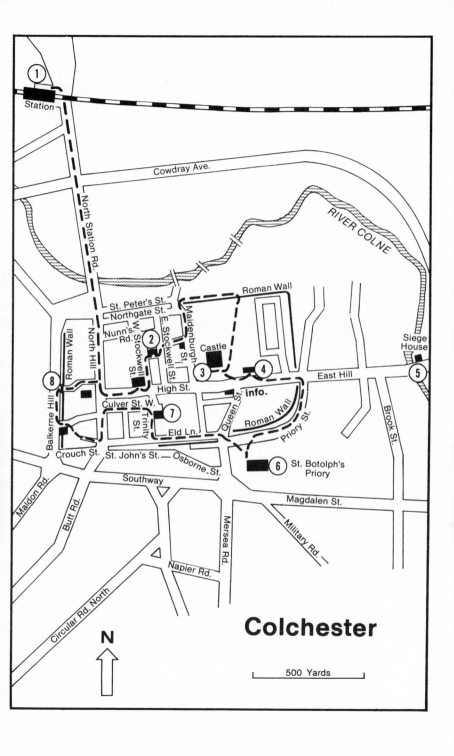

Colchester

N

500 Yards

Holy Trinity Church

near the corner of Priory Street. From here you can make a side trip down East Hill to the half-timbered **Siege House** (5) on the River Colne, which still bears bullet marks from the 17th-century Civil War and is now a restaurant.

A stroll down Priory Street will take you past a fine section of the Roman wall. Turn left into the very romantic ruins of **St. Botolph's Priory** (6), a 12th-century Augustinian foundation destroyed during the siege of 1648. From here follow the map along Eld Lane, passing some inviting pubs, and turn right on Trinity Street.

Holy Trinity Church (7) has a Saxon tower built of Roman bricks. Its 14th-century interior, well worth a visit, is now home to an interesting museum of rural life and crafts. It is open during the same hours as the Holly Trees Museum, above.

Make a left on Culver Street West and follow the map to the **Balkerne Gate** (8), originally built in the late first century A.D. by the Romans. Turn right and stroll down the passageway past the modern Mercury Theatre and the fantastic Victorian water tower, known locally as "Jumbo." From High Street you can walk or take a bus back to the station.

Ipswich

First impressions are often misleading. Step out of the train station at Ipswich and you may wonder what ever brought you there. This old industrial town has little in the way of famous sights, but it does have plenty of character and a peculiar charm that slowly takes hold as you stroll down its ancient streets. A visit to Ipswich will long be remembered by those who place atmosphere above conventional beauty.

Located ten miles inland at the navigable head of the Orwell estuary, Ipswich has been settled since prehistoric times. Then known as *Gipeswic,* it became an important Anglo-Saxon port as early as the 7th century A.D. Trade expanded under Norman rule and the town was granted a charter by King John in 1199. Ipswich flourished until the 16th century, when a decline set in that was not reversed until Victorian days. Since then, it has continued to grow as a prosperous seaport and industrial center.

This trip may easily be combined in the same day with one to Woodbridge or Colchester, or less easily with Bury St. Edmunds. Those traveling by train should watch the schedules carefully.

GETTING THERE:

Trains leave hourly from London's Liverpool Street Station for Ipswich, a journey of about 75 minutes, with return trains operating until late evening. Service is somewhat reduced on Sundays and holidays.

By car, Ipswich is 74 miles northeast of London via the A-12.

WHEN TO GO:

Ipswich should really be seen on a weekday, when its streets bustle with activity. Some sights are closed on Sundays.

FOOD AND DRINK:

Noted for its Tolly Cobbold ales, Ipswich has a number of colorful pubs, and some good restaurants as well. A few choices are:

Great White Horse (Tavern St., near the Town Hall) A 16th-century inn associated with Charles Dickens; pub lunches and a restaurant. $ and $$

Rajasthan (6 Orwell Place, 3 blocks north of the Old Custom House) Noted for fine Indian cuisine. $$

Marno's Restaurant (14 St. Nicholas St., east of the Willis Faber Building) A popular informal vegetarian restaurant. X: Sun. $

Arboretum (High St., near the Ipswich Museum) A lively pub with meals. $

Station Hotel (Burrell Rd., opposite the station) A nice pub for meals. $

TOURIST INFORMATION:

The local tourist office, phone (0473) 58-070, is in the Town Hall at Corn Hill.

SUGGESTED TOUR:

Leaving the **train station** (1), cross the River Orwell and follow Princes Street to Franciscan Way. Use the underground passage to get across this busy intersection, then turn right until you come to the **Willis Faber Building** (2), a spectacular curtain wall of tinted glass. Completed in 1975, this gigantic curved structure is among the most outstanding examples of contemporary architecture in Britain. Take the footpath to the left, which leads past the **Unitarian Meeting House** of 1699, one of England's earliest nonconformist chapels.

Follow the map to Westgate Street. A detour could be made up High Street to the **Ipswich Museum** (3), which features collections of local archaeology, natural history, and the noted Roman Villa gallery. It is open Mondays through Saturdays, from 10 a.m. to 5 p.m.

The pedestrians-only Westgate Street leads to **Corn Hill** (4). Predominantly Victorian in character, this large open square is bounded on the south by the imposing Town Hall.

Stroll down Tavern Street and turn left on Tower Street. The civic church of **St. Mary-le-Tower** (5) has an unusually tall spire and some good carved woodwork inside. Continue on to **St. Margaret's Church** (6), a richly detailed 15th-century flint structure. This is considered to be the finest church in town.

A path leads through a pleasant park to **Christchurch Mansion** (7), an elegant country home dating from 1548 that was twice visited by Queen Elizabeth I. It is now a wonderful museum of local antiquities and fine art, including works by Gainsborough, Constable, and others. Visits may be made Mondays through Saturdays, from 10 a.m. to 5 p.m.; and on Sundays from 2:30–4:30 p.m.; closing at dusk in winter.

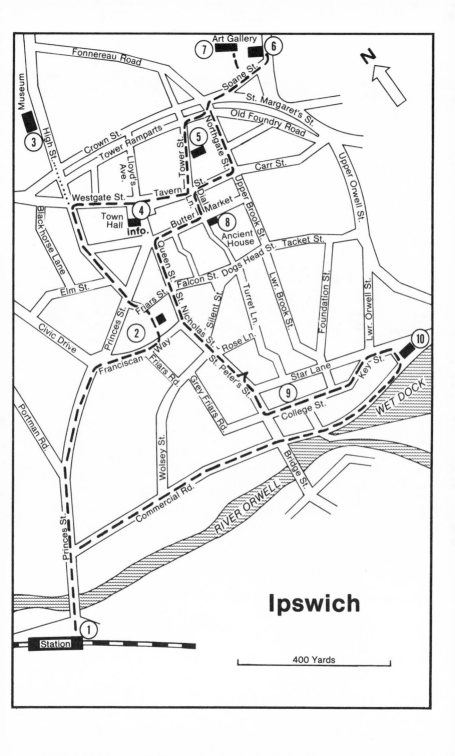

The Ancient House

The most famous sight in Ipswich is the **Ancient House** (8) on Butter Market, which can be reached by following the map. As picturesque as a house could possibly be, this magnificent example of a 16th-century timber-framed building is profusely decorated with extraordinary carvings in high relief. Its interior, now a bookstore, may be visited.

From here, the route leads down towards the river, passing several beautiful old houses en route. The passageway between numbers 9 and 13 on St. Peter's Street is particularly interesting. Turn left on College Street and examine **Wolsey's Gate** (9), all that remains of a college begun in 1528 by Cardinal Wolsey, a local lad who rose to the top, only to fall again when Henry VIII tired of his manipulations. Continue on to the **Old Custom House** (10) on the quay. Always a busy scene, the colorful waterfront is a fascinating place to explore. Return to the station via the route on the map.

Woodbridge

Beautifully situated at the head of a tidal estuary, the little market town of Woodbridge still clings to its Elizabethan past. Unpretentious, unspoiled, and well off the beaten path, it has long been a favorite retreat for artists and poets.

Woodbridge was first mentioned by name in King Edgar's charter of 970, and is described in the Domesday Book of 1086. The name is probably a corruption of the Anglo-Saxon *Udebryge,* most likely meaning Woden's Town, after their pagan deity. A priory was established in the 12th century near the site of the present parish church. Soon afterwards the town acquired the status of being a market place. When the plague subsided in 1349, Woodbridge began to prosper through its wool trade.

During the 17th century the town became an important shipping and shipbuilding center, but this declined as the ever-increasing draft of larger boats made the harbor obsolete. Today, its docks are limited to small pleasure craft, a fact that has spared it the industry of larger ports.

This trip can easily be combined in the same day with one to nearby Ipswich.

GETTING THERE:
Trains leave London's Liverpool Street Station at hourly intervals for Ipswich, where you change to a local for Woodbridge. The total journey takes about 1½ hours, with return trains until mid-evening. Service is reduced on Sundays and holidays.

By car, Woodbridge is 81 miles northeast of London via the A-12.

WHEN TO GO:
Good weather is necessary to enjoy this trip. The outdoor market is held on Thursdays.

FOOD AND DRINK:
Woodbridge has several pleasant country pubs and restaurants, including:

Crown Inn (Thoroughfare, in the town center) Pub lunches and full dinners. $ and $$

Lane O'Gorman Wine Bar (17 Thoroughfare, in the town center) An upstairs wine bar with homemade food. X: Sun., Mon.$

Bull Hotel (Market Hill, by the Shire Hall) A simple country inn with meals. $

Olde Bell and Steelyard (New St. near Market Hill) A 15th-century pub with bar lunches. $

TOURIST INFORMATION:

There is no local tourist office, although you could make inquiries at Ipswich.

SUGGESTED TOUR:

Leaving the **train station** (1), turn right on Quayside and follow it until you come to a sign pointing the way to the Tide Mill. Make a right, crossing the tracks, and walk out to the wonderfully picturesque **Tide Mill** (2), the last remaining example of its kind in England.

A water mill has existed on this spot since the 12th century, while the present structure was erected in 1793 and continued operations until 1957. Tide mills were commonly situated at the heads of estuaries leading from the sea. The Woodbridge mill has been completely restored to working order and is open to the public daily during the season.

From here you can take a beautiful country walk of about 2½ miles by following the route below. Otherwise, you should go directly to Market Hill (6) and carry on from there.

Begin the country walk by strolling past the **docks** (3), which once made Woodbridge a thriving commercial port, and continue along the river wall. This attractive promenade has long been a favorite with artists. In a short while, the trail turns inland and enters the woods at **Kyson Hill** (4). Passing a cross-path, you will come to a junction. Take the macadam path to the right, climbing through the National Trust parkland and crossing the railway on a bridge. By now the trail has become a road that soon turns sharply to the left. Just before the turn you will see a house called Cross Trees on the right. Take the woodland path to the right between the house and the bend in the road. When this emerges on Lane Road make a right and then another immediate right at the intersection.

A few yards beyond this, climb the flight of concrete steps on the left side of the road. This leads to a macadam path between backyards of houses. When you come to a fork, keep to the right. Continue on to Portland Crescent. Follow straight ahead past a cemetery, beyond which Fen Walk keeps to the right of a row of poles. Turn left when

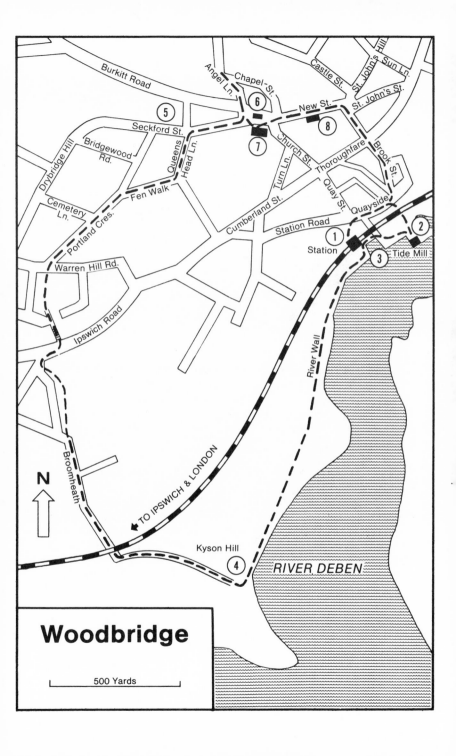

Woodbridge

500 Yards

The Tide Mill

you come to a junction and climb the steps to Seckford Street. To your left is the **Seckford Hospital and Almshouses** (5), built around 1840. Turn right and follow Seckford Street to Market Hill.

The ancient core of the community, **Market Hill** (6) is the site of the present open-air market held on Thursdays. There are several attractive old buildings, including a few pubs, on this square. Dominating all of them is the **Shire Hall**, erected in 1575 and now used as a courthouse. Stroll down charming Angel Lane, which is lined with 17th- and 18th-century cottages.

Returning to Market Hill, visit the **Parish Church of St. Mary** (7), built in the Perpendicular style during the early part of the 15th century. It is an unusually interesting old church, worth an exploration.

New Street leads down to the quay. Following it, you will pass **Ye Olde Bell and Steelyard Inn** (8). Overhanging the road from this is a 17th-century steelyard—a balance scale once used to weigh wagon loads coming to and from the market for toll-collection purposes. It was last used in the 1880s, a rare survival of the turnpike era.

After a sharp turn, New Street intersects with Thoroughfare, the main shopping street of Woodbridge. Continue straight ahead on Brook Street and turn right at Quayside, returning you to the station.

Norwich

Norwich lives in a curious time warp where the past keeps bumping into the present. Essentially a medieval city of great distinction, its twisting, cobbled lanes are charged with the vitality of modern living. It has all the expected features of an English country town; a massive castle, a splendid cathedral, and more ancient churches than anyone would care to count. Its narrow streets run every which way and make about as much sense as the meanderings of a drunken cow. Yet somehow it all seems to work, for Norwich is truly alive and well and ready to step into the next century.

Located in a loop of the River Wensum some 20 miles from the sea, Norwich began as an Anglo-Saxon settlement which by the 9th century was already trading with the Continent. Destroyed by the Danes in 1004, it was soon rebuilt by the Normans and has prospered ever since. When its wool industry declined it took to other pursuits such as brewing, metalworking, food processing, shoe-making, and insurance. Norwich has always adapted to changing times, and in the process has never lost sight of its heritage.

GETTING THERE:

Trains depart London's Liverpool Street Station hourly for the two-hour ride to Norwich, with return trains operating until mid-evening. Service is reduced on Sundays and holidays.

By car, Norwich is 109 miles northeast of London. Take the M-11 to Great Chesterford, then the A-11

WHEN TO GO:

Norwich may be visited at any time of the year, but avoid coming on a Sunday, when some of the sights are closed.

FOOD AND DRINK:

There are numerous pubs and restaurants along nearly all of the walking route. A few choices, in trip sequence, are:

Maid's Head Hotel (Tombland, near the cathedral) In business for over 700 years on the same site, this old hotel has two fine restaurants. $$

Lawyer (12–14 Wensum St., near the cathedral) Lunch in a popular pub. $

Ribs of Beef (24 Wensum St., near the river) An Edwardian pub with river views and lunches. $

Bombay (9–11 Magdalen St., just across the river) Well known for its Indian cuisine. $

Britons Arms Coffee Shop (9 Elm Hill, between the cathedral and St. Peter Hungate) Light lunches in a quaint cottage. X: Sun. $

Marco's (17 Pottergate, near the Market Place) Superb Italian cuisine with homemade pasta. X: Sun., Mon., Aug. $$

Assembly House (Theatre St., south of the Market Place) Inexpensive meals in an elegant Georgian structure. X: Sun. $

TOURIST INFORMATION:

The local tourist office, phone (0603) 66-60-71, is in the Guildhall on Market Place.

SUGGESTED TOUR:

Leave the **train station** (1) and follow the map to Tombland, a delightful open square. Pass through the Erpingham Gate of 1420 and visit the **Cathedral** (2). Begun in 1096, this is, with the exception of Durham, the most completely Norman cathedral in England. Its spire towers to a lofty 315 feet, exceeded in height only by that of Salisbury. The most magnificent view is of its east end, which is supported by majestic flying buttresses.

Enter the exceptionally long **nave** and look up at the marvelous **roof bosses**. These tell the story of both Testaments, but make it clear only to those with eagle eyes or binoculars as they are 70 feet above your head. The **choir** has some extremely good wood carvings, especially on the misericords. The ancient **Bishop's Throne**, behind the high altar, is older than the cathedral itself and probably dates from the 8th century. Stroll past the rounded apse, paying attention to the lovely St. Luke's Chapel, and then go out into the **cloisters**. These contain some wonderfully sculpted bosses, even better than those in the nave.

Leave the cathedral via the south transept and follow the map through its lovely close to **Pull's Ferry** (3). Built in the 15th century, this was once a water gate from which a canal ran to the cathedral. Stroll along the riverside walk past the playing field. There is a beautiful view of the cathedral from here and, with luck, perhaps a cricket

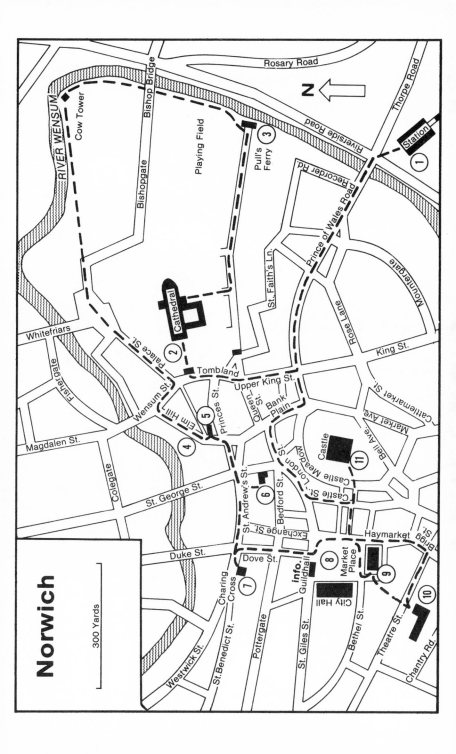

Norwich Cathedral

match in progress. Continue on past the 13th-century **Bishop Bridge**, one of the oldest spans in England still in use. Cow Tower, just as ancient, guards a bend in the river. The path ends at the Adam and Eve pub, which claims to have been here since 1249. Walk down Palace Street and return to Tombland.

Elm Hill (4) is the most delightful street in Norwich. The quaint medieval houses lining this cobbled lane have all been restored and are now used as antique shops, art galleries, restaurants, and the like. Be sure to stroll down the alleyways that lead between the buildings. Probably the oldest structure here is the Briton's Arms, a 15th-century timbered building with a thatched roof. **St. Peter Hungate** (5), at the intersection of Princes Street, is now a museum of church art with fascinating displays of manuscripts, vestments, alabaster carvings, icons, and related treasures. Perhaps the most interesting of these is a 14th-century coffin complete with skeleton. The museum is open Mondays through Saturdays, from 10 a.m. to 5 p.m.

Take a look down Princes Street, then turn right and stroll over to the **Bridewell Museum** (6). Housed in a 14th-century merchant's home later used as a prison for tramps and beggars, the museum features

A Game of Cricket Behind the Cathedral

intriguing displays of local crafts and industries. It is open Mondays through Saturdays, from 10 a.m. to 5 p.m.

Return to St. Andrew's Street and turn left to the **Strangers' Hall Museum** (7), a complex, rambling structure that dates in part from 1320 and was also once a merchant's house. Since 1922 this has been the city's museum of domestic life, with exhibits covering a range of decor and furnishings from early Tudor to late Victorian times. The building itself is well worth the visit, and the displays within are absolutely first rate. It is open Mondays through Saturdays, from 10 a.m. to 5 p.m.

From here walk over to the **Market Place** (8), bounded on the north by the 15th-century Guildhall, home of the tourist office, and to the west by the overpowering City Hall of 1938. A colorful outdoor market has been held here since the Middle Ages, a tradition that continues every day except Sundays. If you visit only one other church besides the cathedral, be sure to make it **St. Peter Mancroft** (9), the most outstanding in Norwich. Located just south of the market, this splendid 15th-century parish church is noted for its fine hammerbeam ceiling and the medieval stained glass in its east window.

It is only a short stroll to the **Assembly House** (10), a graceful Georgian structure whose interior preserves the flavor of the 19th century. Now used for civic and cultural functions it may be visited

Inside Norwich Castle

and is also a wonderful place for inexpensive meals or elegant teas.

Follow the map to the **Castle** (11), begun by Henry I about 1130 on a lofty mound overlooking the city. Heavily restored, it was used as a prison until 1887 and is now a museum of major importance. The superb collections range from art, particularly that of the Norwich School, to local archaeology, natural history, and social history. Allow at least an hour to see this. It is open Mondays through Saturdays, from 10 a.m. to 5 p.m.; and on Sundays from 2–5 p.m. From here it is an easy walk back to the station.

Daytrips in Scotland

Scotland is a very different country from England, and one that never fails to enchant its many visitors. Customs, history, geography, language, laws, attitudes, religion, money, the people themselves, are all quite separate and distinct—sometimes in subtle ways—from what you've encountered south of the border. Those traveling by train will notice that British Rail is called ScotRail here, although the BritRail Pass is, of course, still valid. This is a place to relax and enjoy the celebrated hospitality of the Scots as you explore one of the most beautiful lands on earth.

Because of the relatively great distances between many of its attractions, Scotland may not at first seem to be particularly well suited to daytripping. While this is certainly true of much of the Highlands and the offshore islands, a surprisingly large portion of the country can be comfortably probed on one-day excursions from a base in either Edinburgh or Glasgow. By adopting this strategy you will avoid the need for frequent hotel changes and be able to travel without luggage, returning each evening to the same place in time for dinner and possibly a night's entertainment.

This section begins with a "get acquainted" walking tour of the capital, Edinburgh, considered by many to be among the most delightful cities in Europe. It then describes a broad variety of fascinating daytrips, all of which can be made from either Edinburgh or Glasgow, and ends up with a leisurely one-day rail trip into the spectacular West Highlands.

Edinburgh

It has been called everything from "Auld Reekie" to the "Athens of the North," but no such name can possibly do justice to Edinburgh. One of the world's most likeable cities, the Scottish capital packs an enormous range of sights and sheer beauty between its open spaces and volcanic hills. That, and a certain sense of style born of the Scottish Enlightenment, makes it the top tourist attraction in the country, as well as one of the most popular in all of Britain.

Edinburgh began as a secure fortification atop an extinct volcano, and was known in ancient times as *Dun Eadain*. During the 7th century this was captured by the followers of Edwin, king of the Northumbrians, who built a castle on the rock. By the 11th century a small town began to develop around this and gradually descended the ridge now known as the Royal Mile. Throughout the Middle Ages the population continued to grow, but was always confined by the defensive town wall, resulting in the construction of unusually tall tenement buildings. Appalling housing conditions became so bad that in the mid-18th century Edinburgh finally burst free of its walls and established the elegant New Town on a hill to the north. The valley between the old and new towns, previously a lake, was bridged and then drained, forming the base for Princes Street and the railway line.

The suggested walking tour covers virtually the entire sweep of Edinburgh's history, and passes many of its most outstanding attractions along the way. Since you cannot possibly visit all of them in one day, you may want to plan on returning to some between the one-day adventures that lie ahead.

GETTING THERE:

Trains from England usually leave from London's King's Cross Station and go by way of York, making the hourly run to Edinburgh in as little as 4½ hours. Nearly all of these use the latest InterCity 125 equipment. The very comfortable all-reserved late-night sleeping-car trains, for which there is an extra charge, take longer and always arrive at a civilized hour. Specially equipped coaches are used on the economical reserved-seat "Nightrider" service. There are also a few departures for Edinburgh from London's Euston Station. Whichever train is choosen, BritRail Pass holders will certainly get their money's worth on this run.

Trains from Glasgow leave from Queen Street Station frequently for the 50-minute run to Edinburgh, with returns operating until late evening. Service is somewhat reduced on Sundays and holidays. Slower and less frequent trains also leave from Glasgow's Central Station, with no Sunday service.

By car from London, Edinburgh is 417 miles to the northwest via the M-1 and A-1 highways. A number of other possible routes allow stopovers at such interesting places as York or Chester.

By car from Glasgow, take the M-8 and A-8 highways. The distance is 46 miles.

By air, Edinburgh is connected with London's Heathrow Airport by British Airways' frequent Super Shuttle no-reservation flights, making the hop in 70 minutes.

GETTING AROUND:

Although the suggested tour can easily be covered on foot, Edinburgh itself is a very hilly and spread-out city. It is well served by buses, mostly double-deckers, which run frequently to just about everywhere in town. Fares may be paid to the driver or you can purchase a day pass at the transport office on Waverley Bridge or at 14 Queen Street.

WHEN TO GO:

Edinburgh may be enjoyed at any time, but note that most of the attractions along the walking route are either closed or have shorter hours on Sundays. Never a dull place, the city really comes alive during the annual Edinburgh International Festival, a celebration of the performing arts usually held during the last three weeks of August. Around the same time you can also take in the offbeat Fringe Festival, the Military Tattoo, and other events. Contact the tourist office or the British Tourist Authority for current information.

FOOD AND DRINK:

You'll find nearly all of the world's cuisines in sophisticated Edinburgh. For true Scottish fare, however, you're probably better off waiting until you get to one of the smaller towns. Because of its enlightened licensing laws, pubs in Edinburgh are open for unusually long hours, frequently all afternoon and until late in the evening. Some good restaurant and pub choices are:

Near the Royal Mile:
L'Auberge (56 St. Mary's St., near the Museum of Childhood) An excellent French restaurant with good-value lunch menus. $$ and $$$

L'Alliance Brasserie (7 Merchant St., off George IV Bridge south of St. Gile's) A popular French bistro. X: Sat. lunch, Sun. $$

Beehive Inn (18 Grassmarket, south of the castle) A favorite pub with excellent lunches at the street level. X: Sun. lunch $

Malt Shovel (13 Cockburn St., just north of High Street) Lunch at a thriving pub. $

In the New Town:

Cosmo's (58a North Castle St., near Charlotte Sq.) A very popular and thoroughly Italian restaurant. X: Sat. lunch, Sun., Mon. $$$

Aye (80 Queen St., near Charlotte Sq.) Classical Japanese cuisine. X: Sun. lunch, Mon. $$$

Martin's (70 Rose St., North Lane, between George and Princes St.) Cosmopolitan dining, with set lunch menus available. $$ and $$$

Alp Horn (167 Rose St., near Charlotte Sq.) Swiss cuisine in an Alpine ambiance. X: Sun., Mon. $$

Madogs (38a George St.) Sophisticated American and Continental cuisine. X: Sun. $$

Country Kitchen (4 South Charlotte St., near Charlotte Sq.) Healthy foods in an appealing cafeteria. $

Henderson's (94 Hanover St., near George St.) A cafeteria with imaginative health foods. $

Laigh Kitchen (117a Hanover St., near Queen St.) Light meals, all homemade. $

TOURIST INFORMATION:

An exceptionally good tourist office, complete with an accommodations service and bookstore, is located in the Waverley Market shopping center next to the train station. Entrance is from the Princes Street level, and you can phone them at (031) 557-27-27.

SUGGESTED TOUR:

Begin your day's exploration outside the tourist office on Princes Street, next to **Waverly Station** (1), Edinburgh's well-hidden and half-buried main train station. The adjacent Waverley Market is an unusually fine shopping center of recent date, well worth a visit at a later time. Until the mid-18th century much of this low-lying area was a reedy lake, the *Nor' Loch,* but this was drained and filled when the New Town developed.

To the eternal credit of the city fathers, the south side of Princes Street was reserved for parks and gardens, exposing a dramatic vista of the Old Town and its castle perched high atop a rocky crag. Although the railway runs through the gardens, it is virtually invisible.

View of Edinburgh Castle from the Princes Street Gardens

Continue up Princes Street to the **Scott Monument** (2) of 1840, a 200-foot-high neo-Gothic spire rising above a statue of Sir Walter Scott and his dog. You may climb to its top for a close-up view of the New Town if you happen to be bursting with energy.

Just in line with the foot of Hanover Street is the Royal Scottish Academy, where changing exhibitions of contemporary art are held. Next to this is the **Floral Clock** at the corner of the West Princes Street Gardens, reputed to be the oldest such outdoor timepiece in the world. The nearby **National Gallery of Scotland** (3) packs an exceptionally good collection of fine art into a relatively small space. It is particularly noted for its Italian Renaissance, Dutch and Flemish Old Masters, French Impressionist, and 19th-century English paintings; as well as Scottish works. Admission is free, and visits may be made Mondays through Saturdays, from 10 a.m. to 5 p.m.; and on Sundays from 2–5 p.m. You may prefer to return here on another day, as there is a lot more to cover on this walking tour.

Now follow the map uphill to **Edinburgh Castle** (4), where the town began. Although a fortress existed here since at least the 6th century, the oldest surviving part, St. Margaret's Chapel, dates only from the 12th. Most of the other structures are from more recent times as the castle was frequently rebuilt after several successful conquests by the English. Its commanding position provides an excellent panorama of both the town and the surrounding countryside.

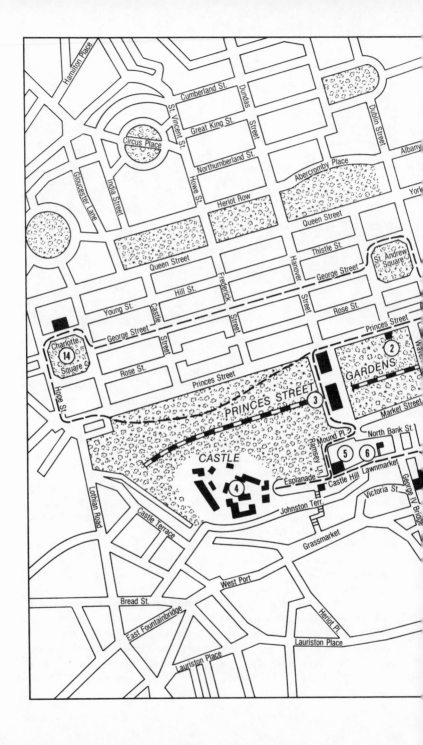

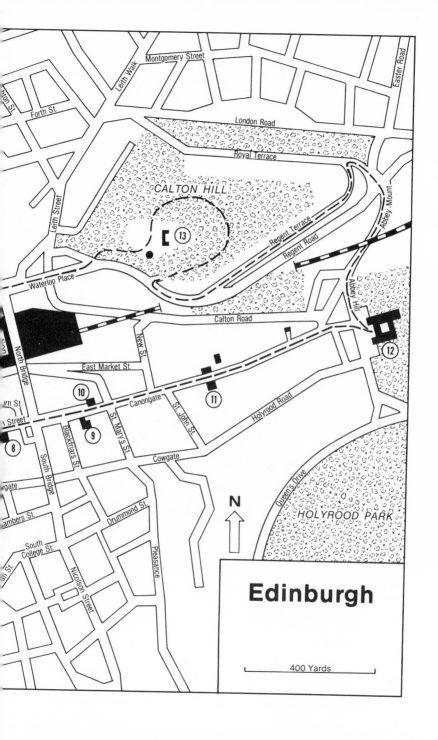

The castle had been used as a royal residence since as early as the 11th century, a role it lost when it was converted into a garrison by Cromwell during the 17th-century English Civil War. Its most famous resident was undoubtedly Mary, Queen of Scots, who gave birth here in 1566 to a son who later became James VI of Scotland and, after the union of the crowns in 1603, James I of England.

The best way to see the castle is to take a guided tour, after which you are free to wander around on your own. You might want to purchase an illustrated guide book at the gift shop inside. In any case, be sure to see the **Royal Scots Regimental Museum**; the dungeons or **French Prison**, complete with an enormous 15th-century artillery piece called *Mons Meg*; the 12th century **St. Margaret's Chapel**; the 20th century **Scottish National War Memorial**; the 15th century **Great Hall**; the **Crown Room** where the "Honours of Scotland" regalia—the oldest in Europe—are displayed; and the **bedroom** of the tragic Mary, Queen of Scots. Edinburgh Castle is open Mondays through Saturdays, from 9:30 a.m. to a last admission at 5 p.m.; and on Sundays from 11 a.m. to 5 p.m. Between October and the end of March the hours are somewhat shorter, especially on Sundays.

Leave the castle and begin your stroll down one of Europe's most fascinating thoroughfares, the **Royal Mile**. Actually a straight succession of several streets, it leads downhill to the Palace of Holyroodhouse, still used as a royal residence but usually open to tourists. During the Middle Ages much of this stretch was an overcrowded slum where the townspeople eked out a living, but after the 18th century expansion of Edinburgh it was considerably improved and today presents a thoroughly delightful mixture of buildings.

The **Esplanade** just in front of the castle was built in the early 19th century as a parade ground and is now used for the famous Military Tattoo. The well against the wall in the northeast corner marks the spot where alleged witches were strangled and then burned as late as the 18th century. This was often used as a pretext to get rid of tiresome people. To the right, next to the steps, is the Cannonball House, which has a ball embedded in its west gable, supposedly fired from the castle during a 1745 rebellion.

The **Outlook Tower** (5) on Castle Hill is from the 17th century but is topped with a marvelous mid-19th-century observatory equipped with a **Camera Obscura**, still a popular tourist attraction after 150 years. Go inside and climb the steep steps for a truly unique optical view of Edinburgh. Along with this show there are also displays of some of the stranger aspects of photography such as pin holes, space, and holography.

On either side of the street you will notice tiny alleyways leading to dark wynds, closes, and courts. These were built as an attempt to squeeze more tenements into an already overcrowded town. Several of them, particularly Semple's Court and Milne's Court, have been restored and are well worth exploring.

Gladstone's Land (6), where Castle Hill becomes Lawnmarket, is a rather comfortable six-story merchant's tenement dating from 1620. Restored and refurnished to its 17th-century condition, it belongs to the National Trust for Scotland and may be visited Mondays through Saturdays, from 10 a.m. to 5 p.m.; and on Sundays from 2–5 p.m. The hours are slightly shorter in winter.

On the opposite side of Lawnmarket is the entrance to **Brodie's Close**, once home of the highly respectable Deacon Brodie who was a town councillor by day and a burglar at night. Hanged in 1788, he provided the inspiration for Robert Louis Stevenson's *Dr. Jekyll and Mr. Hyde*. Across the street you will find the entrance to **Lady Stair's House** on a close of the same name. Greatly restored, this town house of 1622 now serves as a museum for memorabilia of Scotland's greatest literary figures, Robert Burns, Sir Walter Scott, and R. L. Stevenson. Admission is free and visits may be made Mondays through Saturdays from 10 a.m. to 5 or 6 p.m. During the festival it is also open Sunday afternoons.

St. Giles' Cathedral (7) is more correctly known as the High Kirk of Edinburgh although it did serve as a cathedral under Charles I and again under Charles II and James VII/II, all of whom tried to force the English Episcopalian faith on Scotland. Since 1689 it has belonged to the Presbyterian Church of Scotland. Built on the site of earlier churches, the present structure dates from the 15th century but has been much altered over the years. It was here that the 16th-century Protestant reformer John Knox began his fiery sermons aimed at Mary, Queen of Scots, which eventually led to her exile. The interior is rather unusual and features the exquisite **Thistle Chapel**, an early-20th-century addition in the Flamboyant Gothic style. Be on the lookout for a carving of an angel playing the bagpipes.

Behind St. Giles' is the **Parliament House**, begun in 1632. Its legislative function ceased in 1707 when the Scottish Parliament was abolished under the Act of Union with England. Now home to Scotland's supreme courts, it may usually be visited Tuesdays through Fridays.

A few steps down High Street brings you to the **Wax Museum** (8), where Scottish history is re-created with wax figures in realistic settings. As a special treat there is a children's fairy-tale land and a blood-curdling chamber of horrors.

Continue down High Street to the **Museum of Childhood** (9), the first to be devoted to that most important phase of life and often known as the "noisiest museum in the world." A multitude of toys, games,

A Figure of John Knox in his House

dolls, and costumes are displayed along with the more serious aspects of upbringing. The museum is open Mondays through Saturdays, from 10 a.m. to 6 p.m., closing at 5 p.m. from October through May. During the festival it is also open on Sunday afternoons. Admission, happily, is free—so you can afford to join the kiddies.

Just across the street is the **John Knox House** (10), a charming 15th century dwelling in which the famous preacher is alleged to have lived. There is no positive proof of this but the well-restored interior is absolutely fascinating and should not be missed. It is open Mondays through Saturdays, from 10 a.m. to 5 p.m., closing at 4 p.m. in winter.

The Royal Mile now narrows into Canongate and leads downhill past the site of the Netherbow, or lower town gate, at St. Mary's Street. Beyond this is the **Huntly House** (11), a 16th century mansion now used as the **City Museum**. Step inside and amble through its confusing series of rooms and levels, filled with all sorts of bygones and historical objects. Admission is free, and the museum is open Mondays through Saturdays, from 10 a.m. to 6 p.m., closing at 5 p.m. off-season. During the festival it is also open on Sunday afternoons.

Just across the street is the remarkable 16th century **Canongate Tolbooth**, once used as a council room, court, and jail. It now houses temporary exhibitions as well as a brass rubbing center where you can make your own souvenirs. It is open during the same times as the

Huntly House, above, and admission is free. Standing next to it is the **Canongate Church**, in whose yard you will find the grave of Adam Smith, the noted 18th century economist. Near the foot of Canongate is the picturesque **White Horse Close**, a restored 17th-century courtyard whose rear building was once the famous White Horse Inn.

˙At the end of the Royal Mile is the **Palace of Holyroodhouse** (12), which is still a royal residence. You may visit it when the queen is not in Edinburgh. Often just called Holyrood Palace, it began as an Augustinian abbey founded in 1128, parts of which still exist in ruin behind the palace. The abbey's guest house was frequently used as a residence by the Scottish kings in preference to the uncomfortable castle. Intent on making Edinburgh his capital, James IV began transforming the guest house into a proper palace, most of which has since been destroyed. Mary, Queen of Scots lived here for six years starting in 1561, and it was here that she witnessed the brutal butchery of her Italian secretary and probable lover, David Rizzio, most likely at the hand of her jealous husband, Lord Darnley, in 1556.

The palace as it stands today is mostly the result of a 17th century rebuilding ordered by Charles II, although the northwest tower used by Mary is still intact. Guided tours are conducted quite frequently, and last about 40 minutes. Besides the lavishly decorated **State Apartments** and the **Historic Apartments** associated with Mary, Queen of Scots, the tours take in the **Picture Gallery** and its amazing collection of portraits of 89 Scottish kings, all painted by one artist in two years. At the end, you may explore the remains of the **Holyroodhouse Abbey** on your own. The palace is usually open Mondays through Saturdays, from 9:30 a.m. to 5 p.m.; and on Sundays from 10:30 a.m. to 4:30 p.m. During the winter it closes at 3:45 p.m. and all day on Sundays. It is, of course, closed when occupied by the royal family, most often in late May, late June, and early July.

Now follow the map under the railway and up Carlton Terrace, passing the American consulate on Regent Terrace and the Robert Burns Monument. Turn right just beyond the Old Royal High School and climb up **Calton Hill** (13) for some really magnificent views. At its top is the uncompleted **National Monument** honoring the Scottish dead of the Napoleonic wars, intended to be a copy of the Parthenon but abandoned in the early 19th century for lack of funds—or interest. The adjacent **Nelson Monument** to the victor at Trafalgar is over 100 feet tall. Yes, you may climb it if you feel so inclined.

Come down off the hill and onto Waterloo Place, then turn right just beyond North Bridge. The venerable **Café Royal** on West Register Street was built in 1862 and has hardly changed since. This atmospheric old pub is a wonderful place for some liquid refreshment, which you're probably in need of by now.

The Palace of Holyroodhouse

You are now in the **New Town**, an extension of crowded old Edinburgh begun in 1767 and still a masterpiece of civic planning. Stroll across **St. Andrew Square** with its handsome Royal Bank of Scotland building and continue down broad and stately George Street. At each intersection you will be treated to good views in both directions.

Charlotte Square (14), designed in 1791 by Robert Adam, is the most elegant square in town. The splendid **Georgian House** at number 7 on the north side is owned by the National Trust for Scotland and may be visited. Fully restored, it is furnished as it would have been between 1790 and 1810. To help you understand everything, there is also an audio-visual show explaining the development of the New Town. It is open between Easter and the end of October, Mondays through Saturdays, from 10 a.m. to 5 p.m.; and on Sundays from 2–5 p.m. During the rest of the year the house is open on Saturdays and Sundays only, from 10 a.m. to 4:30 p.m.

Now walk down to Princes Street and return to the starting point at the Waverley train station by ambling through the magnificent **Princes Street Gardens**.

St. Andrews

There's a whole lot more to St. Andrews than just a round of great golf, exciting though that may be. This is the home of Scotland's first university, founded in 1412, and of several of Britain's most spectacular and picturesque ruins. The medieval town itself, overlooking the North Sea, is about as attractive as any you'll find in the country. All in all, it's a first-rate daytrip destination.

According to which legend you believe, St. Andrews began in either the 4th or 8th century, when the saint's relics were brought here, possibly as the result of a shipwreck. By the 10th century it had become the major religious center of Scotland, starting work on its great cathedral in 1160 and its castle in 1200. Both of these are now in ruin, but the university continues to flourish, adding a great deal of color to the town.

The Royal and Ancient Golf Club, which sets the rules of the game for the entire world, was founded in 1754. Its Old Course, possibly dating from the 15th century, is the mecca for golfers everywhere. Even if you're not a player, you can still watch as the beginning of the course is practically in the town proper and public footpaths cut right through it.

GETTING THERE:

Trains marked for Dundee leave **Edinburgh's** Waverley Station several times in the morning for the one-hour run to **Leuchars**, the nearest station to St. Andrews. From there you take a bus that runs every half-hour, or a taxi (they meet the trains) into St. Andrews, a distance of 5 miles. Return trains operate until mid-evening, and service is slightly reduced on Sundays and holidays. Those coming from **Glasgow** will have to take a train to Edinburgh first.

By car from Edinburgh, leave westbound on the A-90 and cross the famous Forth Bridge. Once on the north side of the Firth of Forth take the A-92 east to Kirkcaldy, then the A-915 into St. Andrews, 51 miles northeast of Edinburgh by road.

By car from Glasgow, take the M-8 and M-9 east to the Forth Bridge, then carry on as above. St. Andrews is about 75 miles northeast of Glasgow.

WHEN TO GO:

Try to avoid coming on a Sunday, when the major attractions do not open until 2 p.m. Golfers will note that the Old Course is closed on Sundays. Good weather is essential.

FOOD AND DRINK:

St. Andrews has quite a few hotels catering to golfers, many of which have restaurants open to non-residents. There are also several small restaurants and pubs in the town proper. A few choices are:

Russell Hotel (26 The Scores, near the golf course) A small hotel with meals in the bar or restaurant. $ and $$

St. Andrews Golf Hotel (40 The Scores, near the golf course) Pub lunches and full dinners in a small hotel. $ and $$

Pepita's (11 Crails Lane, near the market) A charming place for informal lunches, with fancier evening meals. $ and $$

Victoria Café (St. Mary's Place, near the market) A popular pub with good beer and meals. $

TOURIST INFORMATION:

The local tourist office, phone (0334) 720-21, is on South Street across from Holy Trinity Church. For advance reservations to play golf, call the Links Management Committee at (0334) 757-57 at least eight weeks in advance.

SUGGESTED TOUR:

Leave the **bus station** (1) and follow City Road and Golf Place to the **Royal and Ancient Golf Club** (2). The magnificent old clubhouse is private and cannot be visited, but you can see across the Old Course from here and watch grown people hitting little balls with sticks. Even if you have not made reservations, you just may be able to try this game yourself by asking the Starter. A lottery is held to determine which lucky applicants get to play. There are three other venerable courses nearby, all under the same management as the Old Course, and they are usually less crowded. Clubs may be rented at any of the courses. Closed on Sundays, the Old Course is in a marvelous setting overlooking the North Sea.

Now stroll down a street called The Scores to the **Castle** (3), begun in 1200 as a bishop's palace and eventually used as a prison for religious reformers before falling into ruin. One of these was burned at the stake in front of the castle in 1546, but shortly after that the Protestants seized the stronghold and butchered the ruling cardinal. John Knox, the famous preacher of Edinburgh, joined them until the castle was taken by the French fleet in 1547, after which Knox was sent to the galleys in Nantes. Later released, he spent exile time in England

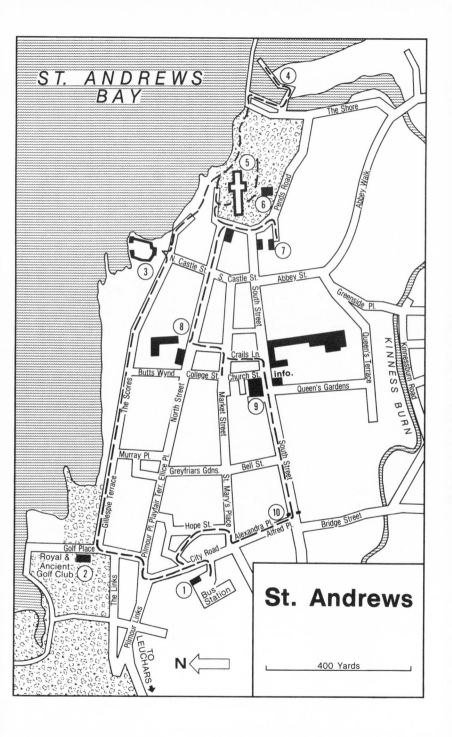

ST. ANDREWS BAY

The Shore

KINNESSBURN

Abbey Walk

Kinnessburn Road

Pends Road

Greenside Pl.

Queen's Terrace

Abbey St.

N. Castle St.

S. Castle St.

South Street

Queen's Gardens

Crails Ln.

info.

Church St.

Butts Wynd

College St.

The Scores

North Street

Market Street

Murray Pl.

Greyfriars Gdns.

Bell St.

Ellice Pl.

Playfair Terr.

Gillespie Terrace

Pilmour Pl.

St. Mary's Place

South Street

Hope St.

Alexandra Pl.

Alfred Pl.

Bridge Street

City Road

Golf Place

Royal &
Ancient
Golf Club

The Links

Pilmour Links

Bus
Station

TO
LEUCHARS

St. Andrews

400 Yards

N

Ruins of the Cathedral

and Geneva before returning to Edinburgh, where he lashed out against Mary, Queen of Scots.

The castle, though in ruin, is quite fascinating. Be sure to see the strange **Bottle Dungeon** and the **Kitchen Tower**. Agile travelers may want to probe the **Mine and Counter Mine**, used in the 16th century taking of the castle. It is a very difficult descent, taken at your own risk. The castle is open Mondays through Saturdays, from 9:30 a.m. to 7 p.m.; and on Sundays from 2–7 p.m.; with shorter hours in winter.

A path from here leads to the delightful little **Harbor** (4), one of the oldest in Scotland. Stones from the castle and cathedral were used in its 17th century reconstruction. Just above it are the 12th century ruins of the Chapel Royal of the Blessed Mary of the Rock.

Follow the map to the **Cathedral** (5), or what's left of it. Begun in 1160 and consecrated in 1318 in the presence of Robert the Bruce, it was the scene of the marriage of James V to Mary of Guise. Its downfall came with the Reformation, when the Catholic decorations were desecrated and anything of value looted. The walls themselves fell prey to both neglect and their use as a handy quarry. Still, enough remains to appreciate what it must have been like.

Close to the southeast angle stands the **Church of St. Regulus**, even older than the cathedral and also in ruin. Its 100-foot-high **tower** has survived intact, however, and may be climbed for the best possible view of St. Andrews. The same ticket admits you to the **Cathedral Museum** (6), which has good collections of local relics. The entire cathedral complex is open at the same time as the castle, above. Except for the tower and museum, admission is free.

The route now leads past **The Pends**, a 14th-century vaulted gatehouse, to the priory precinct. Just down South Street stands the handsome 16th century **Queen Mary's House**, which according to tradition sheltered Mary, Queen of Scots and, later, Charles II. Continue around to **St. Leonard's Chapel** (7), built in 1512 for St. Leonard's College and now well restored. It is open Mondays through Fridays, from 10 a.m. to 4 p.m.

Retrace your steps and turn left on North Street. The first group of buildings on the left is known as **Dean's Court**, dating from the 16th and 17th-centuries and now used as a student residence. A few steps beyond is the small **Preservation Trust Museum**, filled with local bygones. Stop in for a look if it's open.

The entrance arch to **St. Salvator's College** (8) is just down North Street. Go inside and examine this central part of the ancient university. The oldest structure, dating from 1450, is the **Chapel**. Tours of the university are offered from early July to mid-September, at 10:30 a.m. and 2:30 p.m. They start at the porter's lodge in the quadrangle.

Now follow the map through the market with its interesting 19th-century fountain. The very narrow Crails Lane leads to South Street, where the tourist office is located. Across the street is **Holy Trinity Church** (9), founded in 1410 but considerably altered since. It was here that John Knox preached his first sermon in public. Surprisingly, there is an intricate monument to a Catholic archbishop who was brutally murdered nearby in 1679.

Continue down South Street to the **West Port** (10), a magnificent town gate dating from 1589, although altered later. Pass through it and turn right. On the way back to the bus station you may want to make a little detour through **Howard Place**, one of the most delightful little garden squares in the country.

Aberdeen

It may seem like a long way to go for a daytrip, but Aberdeen is easily one of the most interesting and attractive cities in Scotland. Long a major university town and intellectual center with a rich architectural heritage, its economy has been enlivened in recent years with the exploitation of North Sea oil. Yet it remains, like Edinburgh, an eminently likeable place with a remarkably international outlook on life.

There are really two Aberdeens, and both of them are covered on this walking tour. United since 1891, each retains its own distinctive personality. Although the area has been settled since prehistoric times, the city received its first charter in 1179. Old Aberdeen, located at the mouth of the River Don, has been the seat of a college since 1495; while Aberdeen proper, at the mouth of the River Dee, is a prosperous North Sea port noted for its handsome granite buildings.

GETTING THERE:

Trains depart Edinburgh's Waverley Station at about 2-hour intervals for the nearly 3-hour ride to Aberdeen. Service is slightly reduced on Sundays and holidays. Return trains operate until mid-evening.

Trains leave Glasgow's Queen Street Station about every 2 hours for the under-3-hour ride to Aberdeen, with reduced service on Sundays and holidays. Return trains run until early evening.

By car from Edinburgh, take the M-90 north across the Forth Bridge to Perth, then the A-94 and A-92 northeast to Aberdeen. The total distance is 130 miles. You will probably want to use the car to drive to Old Aberdeen instead of taking the bus.

By car from Glasgow, take the M-8 and M-9 east to the Forth Bridge, then carry on as above. The total distance to Aberdeen is 150 miles.

WHEN TO GO:

Aberdeen is best visited on a working day, when the city is alive with energy. Most of its museums are closed on Sundays.

FOOD AND DRINK:

Cosmopolitan Aberdeen abounds in good restaurants and pubs, many serving foreign cuisines. Some choices in the area covered by the walking tour are:

Aberdeen Harbor

Atlantis (145 Crown St., 2 blocks west of the train station) Renowned for its seafood, other dishes available. X: Sun. $$$

Caledonian Thistle (10 Union Terrace, between the art museum and the station) Dining in a luxury hotel. $$$

Aberdeen Rendezvous (218 George St., near Provost Skene's House) A Chinese restaurant with Peking specialties. $$

Poldino's (7 Little Belmont St., just southeast of the art museum) Features Italian cuisine. X: Sun. $$

Nargile (77 Skene St., 2 blocks west of the art museum) A favorite for exotic Turkish food. X: Sun. $$

The Yardarm (40 Regent Quay, on the north side of the harbor) Pub lunches and real ale. $

Dobbies Ale House (22 Guild St., near the train station) Meals in a popular pub. $

Carriages (101 Crown St., 2 blocks west of the train station) A pub with good food. $

Like much of Scotland, the pubs in Aberdeen are often open for unusually long hours.

TOURIST INFORMATION:

The local tourist office, phone (0224) 63-27-27, is in the St. Nicholas House on Broad Street, two blocks northwest of the Mercat Cross. During the summer there is a small branch in the train station.

SUGGESTED TOUR:

Leave the **train station** (1) and follow the map to the nearby **harbor**. Most of this is open to the public and may be explored on foot, allowing unusually close-up views of ships from all over the world as they go about their business of loading and unloading. Just be careful to stay out of the way of moving cranes and vehicles, and not to fall into the water. The modern **Fish Market** (2) is open on Mondays through Fridays, with auction sales beginning at 7:30 a.m.—a treat for those who arrive early enough. About half of the harbor's activities are related to the offshore oil industry, although the liquid gold itself comes ashore elsewhere. The harbor has continually evolved since the 12th century and has been extensively rebuilt during the past two decades, with completely up-to-date facilities today.

Your seafaring mood can be continued by following the map to the nearby **Maritime Museum** (3), located in the interesting 16th-century Provost Ross's House on Shiprow. Exhibits here include ship models, nautical artifacts, paintings, and a history of the local shipbuilding industry along with a fantastically detailed scale model of a North Sea offshore drilling rig, so realistic that it is used by the oil industry for simulating emergency conditions. The museum is open on Mondays through Saturdays, from 10 a.m. to 5 p.m., and admission is free. Don't miss it.

A few more steps up Shiprow will bring you to Castlegate and the 17th-century **Mercat Cross** (4), a small stone shelter in the middle of the open square, embellished with portraits of the Scottish sovereigns from James I to James VII. Once the center of the town's commercial activity, it was also the place of public proclamations. Until the 14th century this square was the approach to Aberdeen's castle, whose site is now occupied by office buildings beyond the turreted Salvation Army Citadel. Just to the northwest stands the castellated **Town House**, incorporating the 17th-century tower of the Tolbooth, a former jail outside of which public executions took place until 1867.

Americans of British descent may be interested in strolling up King Street to **St. Andrew's Cathedral** (5), the Mother Church of the Episcopal Communion in America, where the first bishop of the United States was consecrated in 1784. Note the coats-of-arms of the American states above the north aisle.

Now follow Broad Street past the tourist office to **Marischal College** (6), founded in 1593 and united with King's College in Old Aberdeen since 1860. The present building, dating mostly from about 1905, is a supreme achievement in solid granite architecture, considered lovely by some and hideous by others, but impressive to all. Besides the college, it houses an interesting **Anthropological Museum** covering civilizations throughout the world from ancient to modern times,

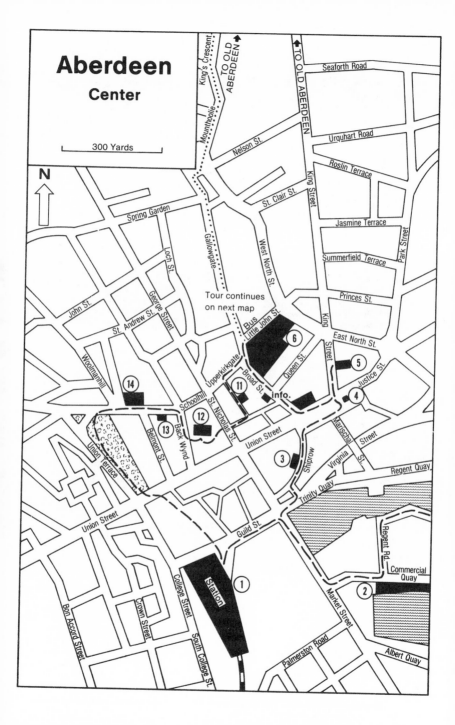

St. Machar's Cathedral in Old Aberdeen

with a focus on Scotland. The museum is open on Mondays through Fridays, from 10 a.m., to 5 p.m.; and on Sundays from 2–5 p.m. Admission is free.

You are now ready to explore Old Aberdeen, until 1891 a separate community, which lies one-and-a-half miles to the north. The easiest way to get there is to take bus number 20 from the corner of Gallowgate and Little John Street, next to Marischal College. Exact fare is required for this. It is also possible to walk by following Gallowgate, Mounthoolie, King's Crescent, Spital, and College Bounds. By car, the easiest route is via King Street.

Begin your amble through **Old Aberdeen** at the rather elegant early-16th-century **King's College Chapel** (7), the oldest surviving structure of the college. Its tower is topped with a truly magnificent crown spire, rebuilt in the 17th century after storm damage. Originally Catholic, then Protestant, the chapel is now nondenominational and is generally open to tourists on weekdays and Saturday mornings. Step inside to see the beautifully carved woodwork, much of which is original, and the 19th- and 20th-century stained-glass windows.

High Street leads past lovely old buildings and cottages now used by the university. At its far end is the **Old Aberdeen Town House** of 1788, once a town hall and presently a library. Continue straight ahead on The Chanonry to **St. Machar's Cathedral** (8), an extremely attrac-

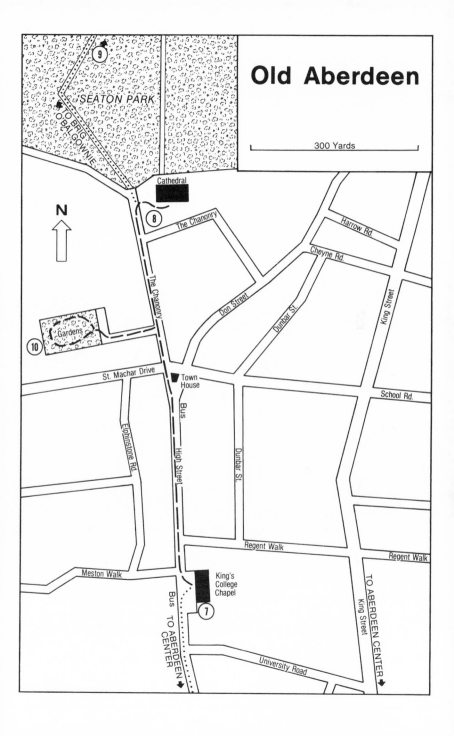

Old Aberdeen

300 Yards

N

SEATON PARK

9

TO BRIG O BALGOWNIE

Cathedral

8

The Chanonry

The Chanonry

Harrow Rd.

Cheyne Rd.

Don Street

Dunbar St.

King Street

Gardens

10

St. Machar Drive

Town House

Bus

School Rd.

Elphinstone Rd.

Dunbar St.

High Street

Regent Walk

Regent Walk

Meston Walk

King Street

King's College Chapel

Bus   TO ABERDEEN CENTER

7

TO ABERDEEN CENTER

University Road

tive stone church from the 15th century. It is named after a saint who first brought Christianity to this area in the 6th century and established a chapel on this site. Since 1688 it has belonged to the Church of Scotland and so is no longer technically a cathedral, but is still called that. Enter from the south porch to examine the renowned heraldic ceiling, emblazoned with the shields of 16th-century leaders.

From here a little side trip could be made through Seaton Park to the 13th-century **Brig o' Balgownie** (9) (off the map, about ¾ mile), Scotland's oldest medieval bridge. Spanning the River Don with one majestic Gothic arch, it was the only way of crossing the stream until the 19th century.

On the way back to town, be sure to visit the **Cruickshank Botanic Gardens** (10) with its extensive collection of rare plants, operated by the university. From the bus stop near the Town House you can board a number 20 bus back to the city center.

Get off in front of Marischal College (6) and stroll around to **Provost Skene's House** (11). First built in the mid-16th century and altered in the 17th, this is Aberdeen's oldest domestic dwelling. Now owned by the city, it is furnished in period style and has highly interesting displays of local history and domestic life as well as a tea shop serving light meals. Visits may be made on Mondays through Saturdays, from 10 a.m. to 5 p.m., and admission is free.

The route now leads to **St. Nicholas Kirk** (12) in its exquisite parklike setting. Dating from the 12th through the 15th centuries and once the largest parish church in Scotland, it is curiously divided into two parts with a common vestibule. The interior is well worth exploring, particularly the medieval crypt of the East Church, where witches were once imprisoned and which was later used as a soup kitchen for Aberdeen's poor. The complex is open on Mondays, Thursdays and Fridays, from noon until 4 p.m.; and on Saturdays from 10 a.m. to noon.

Just a short stroll away, on Schoolhill, is the restored 18th-century **James Dun's House** (13). It is now a museum with varied exhibitions and may be visited on Mondays through Saturdays, from 10 a.m. to 5 p.m. Admission is free.

Continue up the street to the **Aberdeen Art Gallery** (14), which may surprise you with its excellent collection of 18th- through 20th-century art. The emphasis here is on contemporary modern works, with special exhibitions and events keeping the place lively. It is open on Mondays through Saturdays, from 10 a.m. to 5 p.m., remaining open until 8 p.m. on Thursdays; and on Sundays from 2–5 p.m. Don't miss this special treat, especially since it's free.

The best way back to the station is through the Union Terrace Gardens and the modern Trinity Shopping Centre.

Linlithgow

The story of Linlithgow is the story of its massive fortified palace, where Mary, Queen of Scots was born on December 8th, 1542. Long a strategic center in Scotland's epic struggles with England, Linlithgow dominates the east-to-west Lothian passage, an important route to Edinburgh. Although the palace is now in a state of semi-ruin it is still an outstanding attraction that can easily hold your attention for hours with its unusually great amount of ornamental detail. Its dramatic setting at the edge of a small lake, or *loch,* makes it one of the most romantic visions of old Scotland.

Linlithgow itself is quiet today, living with its memories and the many visitors who come to revel in them. The small town that grew up around the palace is a quite pleasant and thoroughly Scottish place, complete with many old and well-preserved houses. Additional interest is added by one of the finest parish churches in the country and by the Union Canal, on which short boat trips can be taken.

This very easy and rather short trip could be combined in the same day with one to Stirling, the subject of the next chapter. There is direct train service between them.

GETTING THERE:

Trains depart Edinburgh's Waverley Station frequently for the 20-minute ride to Linlithgow. Service is slightly reduced on Sundays and holidays, and return trains run until late evening.

Trains leave Glasgow's Queen Street Station at hourly intervals for the 25-minute run to Linlithgow. Service is somewhat reduced on Sundays and holidays, and return trains operate until late evening.

By car from Edinburgh, take the A-8 and M-9 highways west to the Linlithgow exit, then the A-803 into town. The total distance is 19 miles.

By car from Glasgow, take the M-8 east to exit 4, then the A-706 into town. The total distance is 35 miles.

WHEN TO GO:

Linlithgow may be visited at any time, but note that the palace is not open on Sunday mornings or on a few major holidays, while the church is closed on weekends between October and May. Canal boat trips are offered on weekends between Easter and the end of September. Good weather is essential.

FOOD AND DRINK:

There are several pubs and modest restaurants in the town, with an excellent inn two miles away. Some choices are:

Four Marys (67 High St.) A wine bar and bistro in a 16th-century building. $

Coffee Neuk (3 The Cross, near the tourist office) Casual meals. $

Champany Inn (in Champany, 2 miles northeast on the A-803 where it meets the A-904. A popular chophouse with a neighboring formal restaurant under the same management. X: Sat. lunch, Sun. $$ and $$$

TOURIST INFORMATION:

The local tourist office, phone (0506) 84-46-00, is in the Burgh Hall at The Cross, just off High Street.

SUGGESTED TOUR:

Leave the **train station** (1) and stroll down High Street to **The Cross** (2), once a market place and now a square in front of the impressive Town, or *Burgh* Hall. The original structure was destroyed by Oliver Cromwell during the Civil War and the present building finished in 1670, partly paid for from his funds. You may want to stop into the tourist office here for a copy of their *Heritage Trail* booklet, describing the town in greater detail. The **Cross Well**, an elaborate stone fountain built in 1806 as a replica of an earlier well dating from the reign of James V, was carved by a one-handed mason.

Kirkgate leads steeply uphill through the oldest part of town to the splendid 16th-century **gateway** of the palace. The four panels above its arch represent the orders of knighthood to which James V belonged—the Garter, the Thistle, the Golden Fleece, and St. Michael.

Continue through and into the grounds of **Linlithgow Palace** (3). While paying your admission you would do well to purchase a copy of the illustrated guide brochure, which describes all of the rooms and outlines an interesting tour.

A royal residence has stood on this site since at least the 12th century, although the oldest part still remaining, the southwest tower, was built in 1302 by England's Edward I during his campaign against

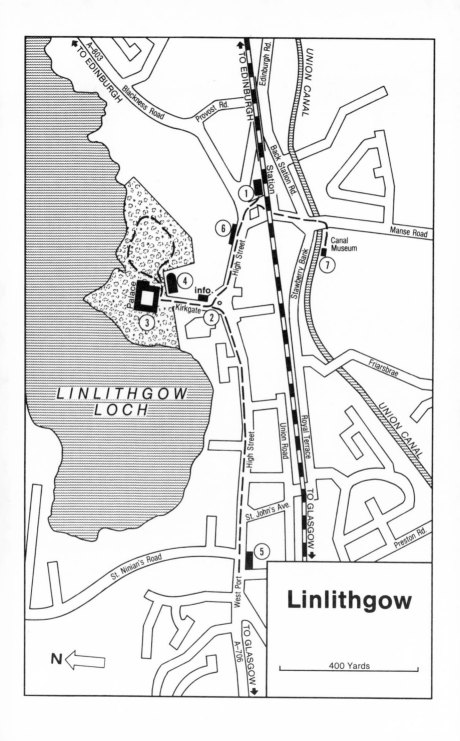

TO EDINBURGH
A-803
TO EDINBURGH
Blackness Road
Provost Rd.
Edinburgh Rd.
UNION CANAL
Back Station Rd.
Station
Manse Road
Canal Museum
High Street
Stawberry Bank
1
6
4
info.
Palace
Kirkgate
2
3
LINLITHGOW LOCH
7
Friarsbrae
UNION CANAL
High Street
Union Road
Royal Terrace
St. John's Ave.
TO GLASGOW
5
Preston Rd.
West Port
St. Ninian's Road
TO GLASGOW
A-706

N

Linlithgow

400 Yards

Linlithgow Palace

the Scots. It was not until 1425 that James I of Scotland began construction of a real palace to replace the former manor house, which had burned down. This became a favored home of James IV and James V, both of whom made extensive additions. The latter's daughter, Mary, Queen of Scots, was born here in 1542. After the union of the crowns in 1603 the court moved to London, and Linlithgow was only occasionally used. It was gutted by an accidental fire in 1745, leaving it in the semi-ruined state you see today.

After exploring its many rooms and paying particular attention to the ornate **stone fountain** in the courtyard, which is said to have once run with wine, you may want to take a walk through the adjacent park for some lovely views. The palace is open on Mondays through Saturdays, from 9:30 a.m. to 7 p.m.; and on Sundays from 2–7 p.m. During the winter it closes at 4 p.m.

St. Michael's Church (4), just south of the palace, is easily among the most interesting parish churches in Scotland. Although consecrated in 1242, it was rebuilt in 1424 and had its modern aluminum spire added only in 1964, by helicopter. Step inside to admire the fabulous window in the south transept, where James IV saw an apparition warning him against war with England. This ghostly advice was ignored, and the king soon fell at the battle of Flodden. Visits may be made from 10 a.m. to noon and 2–4 p.m., but not on Sunday mornings or winter weekends.

View of the Palace from the Park

The town of Linlithgow itself has some interesting old houses. A stroll down High Street to the **West Port House** (5) of 1600 reveals several of these. Returning, note the group of outstanding 16th-century stone houses known as **Hamiltons' Lands** (6) at numbers 40–48.

Now turn right just before the train station and walk under the tracks to the **Union Canal**, which you cross. Linking Edinburgh with Glasgow, it was opened in 1822, remained in commercial service until 1933, and is now used by pleasure boaters. The small **Canal Museum** (7) displays various artifacts and has a short audio-visual show. It is open from Easter until the end of September, on Saturday and Sunday afternoons, from 2–5 p.m. Admission is free. Delightful rides on a colorful little boat are offered at nominal rates. From here it is only a brief walk back to the station.

Stirling

Renowned for its famous castle, the old town of Stirling has several other attractions that help make it a truly outstanding daytrip destination. Located at the very center of Scottish history where many of the great events happened virtually at its doorstep, it is dominated by an enormous rocky crag upon which fortifications have been built since the earliest of times.

Although the site was probably inhabited by ancient Britons and possibly later by Romans and even, according to legend, by King Arthur, the earliest known record of a castle dates from the 12th century. This was taken by the English in 1296 and recaptured by the great Scottish hero Wallace after the Battle of Stirling Bridge. The last place in Scotland to hold out against England's Edward I, it capitulated after an especially bloody siege in 1304 and remained English for ten years before again falling to the Scots following the Battle of Bannockburn.

Much of the castle as it stands today dates from the time of the Stewarts (Stuarts), who made it a royal residence in the 15th century. The infant Mary, Queen of Scots, was crowned here in 1543 at the age of nine months. After the union of the crowns in 1603 it ceased to have much royal function and became a military garrison until recent years.

This trip can easily be combined in the same day with one to Linlithgow as they are both on the same rail line.

GETTING THERE:

Trains leave Edinburgh's Waverley Station frequently for the 50-minute run to Stirling, with greatly reduced service on Sundays and holidays. Return trains operate until mid-evening.

Trains depart Glasgow's Queen Street Station at least hourly for the 40-minute ride to Stirling. Service is greatly reduced on Sundays and holidays, and return trains run until mid-evening.

By car from Edinburgh, take the A-8 and M-9 highways to Stirling, a distance of 37 miles.

By car from Glasgow, the quickest route is via the A-80, M-80, and M-9 highways, a distance of 28 miles.

WHEN TO GO:

Stirling may be visited at any time, although good weather makes it much more enjoyable.

South Face of Stirling Castle

FOOD AND DRINK:

There are quite a few restaurants and pubs along the walking route. A few choices are:

Portcullis Hotel (Castle Wynd, near the castle) A full restaurant with Scottish food as well as a pub, both in a historic building. $ and $$

Barnton Bistro (Barnton St., a block west of the station) Lunch in a popular pub. $

King's Gate Hotel (5 King St., 3 blocks southwest of the station) A simple place with good food. $

TOURIST INFORMATION:

The local tourist office, phone (0786) 75-019, is on Albert Place, Dumbarton Road, southwest of the station.

SUGGESTED TOUR:

Leave the **train station** (1) and follow the map around the modern Thistle Shopping Centre, then turn right on King Street, soon becoming Spittal Street. The continuation of this, St. John Street, leads uphill past some old houses to the interesting Church of the Holy Rude (6), which you can visit later.

For the moment, turn right on Castle Wynd and stroll uphill to **Argyll's Lodging** (2). Now a youth hostel, this magnificent turreted 17th-century mansion was built by Sir William Alexander, the Principal Secretary for Scotland and founder of the Scottish colony of Nova Scotia in the New World. When this was ceded to the French in 1632 Sir William turned his interests southward and took possession of parts of Maine and all of Long Island, which he intended to rename *Isle of Sterlinge*. Fortunately for New Yorkers this did not happen, and Sir William died heavily in debt. His coat-of-arms, above the main entrance, depicts an Indian, a beaver, and a mermaid. The house later passed to the Earl of Argyll, thus the name.

Continue uphill to the **Castle Visitor Centre** (3), where you can learn all about the castle by watching a fascinating audio-visual presentation. It would be a good idea to purchase the official guide brochure along with the ticket, as it explains everything in detail. Thus prepared, you will be taken through **Stirling Castle** (4) itself in a small group led by a knowledgeable guide. After the tour you are free to wander around by yourself, perhaps revisiting the spots that interest you most. Be sure to explore the battlements, especially the **Lady's Hole terrace**, which has fabulous views. The castle is open on Mondays through Saturdays, from 9:30 a.m. to 5:15 p.m.; and on Sundays from 10:30 a.m. to 4:45 p.m. Between October and March the hours are a bit shorter.

Now follow the map down steps and around the Back Walk to the **Guildhall** (5), a lovely 17th-century almshouse for "decayed breithers," as unsuccessful merchants were called. Next to this is the **Church of the Holy Rude** (6), parts of which date from the 15th century. The interior, where the infant James VI (England's James I) was crowned in 1567 along with a sermon preached by John Knox, is well worth a visit.

Turning left behind the apse of the church brings you to a curious ruin known as **Mar's Wark** (7). Begun in 1570 as a palace for the Earl of Mar, it was never really finished and later became a workhouse for vagrants. During a siege of the castle in 1746 it was badly damaged, but the intriguing façade was left standing to serve as a windbreak.

Now stroll down Broad Street, once the market place. The mercat cross in its center, flanked by cannons, marks the spot where public proclamations were made and executions carried out until 1843. On the same square stands the **Tolbooth** (8), an early-18th-century combination town hall and jail. Its rather elegant tower has a nice four-faced clock and a gilded weathercock. From here you can follow the map back to the station.

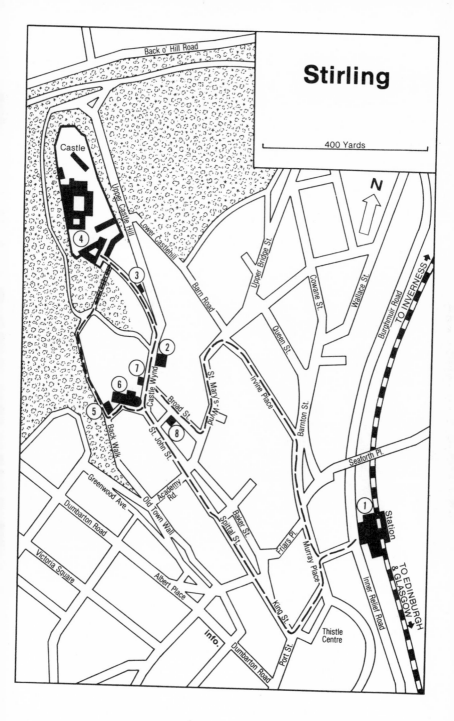

Blair Atholl

Europe's only private army is headquartered at Blair Castle, ancestral home of the Dukes of Atholl and, since 1746, the last castle in Britain to have come under siege. With the strict injunction of *Furth Fortune and Fill the Fetters*—bestowed upon them by James III in 1475—as their motto, the long line of dukes have over the centuries transformed what began as a 13th-century stronghold into the great white baronial mansion you see today. The 32 rooms of it that are open to public view are filled with a sweeping history of Scottish aristocratic life from the 16th century to the present, a treat not to be missed by any visitor to Scotland.

All of this is set in a lovely park adjacent to the tiny village of Blair Atholl, quietly nestled in the Central Highlands. In addition to the castle, there are a few nice attractions in the village itself as well as some very interesting country walks that can be taken, using a map available at the castle as a guide. As to that private army called the Atholl Highlanders, it is the only survivor of the ancient clan system and is now made up primarily of estate workers who also perform ceremonial duties. You may see—or worse, hear—one or more of them playing the bagpipes around 11 a.m. and 2:15 p.m. Their continuation as a "military" organization was authorized by Queen Victoria after a royal visit in 1844.

GETTING THERE:

Trains depart Edinburgh's Waverley Station twice in the morning for the under-2½-hour ride to Blair Atholl. Between early September and late June there is no service on Sundays and holidays. Return trains run until early evening, with a change at Stirling required on Sundays and holidays.

A trains leaves Glasgow's Queen Street Station once each morning for the 2-hour run to Blair Atholl, with additional possibilities by changing at Stirling. On Sundays and holidays a change at Stirling is required, and there is no service between early September and late June on those days. Return trains run until early evening with a change at Stirling.

Blair Castle

By car from Edinburgh, take the A-90 across the Forth Bridge, the M-90 to Perth, then the A-9 to Blair Atholl. The total distance is 78 miles.

By car from Glasgow, take the A-80, M-80, and M-9 past Stirling, then the A-9 past Perth to Blair Atholl, a total distance of 98 miles.

WHEN TO GO:

Blair Castle is open on Easter week, Sundays and Mondays in April, then daily from the third Sunday in April to the second Sunday in October. Good weather is necessary to enjoy this trip.

FOOD AND DRINK:

The tiny village of Blair Atholl has few places to eat or drink, but the following can be recommended:

>**Atholl Arms** (near the train station) A country inn with a pub and a restaurant. $ and $$

>**Castle Restaurant** (in the castle itself) An attractive self-service cafeteria with good food. $

TOURIST INFORMATION:

For all information contact Blair Castle directly, phone (079-681) 207 or 356.

SUGGESTED TOUR:

Leave the **train station** (1) and follow the map to the castle, a distance of less than a mile, going through parkland most of the way. Those with cars can, of course, drive there.

Blair Castle (2) is about as baronial a mansion as you're ever likely to see. Begun in 1269 and vastly altered over the years, it contains an enormous wealth of furniture and decorative arts from the 16th century onwards, as well as armor, tapestries, china, paintings, stuffed animals, and many historical artifacts. You can explore it all at your own pace, more or less following a posted route. A well-illustrated guide booklet, available at the entrance, describes everything of interest in adequate detail. If you do have any questions, there are always informed guards around to ask. The cafeteria on the premises is a fine place for lunch, and there is a well-stocked gift shop worth browsing in. Blair Castle is open during the season (see *When to Go*) on Mondays through Saturdays, from 10 a.m. to 6 p.m.; and on Sundays from 2–6 p.m. During July and August it opens at noon on Sundays. The last admission is at 5 p.m.

The park surrounding the castle is a great place for a short country stroll. One particularly attractive route is shown on the map in this book, while a trail map covering a larger area is available.

Head north from the castle, passing through a gate, and cross the little stream. The path leads to the romantic ruins of **St. Bride's Kirk** and its churchyard. Close to this are the scanty remains of **Old Blair** (3), dating from before the moving of the village to its present site during the 18th century. Turn left on the narrow country lane, again crossing the stream on a stone bridge, then left again through Diana's Grove. From here you can wander back through the woods to the castle and then the village.

Returning to the village, turn left a short distance to the **Atholl Country Collection** (4) in the Old School. Realistic re-creations of local life in bygone times depict a smithy, a crofter's shed, a living room, and the like. There are also fascinating artifacts from the past including farm implements and tools. The small museum is open between late May and mid-October, daily from 1:30–5:30 p.m. During July and August it opens at 9:30 a.m. on weekdays.

Heading back to the station, be sure to turn left and visit **The Mill** (5), where corn is again ground with waterpower. Rebuilt in recent years, it is completely open to visitors, who can watch all of the operations involved. A pamphlet explains it all, and there is a tea room for refreshments. The mill is open between April and October; on Mondays through Saturdays, from 10 a.m. to 6 p.m.; and on Sundays from noon to 6 p.m. From here it is only a few steps to the station.

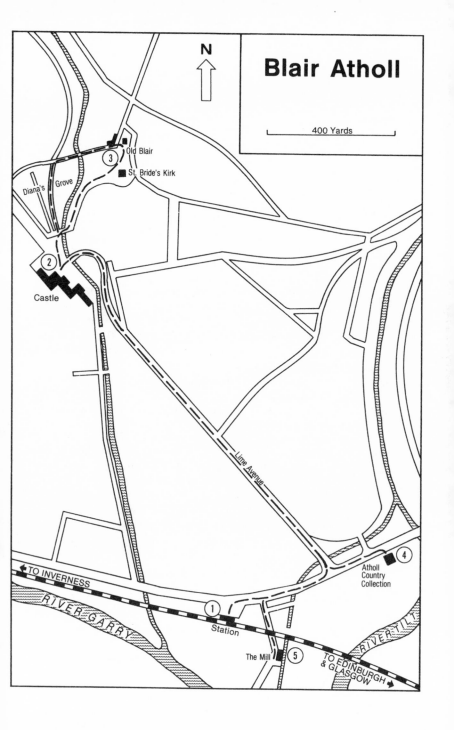

N

Blair Atholl

400 Yards

Old Blair
③
Diana's Grove
St. Bride's Kirk

②
Castle

Lime Avenue

④
Atholl
Country
Collection

← TO INVERNESS

RIVER GARRY

①
Station

RIVER TILT

The Mill ⑤

TO EDINBURGH
& GLASGOW →

Glasgow

Glasgow may not be the prettiest place in Scotland, but it sure is a fascinating city to visit. The dynamic heart of the country, with fully half of the Scottish population within its orbit, just can't be ignored.

Although the city dates from at least the 6th century, it remained a backwater place until the union of the parliaments in 1707, which removed the previous legal obstacles to overseas shipping. Being closer than London to the New World, and well out of pirate-infested waters, it soon grew rich on the tobacco trade with Virginia. The 19th-century Industrial Revolution with its boundless energy eventually created what is surely the supreme Victorian city, whose grandiose solid stone buildings still stand in testimony to an age of unbridled optimism.

Perhaps surprisingly, Glasgow—not Edinburgh—is today the cultural center of Scotland. This began in the 19th century, when boom times brought about an interest in the arts. One of the greatest exponents of the Art Nouveau movement was Glasgow-born Charles Rennie Mackintosh, whose imprint on the city is still highly visible. The Scottish Opera, Ballet, and National Orchestra are based there; and several of its splendid museums rank among the best in Britain.

Although the majority of tourists choose Edinburgh as their base for exploring Scotland, Glasgow is equally convenient for nearly all of the Scottish daytrips in this book. It has a wonderful selection of first-class hotels, some excellent restaurants, and enough night life to keep you busy between probes of the countryside.

GETTING THERE:

Trains from London's Euston Station usually take 5½ hours to reach Glasgow's Central Station. Many of these require reservations. During the evening there is a slower sleeping-car service, arriving at a civilized hour.

Trains depart Edinburgh's Waverley Station frequently for the 50-minute ride to Glasgow's Queen Street Station, with returns until late evening. Service is somewhat reduced on Sundays and holidays. There are also slower and less frequent trains into Glasgow's Central Station, with no Sunday service.

By car from London, take the M-1 northwest to Rugby, then the M-6 to Carlisle, and continue northwest on the A-74 into Glasgow. The total distance is 416 miles.

By car from Edinburgh, take the A-8 and M-8 highways west, a distance of 46 miles.

By air, Glasgow is connected with London's Heathrow Airport by British Airways' frequent Super Shuttle no-reservation flights, making the hop in 70 minutes.

GETTING AROUND:

Although the suggested tour can easily be covered on foot, Glasgow is a very large and spread-out city, with most of its museums well outside the center. These can be reached by city buses, for which exact change is needed. Ask the tourist office for current details. The Underground (subway) is fairly useless for tourists.

WHEN TO GO:

Glasgow can be visited at any time, but it is much more exciting on a working day, when the streets throb with activity.

FOOD AND DRINK:

The city is blessed with an exceptionally wide range of restaurants and pubs in all categories. A few good choices along the suggested walking tour, in trip sequence, are:

Babbity Bowster (16 Blackfriars St., 2 blocks north of Glasgow Cross) Meals in a trendy pub. $

Colonial (25 High St., near Glasgow Cross) A traditional favorite among businessmen. X: Sat. lunch, Mon. eve., Sun., July. $$$

Tolbooth (11 Saltmarket, south of the Glasgow Cross) A restored old Glaswegian pub with meals. $

Café Gandolfi (64 Albion St., 3 blocks east of George Square) Light meals, Italian and otherwise. X: Sun. $

Mitre (12 Brunswick St., south of Hutchesons' Hall) A Victorian pub with meals. X: Sun. $

Le Provençal (21 Royal Exchange Sq., near the Royal Exchange) A contemporary French restaurant. X: Sun. $$$

Rogano (11 Exchange Place, behind the Royal Exchange) A popular sophisticated seafood restaurant. X: Sun., bank holidays. $$$

Danish Food Centre (56 St. Vincent St., near Central Station) Scandinavian dishes in a bright, modern atmosphere. X: Sun. $$

George Square and the City Chambers

Willow Tea Rooms (217 Sauchiehall St., upstairs, near the School of Art) Light meals in an historic 1904 interior by Charles Rennie Mackintosh. $

Loon Fung (417 Sauchiehall St., 2 blocks southwest of the School of Art) A modern Chinese restaurant with Cantonese specialties. $

TOURIST INFORMATION:

The Glasgow tourist office, phone (041) 227-4880, is at 35 St. Vincent Square, one block south of Queen Street Station. They can secure accommodations for you.

SUGGESTED TOUR:

For the convenience of those based in Edinburgh, this walk begins at **Queen Street Station** (1). Just outside this is **George Square** (2), the rather elegant heart of the city. Laid out in the late 18th century, it is surrounded by the type of imposing Victorian structures that lend Glasgow its special character. Although the square is named for George III, its main statue is of Sir Walter Scott, while others represent Queen Victoria, Prince Albert, Robert Burns, James Watt, Gladstone, Peel, *et al.* Across its east end stands the enormous, highly ornate **City Chambers** of 1888, whose opulent interior may be seen by arrangement with the tourist office.

Glasgow Cathedral from the Necropolis

Now turn up John Street past Strathclyde University, a renowned technological school whose former students included John Logie Baird, the pioneer of television in the 1920s. Cathedral Street leads east to what little is left of the medieval town.

Glasgow Cathedral (3), dedicated to St. Mungo who, in the 6th century built the first church here, is an outstanding example of pre-Reformation Gothic architecture. The present structure dates primarily from the 13th century although work on it continued for another 300 years. Having escaped the usual pillaging by Protestant zealots in the 16th century, the interior is especially interesting and well worth a visit. The nave has some superb modern stained glass and is separated from the elevated choir by a magnificent stone rood screen. Be sure to see the **Lower Church**, sometimes referred to as the crypt but actually above ground. A veritable forest of stone pillars surrounds the simple tomb of St. Mungo, the patron saint of Glasgow. The cathedral is closed to visitors on Sunday mornings and usually over the lunch hour.

Cemeteries are not usually tourist attractions, but Glasgow's **Necropolis** (4) is an exception. Set atop a hill overlooking the city, it offers splendid close-up views of the cathedral. The Victorian gingerbread style is carried to extremes on some of the tombs of wealthy merchants, while the memorial to John Knox towers over them all.

The only other holdover from the Middle Ages is **Provand's Lord-**

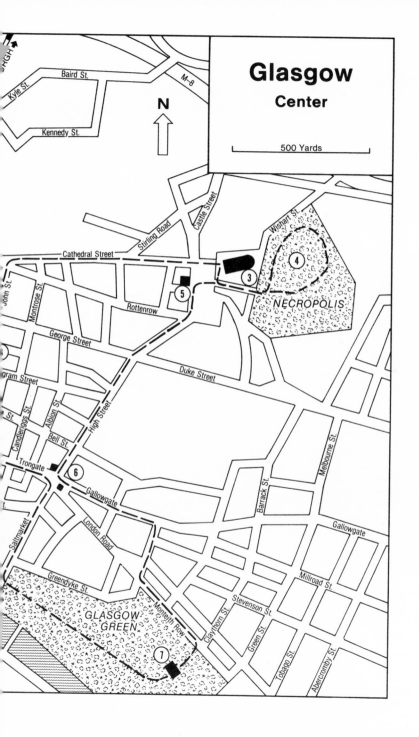

Glasgow
Center

500 Yards

N

Baird St.

Kyle St.

Kennedy St.

M-8

Stirling Road

Castle Street

Cathedral Street

Wishart St.

John St.

Montrose St.

Rottenrow

4

3

5

NECROPOLIS

George Street

gram Street

Duke Street

Candleriggs St.

Albion St.

Bell St.

High Street

St.

Trongate

6

Gallowgate

Barrack St.

Melbourne St.

Gallowgate

London Road

Saltmarket

Greendyke St.

Stevenson St.

Millroad St.

GLASGOW
GREEN

Monteith Row

Claythorn St.

Green St.

Tobago St.

Abercromby St.

1

ship (5), opposite the cathedral. Glasgow's oldest house, it was built around 1471 and is now a small museum with period displays from 1500 to 1918. Visits may be made on Mondays through Saturdays, from 10 a.m. to 5 p.m.; and on Sundays from 2–5 p.m. Admission is free.

Continue down Castle Street and High Street past the railway yards to **Glasgow Cross** (6), once the commercial heart of the city. The mercat cross near its center is a 1929 replica of the medieval original, while the isolated Cross Steeple is all that remains of a 17th-century tolbooth, or town hall and jail. This area is especially rich in local color.

Ambitious walkers may want to make a little side trip at this point. To do so, continue east on Gallowgate, which once led to the gallows but now brings you to the **Barrows**, where a lively flea market is held on weekends. Turn south and into **Glasgow Green**, the city's oldest park. The **People's Palace** (7) was built in 1898 as a cultural center for the East End. Today it serves as a very entertaining museum of the city's colorful past, with frequently changing displays. It is open on Mondays through Saturdays, from 10 a.m. to 5 p.m.; and on Sundays from 2–5 p.m. Admission is free. Return to Glasgow Cross via the park and Saltmarket.

Now follow the map into the merchants' quarter with its wealth of interesting architecture. **Hutchesons's Hall** (8) was built in 1805 to replace an earlier almshouse, and it now serves as the visitor center and regional office of the National Trust for Scotland. You can stop in for a look and perhaps browse through their shop.

Ingram Street leads to the gigantic Corinthian portico of the **Royal Exchange** (9), begun in 1775 as a mansion for one of Glasgow's leading tobacco lords. The equestrian statue in front is of the Duke of Wellington. Later used as a business exchange, this magnificent structure is now a library and may be visited on any day except Wednesdays and Sundays.

A left on the pedestrians-only Buchanan Street brings you to the Argyll Arcade, an enclosed shopping mall from 1827. Just beyond is St. Enoch Square, an open area with an intriguing subway station currently housing the transport information office. Continue on to the Clyde and cross the footbridge for a good view of the famous river that brought Glasgow its shipping prosperity.

Return to the north bank of the river and follow the map to **Central Station** (10), which can be entered from Argyle Street. This enormous old barn of a railway terminal, built in 1870, is constantly busy with departures for the south of Scotland as well as England.

The route now threads its way past some more elaborate buildings and soon leads to the world-famous **Glasgow School of Art** (11) on Renfrew Street. It's hard to believe that this relatively modern structure actually dates from the turn of the century, but then its architect,

Charles Rennie Mackintosh, was way ahead of his time. Although it is a functioning school, visitors are welcome to see the gallery with its collection of Mackintosh furniture, the exquisite library, and some other rooms as well. Informal guided tours can usually be arranged on the spot, and the doors are open on Mondays through Fridays, from 10 a.m. to noon and 2–4 p.m.

If you're not tired yet, you might want to make a short side trip to the **Tenement House** (12) at 145 Buccleuch Street. Miss Agnes Toward, a typist, lived in this 1892 flat from 1911 until 1965 and apparently never changed a thing. Perfectly preserved, gas lights and all, it offers a rare glimpse into the domestic lives of ordinary citizens around the turn of the century. Visits may be made from Easter to the end of October, daily from 2–5 p.m.; and the rest of the year on weekends only from 2–4 p.m. Now follow the map back to your starting point, Queen Street Station.

ADDITIONAL SIGHTS:

Glasgow is noted for its superb museums, most of which lie well outside the center but can easily be reached by bus. Ask at the tourist office for current details. Among the best are:

The Burrell Collection (13) in Pollok Country Park. Opened in 1983, this is simply one of the finest art museums in the world.

The Art Gallery and Museum in Kelvingrove (14) offers a vast collection of art, especially 17th-century Dutch, French Barbizon, Impressionist and Post-Impressionist styles; along with exhibits of armor, archaeology, history, ethnography, natural history, and just about everything else.

The Museum of Transport (15) is scheduled to move into its new Kelvin Hall quarters during 1988. Previously in an old tram depot, it features a fabulous collection of automobiles, streetcars, locomotives, bicycles and the like.

The Hunterian Art Gallery (16) has a large collection of works by Mackintosh along with the Rembrandts, Whistlers, Reynolds, and so on. It is on the grounds of Glasgow University, as is the separate **Hunterian Museum** of archaeology, history, ethnography, geology, and other subjects.

Ayr and the Burns Country

Alas, Ayrshire is no more, having been incorporated into the county of Strathclyde. But its name will live on forever as the home of Robert Burns, Scotland's national bard.

Born on January 25, 1759 in a humble cottage in the village of Alloway, Burns spent his formative years in the vicinity of Ayr, where many of his best-loved stories take place. Later lionized by the literary set in Edinburgh, he was never financially successful, and eventually took a post as a tax collector in the south of Scotland before dying at the young age of 37. His enormous integrity, contempt for tyranny, and love for all humanity have won him a special place in the hearts of Scots and, indeed, of people all over the globe.

This daytrip explores several of the most important sites associated with Burns and the earthy characters he created. Along the way you will be able to pick up more information about other nearby locations along the "Burns Heritage Trail," which you might want to visit at another time.

GETTING THERE:

Trains depart Edinburgh's Waverley Station frequently for the 50-minute ride to Glasgow's Queen Street Station. From there you can walk or take the Rail Link bus one-half mile to Glasgow's Central Station, where you get another train to Ayr, as below.

Trains leave Glasgow's Central Station every half-hour for the 50-minute ride to Ayr, with return service until late evening. Although most of these are marked "Strathclyde Transport," they all accept the BritRail Pass.

By car from Edinburgh, take the A-71 southwest to Kilmarnock, then the A-77 past Prestwick and into Ayr. The total distance is 81 miles. You can drive to Alloway instead of taking the bus.

By car from Glasgow, it's the A-77 southwest all the way to Ayr, 35 miles away. Drive to Alloway instead of taking the bus.

Robert Burns Immortalized

WHEN TO GO:

Most of the attractions are open daily, but the Burns Cottage is closed on Sundays from November through March; and the Tam o' Shanter Museum is closed on Sundays from September through May. Good weather is essential to enjoy this trip.

FOOD AND DRINK:

Being a resort town, Ayr has a good selection of adequate restaurants and pubs. There are also a few in Alloway. Some choices are:

Burns Monument Inn (in Alloway, overlooking the Brig o' Doon) An old inn with both a restaurant and a pub. $ and $$

Marine Court (12 Fairfield Rd. in Ayr, 5 blocks west of the station) Fine hotel dining near the beach. $$

Pickwick Hotel (19 Racecourse Rd., 4 blocks southwest of Ayr Station) Scottish food in a Victorian hotel, with a pub and a restaurant. $ and $$

TOURIST INFORMATION:

The local tourist office in Ayr, phone (0292) 28-41-96, is at 39 Sandgate near the Auld Brig. You could also contact the Land o' Burns Centre in Alloway at (0292) 437-00.

Brig o' Doon

SUGGESTED TOUR:

Leave the Ayr **train station** (1) and stroll over to **Burns Statue Square** (2), where the poet's likeness surveys the scene. From here you can take bus number 205 to Alloway. Those with cars will, of course, drive the three-mile distance.

Get off in front of the modern **Land o' Burns Centre** (3), where a splendid audio-visual show introduces you to the life and times of the bard. Run by the local tourist authorities, it is open daily from 10 a.m. to 6 p.m., closing at 5:30 or 5 p.m. off-season. There is an information desk and a gift shop. Admission is free, but a small charge is made for the show.

Now wander around to the **Burns Monument** (4) of 1823, surely the most horrendously inappropriate shrine ever raised to a simple man of the earth. Looking more like a temple to a Greek god, it contains a small museum of Burns mementoes and is set in a lovely garden, well worth strolling in. The monument is open daily, except on Sundays between November and March. Its admission charge happily includes the Burns Cottage, yet to come.

As you look down from the monument you will notice a particularly attractive old bridge. This is the famed **Brig o' Doon** (5), possibly dating from the 13th century, over which Tam escaped the pursuing witches in Burns' poem *Tam o' Shanter*. Walk down to it and stroll across its graceful single arch for some nice views.

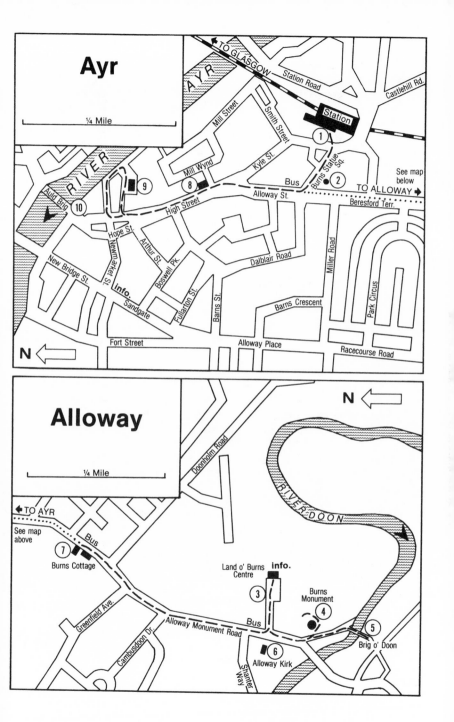

Return to Alloway Monument Road, where there is an inviting pub. Just up the street stands, more or less, the ruined **Alloway Kirk** (6), which has been in that picturesque condition since even before Burns' time. The poet's father, who spelled his name "Burnes," is buried here; and this is where the fictional Tam o' Shanter first encountered the witches in their unholy orgy.

From here it is a pleasant ten-minute walk to the **Burns Cottage and Museum** (7). This "auld clay biggin" with its thatched roof was rebuilt by Burns' father, a market gardener, in 1757. Robert Burns was born here two years later, and lived in the cottage until the family moved to a nearby farm in 1766. After that the simple structure was used for a variety of purposes, including an alehouse and, later, a "temperance refreshment room," whatever that is. In 1881 it was purchased by the Burns Monument Trustees and restored to its 1757 condition.

The cottage today is furnished with period pieces, a very few of which have an association with the Burns family. The small museum in an adjacent building has a superb collection of original works by Burns, including manuscripts, letters, and the like. Visits to the cottage and museum may be made any day, except on Sundays between November and March. During the summer it is open until 7 p.m., closing earlier off-season.

Now board the bus in front of the cottage and ride it back to Ayr, getting off at the **Tam o' Shanter Museum** (8). During Burns' time this was an inn, and is regarded as the place from which the fictional Tam began his wild ride. Fascinating for its period interior, it is now a small museum of Burns mementoes. The museum is open on Mondays through Saturdays, from 9:30 a.m. to 5:30 p.m.; and on Sundays from 12:30–2:30 p.m. During the off-season the hours are shorter and it is closed on Sundays.

Two other structures in Ayr are worth seeking out for their connection with Burns. Stroll over to the **Auld Kirk** (9), a 17th-century church financed by Oliver Cromwell in compensation for an earlier church he had requisitioned. The poet was baptized by its minister, and later worshipped here. Nearby is the **Auld Brig** (10), a 13th-century span immortalized in his poem *Twa Brigs*. From here you can follow High Street back to the station.

Loch Lomond

Here is an easy daytrip with absolutely no cultural sights at all. While it is possible to include an eight-mile hike along the edge of the lake during the high season or make a stopover at one of the villages, most travelers will be perfectly content to just relax on the deck of the cruise boat *Countess Fiona* and enjoy the passing scenery.

Opening the way into the Highlands, Loch Lomond is the largest freshwater lake in Britain, and probably the most popular with vacationers. The hordes thin out, however, as you sail into its spectacular northern reaches. Five miles wide near its southern end, it soon narrows down to considerably less than a mile across. The popular cruise described here covers nearly the entire 23-mile length of Scotland's most famous lake.

GETTING THERE:

Trains depart Edinburgh's Waverley Station frequently for the 50-minute ride to Glasgow's Queen Street Station, from whose lower level you can get a train to Balloch, as below.

Trains leave Glasgow's Queen Street Station (lower level) at about half-hour intervals for the 45-minute ride to Balloch, at the south end of the lake. On Sundays and holidays these leave from Glasgow's Central Station instead, although you can take another train from Queen Street to Partick and change there. Return service operates until late evening. These trains are marked "Strathclyde Transport," but they do accept the BritRail Pass.

By car from Edinburgh, take the A-8 and M-8 west to Glasgow, then the A-82 to Balloch. The total distance is 62 miles.

By car from Glasgow, take the A-82 northwest to Balloch, a distance of 18 miles.

WHEN TO GO:

Cruises on Loch Lomond operate between mid-April and late September, with much better service from late June to late August. You must arrive at Balloch by 10 a.m. at the very latest unless you are taking a simple cruise with no stopover between late June and late August. Good weather is essential to enjoy this trip.

FOOD AND DRINK:

The *Countess Fiona* cruise boat has a bar on board, offering snack meals, draft beer, and other refreshments at pub prices. Ashore, you will find numerous places to eat at Balloch and elsewhere. Some choices are:

> **Balloch Hotel** (Balloch Rd. in Balloch, near the lake) An old inn with both a pub and a restaurant. $ and $$
>
> **Inversnaid Hotel** (by the boat dock near the north end of the lake) A lakeside inn with a great view. $ and $$

TOURIST INFORMATION:

In planning for this trip, it will help to have a current cruise schedule for the *Countess Fiona*. These are usually available at tourist information centers in Scotland, or you can call the company directly at (041) 248-2699. The tourist office in Balloch can be reached at (0389) 53-533.

SUGGESTED TOUR:

Balloch train station (1) is a short walk from **Balloch Pier** (2), where you board the *Countess Fiona* around 10 a.m. for the five-hour cruise to the northern reaches of the lake and back, making stops along the way. Between late June and late August there is also a cruise starting in mid-afternoon and returning in the evening. During these months only it is possible to take the morning cruise, make a stopover, and continue on the later cruise, still seeing the entire lake. The printed schedule makes this all perfectly clear.

The ***Countess Fiona*** was built in 1936 and, under different names, has long been a familiar sight on various lochs and other waterways around Scotland. It was purchased in 1982 by the Alloa Brewery, which operates it today and whose beer flows steadily from the taps in the boat's bar.

If, for some reason, you can't make the *Countess Fiona*'s departure you will be happy to know that there are other companies near the pier offering shorter cruises on the lake.

The first stop for the *Countess Fiona* is at **Luss** (3) on the western bank, opposite several small islands, one of which has a ruined castle. Luss itself is a popular resort village, noted for its mellow stone cottages.

Beyond this the lake begins to narrow as you approach **Rowardennan** (4), above which towers—well, not quite towers—**Ben Lomond** (5), a lovely mountain that peaks out at 3,192 feet. If you have the opportunity to get off here and continue on a later boat, you may want to consider making the relatively easy climb for a fabulous view, allowing about five hours up and down. You can also disembark here

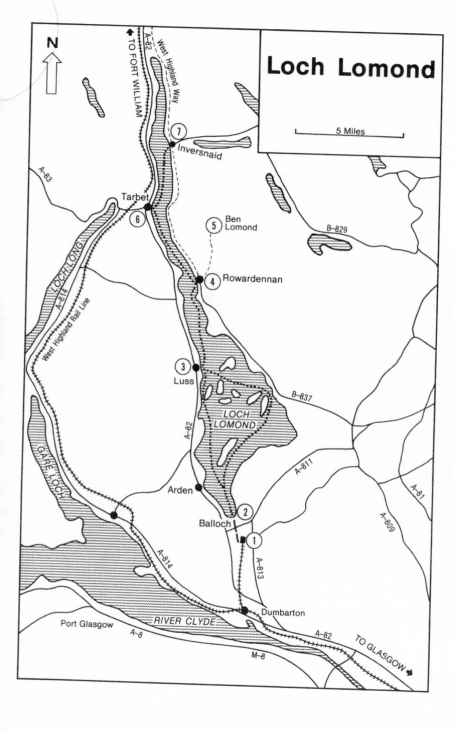

Loch Lomond

N

5 Miles

TO FORT WILLIAM

A-82

West Highland Way

⑦ Inversnaid

Tarbet

⑥

A-83

⑤ Ben Lomond

④ Rowardennan

LOCH LONG

A-814

West Highland Rail Line

③ Luss

B-829

B-837

LOCH LOMOND

A-82

GARE LOCH

Arden

A-811

A-81

Balloch

②

①

A-813

A-809

A-814

Dumbarton

Port Glasgow

A-8

RIVER CLYDE

A-82

TO GLASGOW

M-8

Aboard the Countess Fiona

and hike eight miles to Inversnaid (7), where it is possible to board the later boat during the high season. The attractive lakeside trail between them is part of the famed West Highland Way.

Tarbet (6), the next stop, is another popular resort center. It is remembered in history as the spot where in 1263 the Vikings dragged their galleys overland to Loch Lomond in a last futile attempt to conquer Scotland. This is also a stop on British Rail's West Highland Line, described in the next chapter. It is possible to get a train from here back to Glasgow.

Inversnaid (7), beyond which the lake takes on a fjordlike character, is as far north as the cruise goes. A beautiful but quite isolated spot, it has a famous hotel at the water's edge, next to a waterfall. If you choose to make a stopover here (check the schedule first), you might want to have lunch and then explore **Rob Roy's Cave**, where Robert the Bruce found shelter in 1306.

The *Countess Fiona* now begins its return journey to Balloch, making the same stops along the way.

West Highland Rail Trip

Getting there is more than half the fun on this magnificent one-day rail excursion. The final destination of Fort William, or possibly Mallaig, will certainly add to your enjoyment, but the real star is British Rail's West Highland Line. Climbing mountains, skirting lakes, and traversing wilderness that has never seen an automobile, the train snakes its way through a dramatic landscape that some regard as the finest in Britain.

Completed around the turn of the century, this 164-mile-long rail line opened parts of Scotland that were previously inaccessible. In some remote areas it is still the only means of transport available, and it therefore operates all year round—so you can even delight in gorgeous winter snowscapes from the comfort of a heated train.

Fort William, the primary destination, is a popular resort and the touring center of the southern Highlands. Set at the foot of Britain's highest mountain and the junction of several lochs, it offers more than enough attractions to keep you busy during the four-hour stopover.

Dedicated rail fans may prefer to change trains at Fort William and continue on to Mallaig instead, riding over what is perhaps the most spectacular section of the line. This still allows a return to Glasgow the same day, but with no stopovers at all.

GETTING THERE:

Trains depart Edinburgh's Waverley Station frequently for the 50-minute ride to Glasgow's Queen Street Station, where you change to the West Highland Line, as below.

A train leaves Glasgow's Queen Street Station at around 9:50 a.m. for the four-hour scenic run to Fort William described below. The only practical return train departs Fort William at about 5:30 p.m., arriving back in Glasgow around 9:30 p.m. There is absolutely no workable service on Sundays or some holidays. Check the current schedule before setting out, as changes are always possible.

WHEN TO GO:

This trip may be made in any season, but never on Sundays or some holidays. Clear weather is essential.

FOOD AND DRINK:

Snacks and beverages are available on the train, or you might want to bring lunch. Fort William has a broad selection of restaurants and pubs, including:

>**McTavish's Kitchens** (100 High St., near the museum) Scottish specialties in a self-service downstairs and a full restaurant upstairs. $ and $$

>**Nevis Bank Hotel** (Belford Rd., east of the station) Meals in a popular hotel with a pub and a restaurant. $ and $$

TOURIST INFORMATION:

The tourist office in Fort William, phone (0397) 37-81, is at Cameron Centre near the museum. Current train schedules are available at any station, or by calling (in Edinburgh) (031) 556-2451; or (in Glasgow) (041) 204-2844.

SUGGESTED TOUR:

Board the West Highland Line train at Glasgow's **Queen Street Station** (1), hopefully getting a window seat on the left. Once beyond the metropolis you will follow the Clyde estuary to Gare Loch, then begin heading north alongside Loch Long, a narrow inlet from the sea. The station at Arrochar and Tarbet provides service to the northern part of **Loch Lomond** (2), described in the previous chapter. Across the loch you can see **Ben Lomond**, the highest mountain in the area, and Inversnaid.

Leaving Loch Lomond behind, you soon cross the impressive Glen Falloch viaduct before halting at **Crianlarich** (3), where the line splits. The tracks to the left descend to the delightful little port of **Oban**, which you may want to visit at another time. Meanwhile, the train for Fort William continues its northward climb, leaving civilization behind after stopping at Bridge of Orchy.

The large and hauntingly beautiful **Rannoch Moor**, a desolate wilderness of peat bogs, tarns, streams, and tiny lochs, presented a great challenge to the 19th-century railway engineers, as it has no solid foundation. The problem was solved by "floating" the tracks on a mattress of tree roots and brushwood. You might notice a slight bounce to the ride as the train vibrates the bog. The tiny station at Rannoch is linked to the outside world by a minor road, but after that all is again wilderness. At windswept Carrour the line peaks out at 1,350 feet above sea level, quite a climb for a train to make, and then begins its descent

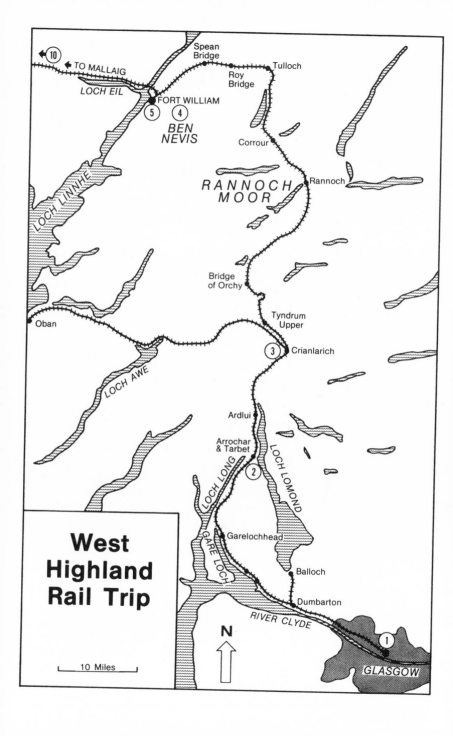

West Highland Rail Trip

Spean Bridge

TO MALLAIG

Roy Bridge

Tulloch

LOCH EIL

FORT WILLIAM

BEN NEVIS

Corrour

LOCH LINNHE

RANNOCH MOOR

Rannoch

Bridge of Orchy

Oban

Tyndrum Upper

LOCH AWE

Crianlarich

Ardlui

Arrochar & Tarbet

LOCH LONG

LOCH LOMOND

Garelochhead

Balloch

GARE LOCH

Dumbarton

RIVER CLYDE

N

GLASGOW

10 Miles

In the Rannoch Moor

to Tulloch and turns westward.

To the left looms the bulky mass of **Ben Nevis** (4), at 4,406 feet the highest mountain in Britain. You can usually see patches of snow on its slopes, even in mid-August. A great many visitors to Fort William make the climb every year, but as that takes about eight hours in all it cannot be done on this daytrip.

You will soon arrive at the **Fort William Station** (5), where you have a choice of either exploring the town during a four-hour stopover before returning to Glasgow, or changing trains and continuing on to Mallaig (10) for a full day of riding the rails without a stopover. Steam locomotives are sometimes used on the run to Mallaig, for which an extra charge is made. Check the schedules carefully.

Those choosing to explore Fort William should head directly for the **West Highland Museum** (6) on Cameron Square, near the tourist office. One of the most delightful little museums in Scotland, it packs its small 18th-century house with local bygones, historical relics, re-created room settings, weapons, archaeological finds, and an amazing range of other collectables. The museum is open on Mondays through Saturdays, from 9:30 a.m. to 5:30 p.m. in June and September and to 9 p.m. in July and August. During the rest of the year the hours are 10 a.m. to 1 p.m. and 2–5 p.m.

Continue down High Street to the **Ben Nevis Centre** (7), a small exhibition of artifacts and displays about the nearby mountain. This is

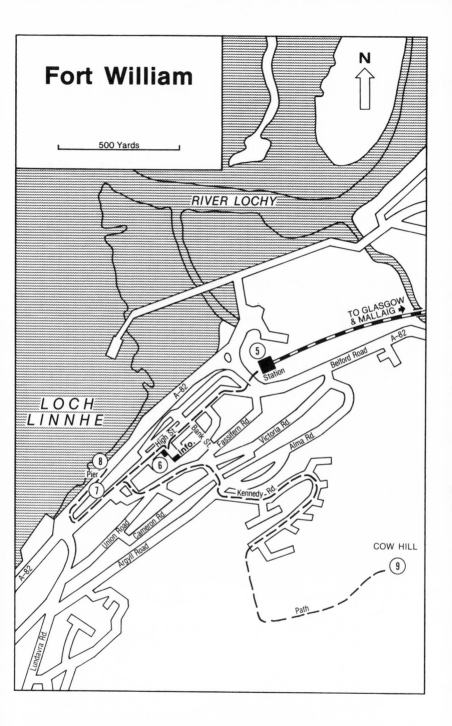

View of Loch Linnhe from Fort William

incorporated into the interesting **Scottish Crafts Exhibition** and gift shop. It is open daily in summer and on Mondays through Saturdays the rest of the year.

Now walk over to the **Town Pier** (8), which offers some outstanding views of Loch Linnhe. The first in a straight line of lochs called the Great Glen, this connects via the Caledonian Canal to Loch Ness, Inverness, and the North Sea; thus providing a boat channel clear across Scotland. The resident monster hasn't swum this far south yet.

Ben Nevis may be right next to Fort William, but you can't see it from the town as an even closer mound blocks the view. This can be overcome by climbing all 942 feet of **Cow Hill** (9) for a sweeping panorama of the area.

Fort William has enough pubs to keep you happy before returning to the station for the only train back to Glasgow. Those who continued on to **Mallaig** (10) will have to turn right around, but the lack of a stopover will be compensated for by the sheer beauty of the ride.

Index

Boat Trips, Castles, Cathedrals, Country Walks, Museums, Railfan Excursions, Roman Relics, and Stately Homes are listed individually under those category headings. *Names of persons are in italics.*

Aberdeen 302–308
Alfred, King (The Great) 108, 113, 175
Alloway 330–334
Anne, Queen 130, 172
Arthur, King 113, 314
Arundel 81–84
Aylesbury 186–189
Ayr 330–334

Balloch 335–336
Bath 19, 130–137
Battle 58, 62–65, 66
Becket, Archbishop Thomas à 34, 36, 124
Bede, The Venerable 110
Blair Atholl 318–321
Blenheim Palace 171–174
Bluebell Railway 71–74
Boadicea, Queen 222
BOAT TRIPS:
    Bath 137
    Bristol 145, 148
    Chester 214, 218
    Greenwich 20
    Guildford 93
    Isle of Wight 102
    Linlithgow 313
    Loch Lomond 335–338
    Oxford 170
    Windsor 128
Bosham 85, 90
Brighton 75–80
Bristol 143–149
Britexpress Card 13
British Airways 14–15, 287, 323
British Rail 9–13, 285, 338, 339
British Tourist Authority 18
BritRail Pass 12–13, 72, 102, 179, 207, 238, 285, 330, 335

Brown, Lancelot "Capability" 74, 172, 176, 230
Brunel, Isambard Kingdom 148
Burns, Robert 293, 324, 330–334
Bury St. Edmunds 253, 263–266
Bus Travel 13

Cabot, John 143, 149
Caerdydd—see Cardiff
Caerphilly 154–155
Cambridge 19, 245–252
Canterbury 34–39, 40
Canute, King 90, 108, 110, 114, 263
Cardiff 150–156
Car rentals 12, 13–14
Carroll, Lewis 94
CASTLES;
    Arundel 82
    Blair 318, 320
    Caerphilly 154–155
    Camber 56
    Canterbury 39
    Cardiff 152
    Castle Rising 262
    Chester 217–218
    Clifford's Tower (York) 243
    Colchester 268
    Dover 41–42
    Edinburgh 289, 292
    Guildford 94
    Hastings 67
    Lincoln 234, 236
    Norwich 284
    Nottingham 224, 226
    Oxford 164
    Rochester 28
    St. Andrews 298, 300
    Shrewsbury 203–204
    Southsea 100
    Stirling 316

CASTLES, continued
  Warwick 176
  Winchester 113
  Windsor 126–128
  Wolvesey 112
CATHEDRALS:
  Aberdeen 304
  Arundel 84
  Bristol 149
  Bury St. Edmunds 264
  Canterbury 35–36
  Chester 218
  Chichester 86, 88
  Clifton 148
  Coventry 192
  Edinburgh 293
  Ely 254, 256
  Exeter 158
  Glasgow 325
  Guildford 96
  Lincoln 234
  Llandaff 156
  Norwich 280
  Old Aberdeen 306–308
  Oxford 169
  Portsmouth 100
  Rochester 28
  St. Albans 220
  St. Andrews (ruins) 300
  Salisbury 119, 121–122
  Wells 139–140
  Winchester 110, 112
  York 242
Charles I, King 100, 204, 212, 214, 224, 230, 260, 293
Charles II, King 22, 29, 100, 129, 260, 293, 295, 301
Charles, Prince of Wales 98
Chester 207, 211, 212–218
Chichester 85–91
Chichester, Sir Francis 22
Churchill, Sir Winston 44, 46, 172
Clifton 148
Coach Travel 13
Coalbrookdale 195
Cogidubnus (Celtic King) 85, 89, 90
Colchester 267–270, 271
COUNTRY WALKS:
  Arundel 82, 84
  Aylesbury 188
  Battle 64
  Blair Atholl 318, 320
  Chichester 90

  Knole 46
  Loch Lomond 336–338
  Oxford 168
  Rye 57
  Shanklin 106
  Wells 140
  Winchester 112
  Woodbridge 276–278
Coventry 175, 190–194
Cromwell, Oliver 24, 34, 112, 154, 156, 188, 254, 292, 310, 334

Darwin, Charles 204
Dickens, Charles 25, 26, 28, 29, 101, 204, 266
Dover 34, 40–43
Dungeness 50

Edinburgh 285, 286–296, 322
Edward the Confessor, King 62, 66, 108
Edward I, King 154, 310, 314
Edward VI, King 202
Egbert, King 108, 110
Elizabeth I, Queen 20, 24, 29, 38, 44, 144, 182, 272
Elizabeth II, Queen 80
Ely 253–256, 263
Epstein, Sir Jacob 156, 165, 192
Ethelred II, King (The Unready) 110, 171
Ethelwulf, King 110
Eton 125, 128–129
Exeter 157–161

Faversham 25, 30–33
Ffestiniog Railway 207–211
Folkestone 48–51
Fort William 339–344

George IV, King 75, 79
Glasgow 285, 322–329
Godiva, Lady 190, 191
Greenwich 19, 20–24, 25
Guildford 92–96, 97

Harold II, King (Godwinson) 62, 64, 90
Hastings 52, 58, 62, 66–70
Henry I, King 82, 171, 284
Henry II, King 36
Henry III, King 154
Henry IV, King 36

Henry VI, King 129, 188, 247
Henry VII, King 97
Henry VIII, King 20, 24, 36, 44, 57, 64, 98, 100, 126, 186, 237, 247, 250, 257, 261, 263, 264, 274
Hereward the Wake 253
Holidays 15
Hythe 49–50

Ipswich 253, 263, 271–274, 275
Ironbridge Gorge 195–201
Isle of Wight 102–107

James I, King (VI of Scotland) 22, 292, 316
James II, King (VII of Scotland) 32, 204, 293, 304
James, Henry 56
John, King 224, 262, 263, 264
Jones, Inigo 22

King's Lynn 253, 257–262
Kipling, Rudyard 80
Knole 44–47, 58, 62, 66
Knox, John 293, 294, 298, 301, 316, 325

Lincoln 232–236
Linlithgow 309–313, 314
Llandaff 154, 155–156
Loch Lomond 335–338, 340

Mackintosh, Charles Rennie 322, 329
Mallaig 339, 342, 344
Marlowe, Christopher 35
Mary I, Queen 20, 24
Mary, Queen of Scots 292, 293, 295, 300, 301, 309, 312, 314
MUSEUMS:
   Aberdeen Art Gallery 308
   Anthropological Museum (Aberdeen) 304–305
   Art Gallery & Museum in Kelvingrove (Glasgow) 329
   Arundel Museum & Heritage Centre (local history) 84
   Ashmolean (art & history, Oxford) 168
   Atholl Country Collection (bygones, Blair Atholl) 320
   Bargate (local history, Southampton) 116

Battle Museum (Battle of Hastings) 64
Blists Hill Open Air Museum (industry, Ironbridge) 197–200
Brewhouse Yard Museum (local life, Nottingham) 226
Bridewell Museum (local crafts, Norwich) 283
Brighton Art Gallery & Museum (art & local history) 79
Bristol City Museum (art & local history) 149
Bristol Industrial Museum 145
British Engineerium (steam engines, Hove) 80
British Road Transport Museum (motor vehicles, Coventry) 192, 194
Buckinghamshire County Museum (local history, Aylesbury) 188
Burns Cottage & Museum (life of the poet, Alloway) 334
Burrell Collection, The (art, Glasgow) 329
Cambridge Folk Museum 251
Camden Works Museum (factory, Bath) 136
Canterbury Heritage Museum (local history) 39
Castle Museum (bygones, York) 243–244
Charles Dickens Birthplace Museum (Portsmouth) 101
Charles Dickens Centre (author's life, Rochester) 26
Chichester District Museum (local history) 89
Christchurch Mansion (arts & antiquities, Ipswich) 272
Clive House (industry & pottery, Shrewsbury) 206
Coalbrookdale Museum of Iron (industry, Ironbridge) 201
Coalport China Museum (Ironbridge) 200
Colchester & Essex Museum (Roman artifacts) 268
Colchester Natural History Museum 268
D-Day Museum (Portsmouth) 100
Dolls' House & Toy Museum (Arundel) 84

MUSEUMS, continued

Dover Museum (antiquities) 42

Edinburgh City Museum (local history) 294

Edinburgh Wax Museum 293

Ely Museum (local history) 256

Exeter Maritime Museum (boats) 158, 160

Fishermen's Muiseum (Hastings) 68

Fitzwilliam Museum (art, Cambridge) 252

Fleur de Lis Heritage Centre (local history, Faversham) 31

Gershom Parkington Collection (clocks, Bury St. Edmunds) 266

God's House Tower (archaeology, Southampton) 116

Grange, The (life of Kipling, Rottingdean) 80

Grosvenor Museum (Roman life & bygones, Chester) 217

Guildford Museum (local history) 94

Guildhall Museum (archaeology, Chichester) 89

Guildhall Museum (local history, Rochester) 26

Hall of Aviation (Southampton) 118

Hastings Museum & Art Gallery 70

Hastings Museum of Local History 68

Herbert Art Gallery & Museum (Coventry) 192

History of Science Museum (Oxford) 165

Holburne of Menstrie Museum (art, Bath) 137

Holly Trees Museum (bygones, Colchester) 268

Holy Trinity Museum (rural life, Colchester) 270

Hunterian Art Gallery (Glasgow) 329

Hunterian Museum (Glasgow) 329

Ipswich Museum (archaeology & local history) 272

Jorvik Viking Centre (York) 243

Kettle's Yard (modern art, Cambridge) 251

King Charles' Tower (Civil War, Chester) 214

Lady Stair's House (literary memorabilia, Edinburgh) 293

Lincoln City & County Museum (archaeology) 326

Lincolnshire Life Museum (local history, Lincoln) 236

Linlithgow Canal Museum 313

Lynn Museum (local history, King's Lynn) 262

Maritime Museum (Aberdeen) 304

Market Cross Art Gallery (Bury St. Edmunds) 266

Mary Rose Exhibition (warship, Portsmouth) 98

Military Museum (Salisbury) 124

Minories Art Gallery (Colchester) 268

Moyse's Hall (local history, Bury St. Edmunds) 266

Museum of Childhood (Edinburgh) 293, 294

Museum of Costume (Bath) 136

Museum of Eton Life 129

Museum of Transport (Glasgow) 329

National Centre of Photography (Bath) 137

National Cycle Museum (Lincoln) 236

National Gallery of Scotland (art, Edinburgh) 289

National Maritime Museum (Greenwich) 22, 24

National Museum of Wales (Cardiff) 152

National Railway Museum (York) 71, 238–239

Norwich Castle Museum (art & antiquities) 284

Nottingham Canal Museum 225

Nottingham Castle Museum (art) 226

Nottingham Costume & Textile Museum 226

Oken's House (toys, Warwick) 176

Oxfordshire County Museum (local history, Woodstock) 174

Pallant House (art, Chichester) 88

People's Palace, The (local history, Glasgow) 328

Portsmouth City Museum (art) 101

Potter's Museum of Curiosity (taxidermy, Arundel) 84

Provost Skene's House (local history, Aberdeen) 308

Roman Baths Museum (artifacts, Bath) 132

Rougemont House Museum (costume & lace, Exeter) 161

Royal Albert Memorial Museum (general interest, Exeter) 161

Royal Greenjackets Museum (military, Winchester) 113

Royal Hampshire Regiment Museum (military, Winchester) 113

Royal Hussars Museum (military, Winchester) 113

Royal Mews Exhibition (carriages, Windsor) 128

Royal Museum & Art Gallery (antiquities, Canterbury) 38

Royal Naval Museum (Portsmouth) 98

Royal Scots Regimental Museum (military, Edinburgh) 292

Royalty & Empire Exhibition (Windsor) 126

Rye Museum (local history) 54

St. Albans City Museum (local history) 223

St. John's House (local crafts, Warwick) 178

St. Nicholas Church Museum (church art, Bristol) 149

St. Peter Hungate Museum (church art, Norwich) 282

Salisbury & South Wiltshire Museum (local history) 122

Shipwreck Heritage Centre (Hastings) 68, 70

Shropshire Regimental Museum (military, Shrewsbury) 204

Social History Museum (King's Lynn) 258

Southampton Art Gallery 118

Southampton Maritime Museum 116

Southsea Castle (military history, Portsmouth) 100

Stained Glass Museum (Ely) 254, 256

Stamford Brewery Museum (beer making) 228, 230

Stamford Museum (local history) 230

Stranger's Hall Museum (local life, Norwich) 283

Stratford Motor Museum 185

Tam o' Shanter Museum (mementoes of Robert Burns, Ayr) 334

Tile Museum (Ironbridge) 200

Tudor House (local history, Southampton) 116

Tunbridge Wells Museum (local history) 60

Usher Gallery (art, Lincoln) 236

Verulamium Museum (Roman artifacts, St. Albans) 222

Victoria Art Gallery (Bath) 137

Virconium Museum of Roman Artifacts (Shrewsbury) 204

Warwickshire County Museum (local history, Warwick) 178

Wells Museum (local history) 140

Welsh Folk Museum (traditional buildings & crafts, St. Fagan's) 155

Westgate Museum (armor, Canterbury) 38

Westgate Museum (armor, Winchester) 110

West Highland Museum (local history, Fort William) 342

Winchester City Museum (local history) 110

Yorkshire Museum (archaeology, York) 239

Nash, John 80

Nash, Richard "Beau" 58, 130, 133

Nelson, Horatio Lord 24, 97, 98

New Romney 50

North Wales 207–211

Norwich 279–284

Nottingham 224–227

Old Sarum 119, 121

Oxford 162–170, 171, 245

Palaces—see Stately Homes

Pepys, Samuel 251

Portmadog 208–210
Portsmouth 92, 97–101

RAILFAN EXCURSIONS:
  Romney, Hythe & Dymchurch
    48–51
  Bluebell 71–74
  Volk's Railway (Brighton) 76
  Bristol 145
  North Wales 207–211
  West Highland Rail Trip 339–344
Rail travel 9–13
Restaurants 16
Richard I, King (Lionheart) 97, 114
Rochester 20, 25–29, 30
ROMAN RELICS:
  Bath 132
  Canterbury 38
  Cardiff 152
  Chester 217, 218
  Colchester 267, 268
  Dover 42
  Fishbourne Roman Palace 90
  Lincoln 232, 236
  St. Albans 219, 222–223
  York 239, 242
Romney, Hythe & Dymchurch 48–51
Rottingdean Village 80
Royal Tunbridge Wells 58–61
Rye 19, 52–57, 66

St. Albans 219–223
St. Andrews 297–301
St. Augustine 35, 36, 38
St. Fagan's 154, 155
Salisbury 119–124
Sandown 106
Scott, Sir Walter 289, 293, 324
Sevenoaks 44–47
Shakespeare, William 179–185, 258, 267
Shanklin 102–107
Sheffield Park Garden 71, 74
Shrewsbury 195, 202–206, 207, 208
Southampton 108, 114–118
Stamford 228–231
Stanmer Village 80
STATELY HOMES & PALACES:
  Arundel Castle 82
  Blair Castle 318, 320
  Blenheim Palace 171–174
  Burghley House 228, 230

Chartwell 44–46
Georgian House (Bristol) 149
Georgian House (Edinburgh) 296
Holyrood Palace (Edinburgh) 295
Ightham Mote 45–46
Knole House 44, 46
Linlithgow Palace 309, 310–312
Mompesson House 121
Preston Manor 80
Royal Crescent (Bath) 136
Royal Pavilion (Brighton) 79–80
Sandringham 262
Stirling Castle 316
Treasurer's House (York) 242
Waddesdon Manor 186, 188
Warwick Castle 176
Wilton House 124
Windsor Castle 126–128
Stephen, King 82
Stevenson, Robert Louis 293
Stirling 309, 314–317
Stonehenge 119–121
Stratford-upon-Avon 19, 175, 179–185

Telford, Thomas 204
Thames Barrier 24
Tourist information 17–18
Train travel 9–13
Tunbridge Wells, 44, 58–61, 62, 66

Victoria, Queen 24, 28, 58, 60, 80, 82, 102, 126, 176, 214, 318, 324

Warwick 175–178, 179, 190
Wells 138–142
West Highland Rail Trip 339–344
William I, King (The Conqueror) 28, 62, 64, 66, 67, 85, 108, 112, 175, 212, 224, 232, 234, 237, 243, 253, 267
William II, King (Rufus) 110, 112
William IV, King 80
Winchester 108–113, 114
Windsor 125–129
Woodbridge 271, 275–278
Woodstock 162, 171–174
Wookey Hole 138, 140, 142
Wren, Sir Christopher 22, 24, 112, 128, 164, 234, 250

York, 19, 237–244

DayTrips

TRAVEL GUIDES BY EARL STEINBICKER

● **OTHER TITLES NOW AVAILABLE** ●

DAYTRIPS IN GERMANY
55 of Germany's best attractions can be enjoyed on daytrips from Munich, Frankfurt, Hamburg, and Berlin. Walking tours of the big cities are included, as are glossaries. 62 maps and 94 photos. 3rd edition, 336 pages.

DAYTRIPS IN FRANCE
Describes 45 great one-day excursions—including 5 walking tours of Paris, 23 daytrips from the city, 5 in Provence, and 12 along the Riviera. Glossaries, 55 maps, 89 photos. 2nd edition, 336 pages.

DAYTRIPS IN HOLLAND, BELGIUM AND LUXEMBOURG
There's more to the Low Countries than just Amsterdam, Brussels, and Luxembourg City. Many unusual destinations are covered on the 40 daytrips described in this guidebook, along with all of the favorites including the 3 major cities. Glossaries, 45 maps, 69 photos, 288 pages.

DAYTRIPS IN ITALY
Features 40 one-day adventures in and around Rome, Florence, Milan, Venice, and Naples. It includes walking tours of the major cities as well as many smaller destinations such as the hill towns of Tuscany. Glossaries, 45 maps, 69 photos, 288 pages.

DAYTRIPS IN EUROPE
75 one-day excursions from the great cities of a dozen European countries. Heavily illustrated with maps and photos.

"Daytrips" travel guides by Earl Steinbicker describe the easiest and most natural way to explore Europe on your own. Each volume in the growing series contains a balanced selection of enjoyable one-day adventures that can be taken from a major base city, or even within that city. Some of these are to famous attractions, while others feature little-known discoveries.

For every destination there is a suggested do-it-yourself tour, a local map, full travel directions, time and weather considerations, restaurant recommendations, photos, and concise background material.

Since all of the daytrips can be made by public transportation, the books are especially useful to holders of the various popular railpasses. Road directions are also included. These guides are ideal for business travelers as they make the most of limited free time.

SOLD AT LEADING BOOKSTORES EVERYWHERE

Or, if you prefer, by mail direct from the publisher. Use the handy coupon below or just jot down your choices on a separate piece of paper.

Hastings House
141 Halstead Avenue
Mamaroneck, NY 10543

Please send the following books:

_____copies	**DAYTRIPS LONDON** @ $12.95 (0-8038-9329-9)	_____
_____copies	**DAYTRIPS IN BRITAIN** @ $12.95 (0-8038-9301-9)	_____
_____copies	**DAYTRIPS IN GERMANY** @ $12.95 (0-8038-9327-2)	_____
_____copies	**DAYTRIPS IN FRANCE** @ $12.95 (0-8038-9326-4)	_____
_____copies	**DAYTRIPS IN HOLLAND, BELGIUM AND LUXEMBOURG** @ $12.95 (0-8038-9310-8)	_____
_____copies	**DAYTRIPS IN ITALY** @ $10.95 (0-8038-9293-4)	_____

New York residents add tax: _____

Shipping and handling @ $1.50 per book: _____

Total amount enclosed (check or money order): _____

Please ship to: _____

_____

_____